The Mystery in Ancient Egypt

The Exodus in the Qur'an, the Old Testament, Archaeological Finds, and Historical Sources

Louay Fatoohi   **Shetha Al-Dargazelli**

Luna Plena Publishing   Birmingham

© 2008 Louay Fatoohi and Shetha Al-Dargazelli

All Rights reserved. No part of this book may be reproduced, translated, stored in a retrieval system, or transmitted by any means, electronic, mechanical, photocopying, recording, or otherwise, without written permission from the author.

All Biblical quotes are from the *New English Translation* (NET) Bible, so the designation "NET" was not necessary to use. All quotations from the NET Bible are published under this copyright notice:

Scripture quoted by permission. Quotations designated (NET) are from the NET Bible® copyright ©1996-2006 by Biblical Studies Press, L.L.C. www.bible.org All rights reserved.
This material is available in its entirety as a free download or online web use at http://www.nextbible.org/.

First published: November 2008

Production Reference: 1061108

Published by:
Luna Plena Publishing
Birmingham, UK.
www.lunaplenapub.com

ISBN 978-1-906342-03-6

Cover design by:
Mawlid Design
www.mawliddesign.com

Cove image:
The image is of a statue of Ramesses II at the Temple of Luxor. It has been edited to show the Pharaoh of the exodus drowning.

About the Authors

Louay Fatoohi is a British scholar who was born in Baghdad, Iraq, in 1961. He converted from Christianity to Islam in his early twenties. He obtained a BSc in Physics from the College of Sciences, University of Baghdad, in 1984. He obtained his PhD in Astronomy from the Physics Department, Durham University, in 1998.

The author of several books and over forty scientific and general articles in Arabic and English, Dr Fatoohi is particularly interested in studying historical characters and events that are mentioned in the Qur'an and comparing the Qur'anic account with the Biblical narratives and historical sources. His most recent books are *The Mystery of the Crucifixion: The Failed Attempt to Kill Jesus in the Qur'an, the New Testament, and Historical Sources*, *The Mystery of the Historical Jesus: The Messiah in the Qur'an, the Bible, and Historical Sources*, and *The Prophet Joseph in the Qur'an, the Bible, and History: A new detailed commentary on the Qur'anic Chapter of Joseph*.

Shetha Al-Dargazelli is a British scholar who was born in Baghdad, Iraq, in 1946. She graduated from the Physics Department, the College of Sciences, University of Baghdad, in 1966. She completed an MSc in 1970, and obtained a PhD in Physics from the Physics Department, Durham University, in 1979.

Dr Al-Dargazelli taught at Universities in Iraq where she was appointed professor in 1991. She moved with her husband Louay to the United Kingdom in 1992, where she worked at Durham University and Aston University. She has published several books, including four university Physics textbooks, one book on Sufism, and another on the status of woman in Islam.

Ancient Egypt

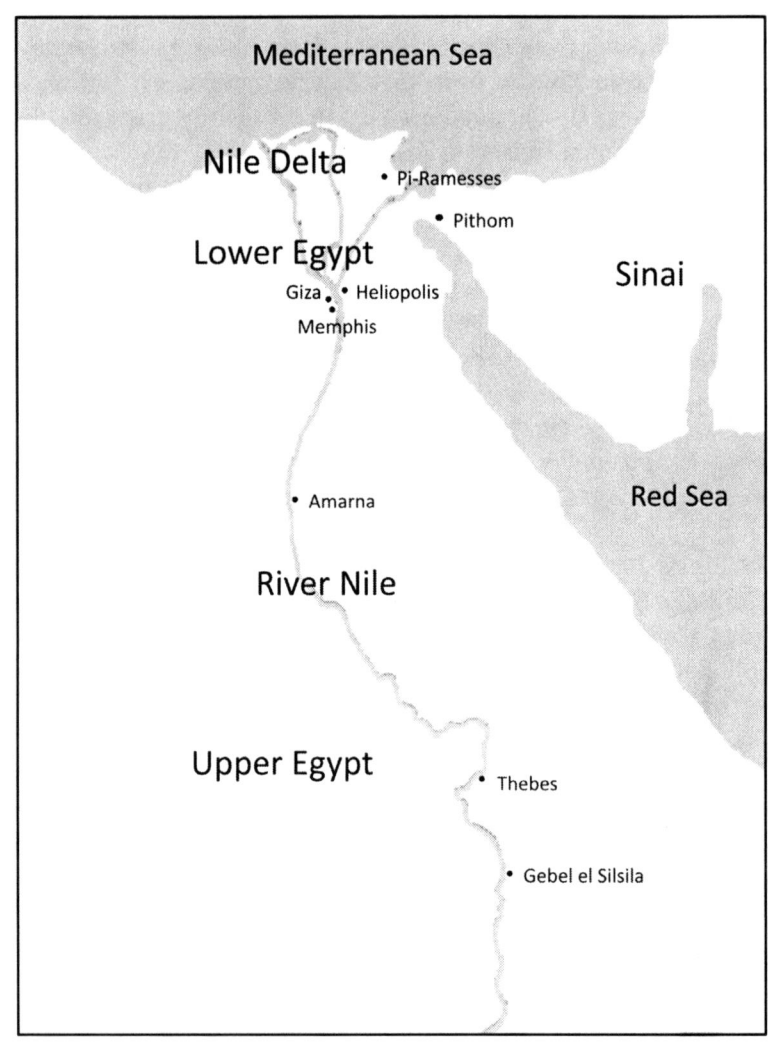

Contents

Preface 9
Introduction 13

1. Joseph: The First Israelite in Egypt 17
1.1 The Biblical Story of Joseph 17
1.2 The Qur'anic Story of Joseph 20
1.3 Joseph's Age 22
1.4 Problems in the Biblical Story of Prophet Joseph 23

2. Locating and Dating Israel's Entry into Egypt 31
2.1 The Silence of History on Joseph 31
2.2 The Biblical Location of Israel's Entry into Egypt 33
2.3 The Biblical Dating of Israel's Entry into Egypt 35
2.4 The Qur'anic Location and Dating of Israel's Entry into Egypt . 38
2.5 What Position Did Joseph Occupy? 42

3. The Exodus in the Bible 47
3.1 The Biblical Narrative 47
3.2 Problems in the Biblical Exodus 50
   3.2.1 The Length of the Israelites' Sojourn in Egypt 51
   3.2.2 The Number of Israelite Generations in Egypt 53
   3.2.3 The Israelite Population 57
   3.2.4 Controlling the Israelite Population by Slavery 62
   3.2.5 Controlling the Israelite Population by Massacre 63
   3.2.6 The Etymology of "Moses" 65
   3.2.7 Moses' Father-in-law 66
   3.2.8 The Command to Return to Egypt 66
   3.2.9 Moses' Age 67
   3.2.10 Other Contradictions 68

4. The Exodus in the Qur'an 69
4.1 The Qur'anic Account 69
4.2 Biblical Claims Unsupported by the Qur'an 72
4.3 The Bible's "Israelization" of God and Religion 75

5. Biblical Dating of the Exodus 81
5.1 The Silence of History on Moses 81
5.2 The Pharaoh of Oppression and the Pharaoh of the Exodus 82
5.3 Historical Egyptian Elements in the Biblical Narrative 86
5.4 Contradictions in the Biblical Dating of the Exodus 91
5.5 Liberal consideration of the Biblical Narrative 93

6. The Qur'anic Identification of Pharaoh 97
6.1 One Pharaoh Not Two 97
6.2 A Long-Reigning Pharaoh 101
6.3 The Pharaoh "of the awtād" 107

    6.4 A Mummified Pharaoh..111
    6.5 Miscellaneous Notes..114

7. Who Was Hāmān? 119
    7.1 The Qurʾanic Egyptian Hāmān 119
    7.2 The Biblical Persian Hāmān 124

8. Leaving Egypt...127
    8.1 Dispersed Enslaved Israel 127
    8.2 Gathering Israel for the Exodus... 130
    8.3 A Night Escape 135
    8.4 Going East 137
    8.5 A Small Isolated Group 140

9. Post Exodus..143
    9.1 Polytheistic Behaviors 143
    9.2 Inscription of the Tablets 149
    9.3 The Holy Land..151
    9.4 The Failure to Enter the Holy Land 153
    9.5 Entering the Holy Land... 155
    9.6 Miracles 159
    9.7 Merneptah's "Israel Stela"..161

10. Pharaonic Massacres..167
    10.1 The Motive of Pharaoh's First Massacre 167
    10.2 The Second Massacre 169
    10.3 The First Massacre: History or Literary Motif? 172

11. Scriptural Names of the Israelites 177
    11.1 Who Were the ʿApiru/Habiru? 177
    11.2 Hebrews Hijack ʿApiru 179
    11.3 Jews: Moses' Followers 184

12. The Historical Exodus...189

Appendix A: Qurʾanic Verses on Moses 193
    A.1 The Chapter of al-Aʿrāf (the Heights) (7.103-137, 7.159-166) .. 193
    A.2 The Chapter of ṬāHā (20.9-97) 196
    A.3 The Chapter of al-Qaṣaṣ (the Stories) (28.2-46)......................... 199
    A.4 The Chapter of ash-Shuʿarāʾ (the Poets) (26.10-66) 202
    A.5 The Chapter of Baqara (The Cow) (2.47-71)............................... 203
    A.6 The Chapter of Ghāfir (Forgiver) (40.23-46)............................. 204
    A.7 The Chapter of Yūnus (Jonah) (10.75-93).................................. 206
    A.8 The Chapter of Isrāʾ (The Night Journey) (17.4-7, 17.101-104)207
    A.9 The Chapter of Dukhān (Smoke) (44.17-33)...............................207
    A.10 The Chapter of Zukhruf (Ornaments) (43.46-55).................... 208
    A.11 The Chapter of Maʾida (The Table) (5.20-26).......................... 208
    A.12 The Chapter of Naml (Ants) (27.7-14) 208
    A.13 The Chapter of An-Nāziʿāt (The Snatchers) (79.15-25).......... 209

Appendix B: Egyptian Dynasties and Kingdoms..............................211

References 213
    Works in English 213
    Works in Arabic 216
Index of Qur'anic Verses 219
Index of Biblical Passages 223
Index of Names and Subjects 227

Preface

This is a rewrite of our book *History Testifies to the Infallibility of the Qur'an: Early History of the Children of Israel* whose first edition came out 10 years ago and which has been translated into Arabic and Indonesian. The rework is so substantial that we had to call it a new book rather than a new edition of the earlier work.

We decided to rewrite the original book because we felt that it needed a number of improvements. **First**, feedback on the first book indicated that it was not easy to read. Some informed readers had to read the book twice to fully understand it. Clearly, it was not reader friendly. One major reason was the way the book was structured.

Second, the original book covered some topics that were not completely needed for a book that focused on the exodus. While those topics remain as interesting as they were, they are not as relevant to the subject of Israel in ancient Egypt, so we removed them from this book. For instance, the first book covered aspects of Jesus' story that have some subtle links to elements of the story of the exodus. These have now been covered far more comprehensively by one of us in a book that focuses on Jesus: *The Mystery of the Historical Jesus: The Messiah in the Qur'an, the Bible, and Historical Sources.*

Third, the text itself was also at times not easy to read, so we also focused on improving the language and readability of the text.

These changes have meant that the new book has almost a completely different structure. However, not everything has changed. The main arguments and conclusions of the book remain the same. Some sections of the new book still look similar to the corresponding sections in the older book, but even in these cases the text had to be substantially edited and improved. We believe that the new book is much better written, considerably easier and enjoyable to read, and completely accessible to the general reader.

We have also decided this time not to include the Arabic text of the Qur'anic verses. While the inclusion of the Arabic text was not an issue for the earlier book, most of the target readership of the book do not read Arabic and would find the text redundant. Furthermore, those who can read Arabic can easily check the Arabic origin of the translated Qur'anic verses should they wish to use a paper or electronic copy of the Qur'an.

This is why we have rewritten the book. But why did we write the original book in the first place?

Not many events in history have captured the imagination of the layperson and the scholar as much as the exodus. The scholarly interest in the history of Israel in ancient Egypt, in general, and the exodus, in particular, has triggered an enormous amount of research by historians, Biblicists, and archaeologists. Researchers have desperately clung to a shred of pottery unearthed from an ancient site or argued the reading or translation of a few hardly legible words from an ancient inscription to prove a point or another.

This interest of scholars in extra-Biblical data in the form of archaeological finds and ancient scriptural sources is in total contrast to their persistent neglect of the Qur'an. It is true that the Qur'an is not a traditional historical book like the Bible and that it gives only very brief information on ancient history of the Israelites. But the information it contains is significant in terms of both quality and quantity.

This attitude toward the Qur'an underlines two different assumptions. **First**, the Bible represents a perfectly or largely true account of history, so any book that contradicts or challenges it, as the Qur'an does, cannot be reliable. This is an assumption of faith, but it is one that influences many. **Second**, the Qur'an has unfaithfully copied much of its material from the Bible and other Jewish and Christian sources. This makes the Qur'an not an original, let alone credible, source of information. This view of the Qur'an is as old as the Qur'an itself. It was first held by Jews and Christians at the time of its revelation, and it remains faithfully subscribed to 14 centuries later.

It is true that a cursory look at the Qur'an would reveal similarities with the Bible. But the Qur'an implies that since Jewish writings, such as the Bible, are partly based on revealed scriptures and given that the Qur'an is revealed by the same and one God, these similarities are only to be expected. Additionally, these similarities are very limited and the differences between the Qur'an and the Bible are much greater in number and details. This general statement applies to the Qur'anic account and its Biblical counterpart of the history of Israel.

The right approach to assessing history in the Qur'an is to investigate it carefully and thoroughly and give it at least a small fraction of the time and energy that has been generously allocated to the Bible. If those interested in the historicity of the exodus had done so, they would have found a picture that is, unlike the Bible's, internally consistent and in line with external evidence. The Qur'an does not contradict itself, and it is free of those Biblical claims, or any other claims, that fly in the face of external evidence. Furthermore, the Qur'an reveals a number of facts about the exodus that lead to an unambiguous identification of Pharaoh.

We wanted to write a book that demonstrates that keeping the Qur'an completely out of the research into the exodus was unjustifiable. Muslims in particular would also be interested in this book's attempt to show that the accuracy of the Qur'an confirms its claim to divine origin and inerrancy. This is why we wrote this book.

When we published the first book, we hoped that it would create interest in the Qur'anic account of the history of Israel in ancient Egypt. We firmly believe that we made a strong case for further contributions to this subject and to the study of other parts and aspects of the Qur'anic text. Unfortunately, but also unsurprisingly, this has not happened yet. We still believe that this dismissive attitude toward the Qur'an will change, and our publication of this book is a confirmation of this belief.

We would like to thank our close friend Tariq Chaudhry whose comments on an earlier draft of the book helped us improve it considerably.

Introduction

The sojourn of the Israelites in Egypt and their subsequent exodus and settlement in Palestine have been among the most celebrated events of Biblical times. History, as related in the Bible, is very much the history of the Israelites who are portrayed as the "chosen people" of God and the center of His plans. It is just natural, then, to find that such eminence has been given to the sojourn, exodus, and settlement as these events represent the birth of the nation of Israel.

Not only Jewish and Christian lay believers have shown exceptional interest in the sojourn, exodus, and settlement. Scholars have been investigating every aspect of each of these episodes of the history of the Israelites. Thousands of popular and academic books and articles have been and are still being published and many scholarly lectures, seminars, and conferences have been organized to address every detail of these events. The scholarly interest in these triangular events may be divided into theological and historical. It is the historical aspect of these events that concerns us in this book.

While theologians are interested in the religious significance and implications of the sojourn, exodus, and settlement, historians' main concern is the historical value of these incidents. The question for the historian is not what these events meant in religious terms but rather whether they occurred at all and if so whether they occurred as the Bible describes them. Ultimately, historical research into the sojourn, exodus, and settlement has significant implications for the theology of these episodes.

The investigation of the historicity of the sojourn, exodus, and settlement was boosted from the late 19th century by the growing amount of information unearthed by archaeological excavations in Egypt, Palestine, and Jordan, in particular, and the Near East, in general. Historians needed no more to rely only on the Bible and other ancient Jewish sources as their only sources. Scholars interested in the historicity of Biblical events finally have in archaeological finds independent sources. The Biblical account, thus, started to be examined in the light of the new data. In the eyes of many, a totally new field of research has thus developed: "Biblical archaeology."

We will be examining the Biblical account and archaeological finds. But this book's main new contribution to the literature is its detailed investigation of the Qur'anic story of the exodus and its demonstration of the harmony of this account with external evidence. This book is a modest attempt to create what might be called "Qur'anic archaeology."

This book does not follow the trend common among scholars of trying to *rationalize* miracles and present them as normal events to convince the disbeliever and the skeptic reader that they did occur. It rather focuses on determining the historical contexts within which miracles took place. It is true that history consists, largely, of normal and natural events, but miracles also have influentially contributed to what history came to be and they will continue to do so. The crossing of the sea was one of those miracles without which the history of the world would have been totally different.

We need to explain some of the stylistic choices in the book. Each Qur'anic verse has been followed by a combination of two numbers identifying its *sūra* or "chapter" and its position in that chapter. For instance, the combination 28.3 refers to the 3rd verse of the 28th chapter.

We have consulted some English translations of the Qur'an, but the translations used are ours. We always use our own translations of the Qur'an because translation is an act of interpretation, reflecting the translator's understanding of the text.

Square brackets have been used to enclose explanatory texts that are needed to clarify the translation. Alternative texts, such as the English meaning of a term that is cited in its Arabic origin, are enclosed in round brackets.

A number of different printing styles are used in the book. A special font has been used for the Qur'anic text and another for Biblical passages. Roman transliterations of Arabic terms are in italics.

Let's now take a quick look at the contents of the book. **Chapter 1** presents the story of Joseph's entry into Egypt in the Bible and the Qur'an. It then discusses some of the problems in the Biblical account.

In **Chapter 2** we first explain why the absence of any mention of Joseph and Moses in ancient non-scriptural sources has no implication for the historicity of these characters and their stories. The chapter then uses the Bible, the Qur'an, and information from archaeological finds and historical sources to date the entry of the early Israelites into Egypt and identify the area where they lived. We also discuss the nature of the high position that Joseph held.

The story of Moses, and thus the exodus, according to the Bible is summarized in **Chapter 3**. This chapter also discusses problems in the Biblical account. These consist of discrepant passages, unrealistic claims, and statements that contradict established facts.

Chapter 4 first reviews the Qur'anic story of Moses. It then discusses a number of Biblical claims that are not supported by the Qur'an.

In **Chapter 5**, references in the Biblical account of the exodus that can be used, with the help of archaeological findings, to date that event are examined. The chapter also considers Biblical inconsistencies and discusses which references are more likely to be accurate.

Identifying Pharaoh according to the Qur'an is the focus of **Chapter 6**. The Qur'an contains information that allows us to identify this Pharaoh unambiguously.

Chapter 7 then studies in detail an important character in the Qur'anic story of the exodus called Hāmān. A Persian Hāmān is also mentioned in the Bible, but the chapter shows that the Egyptian Hāmān was historical whereas the Biblical Hāmān is unhistorical and the result of changing the story of the original Hāmān in the editorial work that the Biblical text went through over the centuries.

How Moses prepared the Israelites for the exodus and how they left Egypt are the subjects of **Chapter 8**.

In **Chapter 9**, the limited information in the Qur'an about Moses and the Israelites after the exodus is covered. The chapter also examines the earliest mention of the Israelites in an ancient record and its ramifications for the exodus.

Chapter 10 examines the Biblical and Qur'anic stories of Pharaoh's massacre of Israelites infant males at the time of Moses' birth. It also discusses the Qur'anic statement that Pharaoh ordered a second massacre of Israelites males after Moses' return to Egypt. The chapter concludes with a critical study of a misleading approach that reduces many historical stories, scriptural and non-scriptural, to motif works.

In **Chapter 11**, we discuss the various names given to the Israelites in the Bible and the Qur'an. We show how the Biblical term "Hebrew" is a misnomer that was used by the Biblical authors for a certain purpose. We also discuss the different etymologies that the Qur'an and the Bible give to the term "Jew."

Chapter 12 summarizes the findings of this book, telling the story of the exodus using the Qur'an and archaeological and historical sources.

The book has two appendices for reference. **Appendix A** compiles the longest accounts of Moses' story from various Qur'anic chapters.

Appendix B lists the Kingdoms of ancient Egypt. It gives a chronology for all Periods and the Dynasties that are more relevant to the book. It also contains a listing of all Pharaohs of the 19th Dynasty, which is when the exodus took place.

For the reader's convenience, the book has three indexes for Qur'anic verses, Biblical passages, and general names and subjects.

1

Joseph: The First Israelite in Egypt

Both the Bible and the Qur'an present prophet Joseph as the first Israelite to enter Egypt. In this chapter, we will study Joseph's story in both scriptures and then discuss some of the problems in the Biblical account. Relevant extra-scriptural information will be left to the next chapter.

1.1 The Biblical Story of Joseph

The story of Joseph occupies sections 37-50 of Genesis, the first book of the Bible.

Jacob, one of Abraham's grandsons, had twelve sons from four wives. He fathered 6 sons from Leah; 2 from her sister Rachel; two from Bilhah, Rachel's maidservant; and 2 from Leah's maidservant, Zilpah. Jacob loved one of Rachel's sons, Joseph, more than his brothers, because he fathered him in old age. In one expression of this love, Jacob made for Joseph a richly ornamented robe. Jacob's special love for Joseph made his other brothers hate him. Joseph used to report to his father any bad thing the sons of Bilhah and Zilpah did when he was out with them tending the flocks, and that did nothing to endear him to his brothers.

Joseph's brothers were further angered when their 17 years old brother recounted to them a dream he saw. Joseph saw himself and his brothers binding sheaves of grain in the field, when his sheaf rose up and stood upright while his brothers' sheaves surrounded and bowed down to it. Joseph's brothers disliked him because the dream suggested that he would rule over them.

Joseph then told his father and brother about a second dream in which the sun, the moon, and eleven stars bowed down to him. This dream angered not only his brothers but also his father who, having understood what the dream meant, rebuked him for suggesting that he, Joseph's mother, and all his brothers would prostrate to him.

One day Jacob sent Joseph to see whether all was fine with his other sons whom he had sent to graze the flocks. When Joseph's brothers saw him in the distance, they planned to kill him. One of them convinced his brothers not to do so but to throw Joseph instead in an empty cistern, which they did, after stripping him of his ornamented robe. Joseph's brothers then changed their minds and sold him for 20 shekels of silver to a caravan of Midianite merchants. They smeared Joseph's robe with goat blood and took it back to their father as evidence that Joseph was killed by an animal. The Midianite merchants then sold Joseph to Potiphar, Pharaoh's captain of Guard, in Egypt.

Joseph earned the trust of his new master who put him in charge of his household. Potiphar's wife then tried to seduce the handsome Joseph, but he refused to obey her. One day she was alone with him in the house so she tried her luck once again. She caught him by his cloak, but he ran out of the house, leaving the clock in her hand. In an act of revenge, she complained to her husband when he came back that Joseph tried to sexually assault her. Angry at what the slave tried to do, Potiphar put Joseph in jail.

At some point, the cupbearer and the baker of the king, who had angered their master, joined Joseph in the prison. Each of the two officials saw a dream which Joseph interpreted successfully. The cupbearer was going to be restored to his job in three days time while the baker's dream meant that he will be executed. Joseph asked the cupbearer to mention his case to Pharaoh, but the cupbearer forgot to do that.

Two years later, Pharaoh saw two strange dreams. In the first, he saw seven good looking fat cows that had come out of the Nile being eaten by seven ugly thin cows which emerged after them from the river. In the second, Pharaoh saw seven thin heads of grain swallow seven healthy and full ones. As Pharaoh looked for an interpretation for his dream, the cupbearer remembered Joseph so he recommended him to Pharaoh. Joseph told Pharaoh that the dreams meant that Egypt will soon have seven years of great abundance of harvest followed by seven years of famine.

Joseph also advised Pharaoh that he should appoint commissioners to collect a fifth of the harvest in each of the seven good years to store it for the years of hardship. Having been impressed by the now 30-year-old Joseph, Pharaoh put him in charge of implementing the food storage plan and made him second only to him. In the good seven years, Joseph gathered all surplus food from each city and stored it in fields around it. When the famine arrived, Joseph started selling grain to the Egyptians and others who came from abroad.

Like people in Egypt and nearby regions, Jacob and his family were hit by the famine. Having heard that there was grain in Egypt, he sent ten of his brothers to buy some. The only son that he did not send was Benjamin, Joseph's full brother, because he was concerned that he could be harmed. When the ten brothers came to buy grain from Joseph he recognized them, but they did not know him. Joseph devised a plan to bring Benjamin to Egypt. He accused his brothers of being spies, kept one of them in Egypt, and told them that they should not come back without bringing their youngest brother from Canaan as proof that they were telling the truth that they had come only for the food. He kept one of his brothers as a hostage, filled the bags of his other brothers with grain, secretly put the silver they paid for the grain back in their luggage, and let them go back to their land.

Having consumed all the grain they brought from Egypt, Jacobs' sons needed to go back to Egypt in the second year of the famine, but this time they took with them Benjamin, as Joseph had stipulated. After having the sacks of his brothers filled with food and the silver they paid for it also put back, Joseph instructed his steward to put his silver cup in Benjamin's sack. Shortly after starting their journey back to Canaan, Joseph's brothers were stopped by the steward who accused them of stealing Joseph's cup. After finding the stolen cup in Benjamin's luggage Joseph decided to keep him as a slave. One of his brothers then offered to become a slave to Joseph instead of Benjamin as he feared the impact of losing Benjamin on his father. During these exchanges Joseph decided to reveal his identity to his brothers. He then asked them to bring their father and families to settle in Egypt.

Jacob took with him to Egypt his sons, grandsons, daughters, and granddaughters — that is, all his offspring:

> All the direct descendants of Jacob who went to Egypt with him were sixty-six in number. (This number does not include the wives of Jacob's sons.) Counting the two sons of Joseph who were born to him in Egypt, all the people of the household of Jacob who were in Egypt numbered seventy. (Gen. 46:26-27)

Joseph continued to manage the distribution of food during the remaining famine years, buying from the Egyptians their property and ultimately buying them as slaves in return for food.

The offspring of Jacob, who by then had become known as "Israel," settled in Egypt in an area known as Goshen. The Israelites acquired property and their numbers grew greatly. Jacob lived the last 70 of his 147 years in Egypt. Like his father, Joseph also lived long — 110 years. When he died he was embalmed and buried in Egypt. Before his death, Joseph assured his brothers of God's promise to them: "God will surely come to you and lead you up from this land to the land he swore on oath to give to Abraham, Isaac, and Jacob" (Gen. 50:24). The Biblical story then ends with the dying Joseph asking his brothers to ensure that his bones are carried in the future to the promised land.

1.2 The Qur'anic Story of Joseph

Joseph' story in the Qur'an is mentioned in its entirety in one chapter which is named after him. The chapter of Joseph is the 12th chapter of the 114 Qur'anic chapters. It consists of 111 verses with the story of Joseph occupying 98 verses.

Joseph is mentioned only twice outside this Qur'anic chapter: once with a number of other prophets in a verse that talks about his great grandfather Abraham, and another when a believer in Egypt at the time of Moses reminded his people of Joseph who lived there centuries earlier:

> And We gave Isaac and Jacob to him (Abraham), each of whom We did guide; and Noah did We guide before; and his (Abraham's) descendants David, Solomon, Job, Joseph, and Aaron; and thus do We reward the good-doers (6.84).
>
> Surely Joseph came to you in times gone by with clear proofs, but you ever remained in doubt about what he brought to you. When he died, you said: "Allah will not send a messenger after him." Thus does Allah cause to err him who is an extravagant doubter (40.34).

The chapter of Joseph was revealed in Makkah, i.e. before the immigration of Prophet Muhammad to the city of al-Madīna. Some scholars think that the first three verses and the seventh verse of this chapter were revealed in al-Madīna, but there is nothing in those verses that supports this assumption.

The story starts with little Joseph recounting to his father a visionary dream in which he saw eleven stars, the sun, and the moon prostrating to him. Jacob instructed his son not to talk to his half brothers about the dream. They were envious of Joseph because they thought that their father loved him more than them. The Qur'an then tells us about a plan that Joseph's brothers worked out to get rid of Joseph. After obtaining their father's permission to take Joseph with them to where they graze their cattle, they threw him in a well.

Joseph's brothers thought that some travelers would find their young brother and take him far from the land of their father. Pretending to cry for losing Joseph, they returned to their father carrying their brother's shirt which they had smeared with some blood. They claimed that a wolf devoured Joseph after they left him unattended. As for little Joseph, caravan travelers found him, took him away, and sold him in Egypt. The person who bought Joseph is seen a few years later occupying the high position of the "'Azīz," which means "invincible" ...etc.

Joseph grew up into an extremely handsome young man, and the 'Azīz's wife tried to seduce him, but he rejected her advances. Women in the city then started to talk about the woman's fondness of Joseph. She invited them to her house, and in their presence threatened Joseph with imprisonment if he would not obey her. The chaste Joseph preferred being thrown unjustly in jail to committing fornication, so the 'Azīz's wife and her accomplices put him in prison.

At some point, Joseph was joined in prison by two men. Having seen in their inmate signs of righteousness and paranormal abilities, the two prisoners asked him to interpret two dreams they saw. Joseph successfully interpreted the dreams: one prisoner would be killed, and the second would be freed and returned to work as the king's cupbearer. Joseph asked the latter to tell the king, after rejoining his service, about the injustice that he suffered. Satan made the cupbearer forget about Joseph, so he stayed in jail.

A few years later, the king saw a dream and asked his court for an interpretation, but they could not help. This time the cupbearer remembered Joseph, so he asked for permission to go and ask his former prison mate for the interpretation. Joseph told him that there was going to be seven years of plenteous crops, followed by seven years in which there will be little harvest, before a year of copious rain sets in.

Having heard the interpretation, the king asked for Joseph to be brought to him. Joseph, while still in prison, requested through the messenger that the king questions the women who conspired against him. The 'Azīz's wife confessed to what she did to Joseph and acknowledged her guilt.

After setting Joseph free, the king wanted him to join his close circle and appoint him in a high position. Joseph asked to be put in charge of the storehouses of the land, and the king granted him his request.

During the years of famine, which Joseph had predicted, his brothers came to Egypt asking for food. They were allowed into Joseph's office, and he recognized them, but they did not recognize him. He gave them provisions but told them not to come back asking for more without bringing their half brother.

When they returned to their father, they told him about Joseph's decision and asked him to send their half brother Benjamin with them to get more provisions. Jacob, who had agreed to send Joseph with them years earlier, first refused. He then agreed to their request provided that they would take an oath to return Benjamin unless something out of their control would prevent them from doing so. They took the oath, so Benjamin went with his brothers to ask for provisions in Egypt. This time

Joseph secretly revealed his real identity to Benjamin who was being mistreated by his older brothers.

With the collusion of Benjamin, Joseph worked out a plan to keep his brother with him in Egypt, but without revealing his real identity to his ten half brothers. He accused Benjamin of stealing the drinking cup of the king and, consequently, took him as a slave and refused to allow him to return with his brothers.

Joseph's brothers' first reaction to this development was to claim that their other half brother, i.e. Joseph, had also committed a robbery. Later, they tried to convince Joseph to allow Benjamin to go back with them and take one of them as a slave instead. This offer, which Jacob's sons put forward because they had promised their father to bring back Benjamin, was turned down by Joseph. Jacob, who was still very sad for the disappearance of his son Joseph, though well aware through divine knowledge that he was still alive, lost his sight as a result of his unceasing sorrow for losing Joseph.

Jacob sent his sons for the third time to Egypt, this time to look for both Joseph and Benjamin. When Joseph's brothers met him, he revealed his identity to them. Completely stunned by the revelation, they showed genuine regret for what they had done and repented for their sinful behavior.

Joseph then asked them to take his shirt and put it on his father's face in order to restore his sight. He also asked them to bring his parents and their families to Egypt. When Joseph's shirt was put on Jacob's face, his sight was restored. Jacob's sons asked their father to pray to God to forgive them for what they had done.

In Egypt, Jacob, Joseph's mother, and his brothers prostrated in respect to Joseph who was occupying a high position. Joseph then drew his father's attention to the fact that this was the realization of the dream that he saw when he was still a young boy. In the last verse of the story of Joseph, we see this noble prophet in a magnificent thanksgiving prayer to God for the favors that He conferred on him and his family.

After the story of Joseph, the chapter concludes with ten general verses.

Readers interested in a detailed study of the Qur'anic story of Joseph may consult our book *Joseph in the Qur'an, the Bible, and History* (Fatoohi, 2007a).

1.3 Joseph's Age

The Bible states that Joseph was 17 (Gen. 37:2) when he was taken to

Egypt and that he was 30 (Gen. 41:46) when he was freed from jail and promoted by the king.

According to the Qur'an's account, when Joseph was abandoned in the well by his brothers and then found by caravan travelers he was only a "young boy" — probably 6-10 years old (also 12.11-12):

> And there came travelers in a caravan and they sent their water drawer and he let down his bucket; he said: "O good news! This is a young boy"; and they concealed him as an article of merchandise, and Allah knew what they were doing (12.19).

Then he lived in his lord's house until he became a young man:

> And when he attained his full strength, We gave him Wisdom and Knowledge; and thus do We reward the good-doers (12.22).

This age may be estimated to be 16-18 (Fatoohi, 2007a: 248), which means that Joseph lived in the 'Azīz's house for 6-12 years.

Then his master's wife tried to seduce him, and when he turned her down, she put him in jail, where he stayed for "several years" (from 12.42). This may have lasted for 4-6 years, though it may have been longer.

When the king released him from jail and put him in charge of the storehouses of the land, Joseph was then 20-24 years old. Thus, Joseph's rise to power happened possibly 10-18 years after his entry into Egypt.

Joseph had been in charge of the storehouses for at least the seven prosperous years when his brothers came to him at some point in the following seven years of hardship asking for provisions. Therefore, when Joseph met his brothers in Egypt, he was at least 27-31 years old, as we do not know in which of the famine years this meeting took place.

Joseph's reunion with his father took place after the third visit of his brothers to him. It is possible, therefore, that Joseph's separation from his father lasted 17-25 years. Jacob's entry into Egypt occurred some 20 years after Joseph's entry, or even longer if Joseph's brothers visited him later in the famine years.

1.4 Problems in the Biblical Story of Prophet Joseph

The relatively brief Qur'anic story has a lot of similarity with its much longer Biblical equivalent. However, there are also significant differences between the two accounts. In our detailed analysis of the Qur'anic story of Joseph in *Joseph in the Qur'an, the Bible, and History* we noted that, unlike the Biblical account, the Qur'anic story is consistent. The latter also contains many allusions which, although subtle, are essential to observe for understanding details of that story. The story of the Bible ignores such allusions and their significance, and this explains some of the inconsistency in that account. The lack of consistency and cohesion in the Biblical account is perfectly explained by the fact that the current surviving text is based on an original story that was subjected to a long editorial process that involved many people, which is how the text of the Bible in general came into being.

We will briefly identify here some of the flaws in the Bible's account of Joseph's story. These differ in significance. Some may be seen as weaknesses, but the majority are fundamental problems. The order in which they are listed here does not reflect the relative significance of each point, but often the order in which they occur in the Bible:

(1) The Bible claims that the seventeen-year-old Joseph was well aware of his brothers' envy of him, yet that did not prevent him from recounting his dreams to them. Even their bad reaction to hearing the details of the first dream did not make him refrain from relating the second dream to them.

(2) When describing Joseph's dream, the Qur'an mentions the eleven stars before the sun and moon: "O my father! I saw eleven stars, the sun, and the moon; I saw them prostrating to me" (12.4). This reflects the fact that the prostration of Joseph's brothers before him was going to happen before his parents', as shown in the Qur'anic story. Having failed to notice this subtle reference in the original tradition, the Biblical writers used the typical style of mentioning the two luminaries before the planets: "I had another dream. The sun, the moon, and eleven stars were bowing down to me" (Gen. 37:9). They did that despite their explicit statement that Joseph's brothers prostrated before him in both visits they made to Egypt to buy corn, i.e. before Jacob's arrival to Egypt: "Joseph's brothers came and bowed down before him with their faces to the ground" (Gen. 42:6), and "when Joseph came home, they presented him with the gifts they had brought inside, and they bowed down to the ground before him" (Gen. 43:26).

(3) One serious weakness in the Biblical account of the story of Joseph is its complete omission of the prostration of Joseph's parents to their son, although it is mentioned in the dream and in Jacob's interpretation! This omission is significant, because dreams play such a major role in the story of Joseph. The failure of the Biblical writers to mention the realization of a major element in a dream represents a failure to recount essential details of the original story.

(4) The Bible states that Jacob reprimanded Joseph for his dream, as if he was responsible for seeing it: "When he told his father and his brothers, his father rebuked him, saying, 'What is this dream that you had? Will I, your mother, and your brothers really come and bow down to you?'" (Gen. 37:10)!

This accuses Jacob, implicitly, of being ignorant of the fact that such dreams are divine visions, and that the person has no control over seeing them, or indeed seeing dreams in general. At the same time, the Bible points out that Jacob understood from the dream that the sun stood for himself and the moon for Joseph's mother, so he realized the truthfulness of that dream and knew its interpretation. The Biblical writers have fallen in an obvious contradiction.

(5) In the Qur'an, the decision of Joseph's brothers to cast him down the well represented a rejection of the suggestion to kill him. They adopted the alternative plan of abandoning him in a land far from where his father lived, thinking that some caravanners would pick him and take him away. Joseph's brothers cast him in the well instead of trying to give or sell him directly to those travelers because he was bound to resist such a plot and expose his brothers in front of the potential buyers. This was going to undermine Joseph's brothers' plan, and perhaps land them in trouble. The Qur'anic story is consistent.

In the Bible, we find one of Joseph's brothers convince the others not to kill their brother and to cast him in the well instead: "When Reuben heard this, he rescued Joseph from their hands, saying, 'Let's not take his life!' Reuben continued, 'Don't shed blood! Throw him into this cistern that is here in the wilderness, but don't lay a hand on him.' (Reuben said this so he could rescue Joseph from them and take him back to his father)" (Gen. 37:21-22). The Bible does not explain why the rest of Joseph's brothers agreed to Reuben's suggestion. When a group of merchants passed by that place, one of Joseph's brothers said: "What profit is there if we kill our brother and cover up his blood?" (Gen. 37:26), which indicates that although they threw Joseph in the well, they were still thinking of killing him. This clear contradiction prompts the question about their acceptance to cast Joseph in the well in the first place!

Joseph's brothers then sold him to Midianite merchants. This is another contradiction with the fact that they threw him in the well.

The cause of these contradictions and weaknesses is simple. The Biblical writers knew from the original story that Joseph was put in the well and that he was picked up by the caravanners. They did not understand, however, the causes of these events and their connection with each other. When they mentioned them and tried to link them to each other as they thought fit, the narrative came out weak and discrepant.

(6) According to the Qur'an, this was Jacob's reaction to seeing the blood-stained shirt: "[No,] rather your souls have suggested to you [doing] something [evil]; so, [my course is] perfect patience. And it is Allah whose help is sought

against what you describe" (from 12.18). In contrast, this was Jacob's reaction according to the Bible: "He recognized it and exclaimed, 'It is my son's tunic! A wild animal has eaten him! Joseph has surely been torn to pieces!' Then Jacob tore his clothes, put on sackcloth, and mourned for his son many days. All his sons and daughters stood by him to console him, but he refused to be consoled. 'No,' he said, 'I will go to the grave mourning my son.' So Joseph's father wept for him" (Gen. 37:33-35). The immense difference between the Qur'anic account and its Biblical counterpart reflects the great difference between the images of Jacob in the two books.

Jacob's reaction in the Qur'an reflects his *knowledge* that his sons have plotted an evil scheme and that their account was untrue: "[No,] rather your souls have suggested to you [doing] something [evil]"; his perfect, prophetic *patience*: "[my course is] perfect patience"; and his *reliance* on God to reveal the truth: "And it is Allah whose help is sought against what you describe."

Conversely, the Bible portrays Jacob as being *ignorant* of the truth of what his sons claimed. It even claims that Jacob did not believe his sons at the beginning when they came back from Egypt with the news that Joseph was still alive: "So they went up from Egypt and came to their father Jacob in the land of Canaan. They told him, 'Joseph is still alive and he is ruler over all the land of Egypt!' Jacob was stunned, for he did not believe them. But when they related to him everything Joseph had said to them, and when he saw the wagons that Joseph had sent to transport him, their father Jacob's spirit revived. Then Israel said, 'Enough! My son Joseph is still alive! I will go and see him before I die'" (Gen. 45:25-28).

(7) The Qur'an is absolutely clear about the reason behind the false complaint of the 'Azīz's wife to her husband that Joseph tried to seduce her. Her husband arrived to the house when she was trying to seduce Joseph. He saw how his wife and Joseph looked, and noticed that Joseph was trying to escape from the house with a torn shirt. This exposed what was happening, so the 'Azīz's wife rushed to accuse Joseph in order to repel the charge away from herself: "They raced with one another to the door, and she tore his shirt from behind; and they met her lord at the door. She said: 'What is the punishment of he who intends evil for your wife other than imprisonment or a painful torment?'" (12.25).

The imprisonment of Joseph was mainly intended to force him to obey the calls of the 'Azīz's wife and the other women: "Then it occurred to them after they had seen the signs that they should certainly imprison him for a while" (12.35). The 'Azīz also had an interest in putting Joseph in prison.

The Biblical account does not explain at all why Potiphar's wife accused Joseph of making advances toward her. It only says that she tried one day to seduce Joseph when "none of the household servants were there in the house" (Gen. 39:11), and that he fled the house leaving his shirt in her hands. Unlike her role in the Qur'anic story, Potiphar's wife was not under any pressure to explain away a situation that involved her and Joseph to have to accuse him in defense of herself. She looks to have accused him with no reason! Again, the Biblical writers were aware from the original story that the woman accused Joseph of trying to assault her, but because they did not mention the husband's unexpected return, the wife's action appears unexplained and aimless.

(8) The Qur'an explains why Joseph returned to his brothers their goods in the following verse: "He said to his servants: 'Put their goods in their luggage so that they may recognize them when they return to their family, so that they may come back'" (12.62). Joseph had two goals. **First**, he wanted to give his brothers goods that they can exchange for grain to enable them to return to him quickly. **Second**, he used that to influence his father so that he would allow his sons to bring Benjamin to Egypt. Witnessing the unplanned situation of his sons finding their goods gave Jacob more confidence in them and in their words about the kindness of the 'Azīz. This made him overturn his earlier decision and agree to let Benjamin go with his brothers: "When they opened their baggage, they found that their goods had been returned to them. They said: 'O our father! What more can we ask for? Our goods have been returned to us, and we shall bring grain for our family, protect our brother, and have an additional measure of a camel load; this is an easy measure to get' (12.65). He said: 'I will not send him with you until you give me a firm covenant in Allah's name that you will certainly bring him back to me unless you become completely powerless.' And when they gave him their covenant, he said: 'Allah is in charge of what we have said' (12.66)."

The Bible says: "Then Joseph gave orders to fill their bags with grain, to return each man's money to his sack, and to give them provisions for the journey" (Gen. 42:25), but without explaining why Joseph did that! Note also the following Biblical statement: "When they were emptying their sacks, there was each man's bag of money in his sack! When they and their father saw the bags of money, they were afraid" (Gen. 42:35). This means that the writers were aware that there was a link between Joseph's returning of the goods to his brothers and the latter's finding of the goods at home in the presence of their father. It is equally clear that the Biblical writers did not know Joseph's aim, so they did not say that Joseph wanted his brothers to find the goods *at home*. Joseph's decision to return his brothers' goods stayed in the text, but in the absence of any mention of the fact that it was part of Joseph's plan and of its role in that plan.

(9) The Bible claims that Joseph kept one of his brothers as a hostage so that his brothers would bring Benjamin to him: "he had Simeon taken from them and tied up before their eyes" (Gen. 42:24). It also mentions Jacob's sorrow for losing that son: "Their father Jacob said to them, 'You are making me childless! Joseph is gone. Simeon is gone. And now you want to take Benjamin! Everything is against me'"(Gen. 42:36). The Biblical writers, however, ignored this major event completely afterward!

Genesis 43 starts as follows "Now the famine was severe in the land. When they finished eating the grain they had brought from Egypt, their father said to them, 'Return, buy us a little more food.' But Judah said to him, 'The man solemnly warned us, "You will not see my face unless your brother is with you"'" (Gen. 43:1-3). Note how Jacob and his sons, or more appropriately the Biblical writers, overlooked the fact that Simeon was kept as a hostage by Joseph! In fact, Jacob ordered his sons to go to Egypt only to bring more provisions after they finished their stock!

(10) Jacob sent his sons again to Egypt because "the famine was severe in the land" (Gen. 43:1), yet the presents that he sent to Joseph do not suggest that they had a famine: "Take some of the best products of the land in your bags, and take a gift down to the man — a little balm and a little honey, spices and myrrh, pistachios and almonds" (Gen. 43:11)!

(11) The following two verses indicate that Joseph had a place to which he admitted special guests: "When they entered Joseph's place, he admitted his brother to his private place and said: 'I am your brother, so do not be grieved at what they have been doing'" (12.69), and "then when they entered Joseph's place, he admitted his parents to his private place and said: 'Enter into Egypt, Allah willing, secure'" (12.99).

This private room is referred to in the Biblical account, but in a different context: "When Joseph looked up and saw his brother Benjamin, his mother's son, he said, 'Is this your youngest brother, whom you told me about?' Then he said, 'May God be gracious to you, my son.' Joseph hurried out, for he was overcome by affection for his brother and was at the point of tears. So he went to his room and wept there" (Gen. 43:29-31). The Biblical writers knew that Joseph's private room played a role in the story, but they had no clue what that role was. They assigned to it the completely insignificant role of being the place in which Joseph wept.

(12) In the Qur'anic story, Joseph's plan to keep Benjamin with him aimed at ensuring that he would not lose contact with his father and brothers should the latter discover his identity and decide not to come back to him. In the Biblical story also, Joseph carries out the plan of accusing Benjamin of robbery. But the plot ends with him revealing his real identity to his brothers during the same visit! The Bible portrays Joseph's plan to accuse Benjamin as completely goalless. This is another real event that the Biblical writers knew of but did not know its role and

significance, so they ended up mentioning it as an aimless event!

(13) The Qur'an points out that Joseph's brothers asked him to take one of them as a slave instead of Benjamin, so that they could return the latter to their father and not break their covenant with him: "They said: 'O 'Azīz! He has a father who is a very old man, therefore retain one of us instead of him; surely we see you to be one of the good-doers'" (12.78). The Bible indicates that Joseph's brothers asked him to take them "all" as slaves "in addition to Benjamin": "So Judah and his brothers came back to Joseph's house. He was still there, and they threw themselves to the ground before him. Joseph said to them, 'What did you think you were doing? Don't you know that a man like me can find out things like this by divination?' Judah replied, 'What can we say to my lord? What can we speak? How can we clear ourselves? God has exposed the sin of your servants! We are now my lord's slaves, we and the one in whose possession the cup was found'" (Gen. 44:14-16)! The offer of Joseph's brothers was not only of no benefit whatsoever for them, but was also an invitation to Joseph to harm them!

The Bible then refers to a later event in which Judah asked Joseph to take him as a slave instead of Benjamin so that the latter can return to his father: "Please let your servant remain as my lord's slave instead of the boy. As for the boy, let him go back with his brothers" (Gen. 44:33). This is clearly closer to the real event than the earlier account.

(14) The Biblical story does not mention at all Jacob's loss of sight and Joseph's miracle of restoring it. There are references in the Bible, however, that could have originated from that ignored part of the original story. These references are God's promise to Jacob: "Joseph will *close your eyes*" (Gen. 46:4); Jacob's words to Joseph after they met: "Now let me die since I have *seen your face*" (Gen. 46:30); and the clause "Now *Israel's eyes were failing* because of his age; he was not able to see well" (Gen. 48:10).

There are more contradictions and inaccuracies in the Biblical story of Joseph. Its feeble structure is also all too evident to require highlighting.

2

Locating and Dating Israel's Entry into Egypt

We will first explain why the unavailability of any mention of Joseph and Moses in ancient non-scriptural sources has no implication for the historicity of these characters and their stories. We will then study how the entry of Joseph and the early Israelites into Egypt has been dated and how the place of entry has been identified. Arguments from the Bible, the Qur'an, and historical sources will be considered. We will conclude the chapter with a discussion of the nature of the high position that Joseph held.

2.1 The Silence of History on Joseph

There is no mention in the available ancient Egyptian texts and artifacts of Joseph or Moses and their stories. Egypt is dead silent on the Israelites' entry into Egypt and their exodus. More than a century of archaeological excavation in Egypt and Palestine has failed to unearth any evidence that explicitly and directly substantiates the history of the Israelites in Egypt. This has made some scholars deny the historicity of these characters and their stories. More generally, the absence of Biblical characters, places, and events outside the Bible has been used as evidence that they never existed and are mere inventions of the Biblical authors.

The fact that archaeology has nothing to say about a certain historical claim — whether Biblical or not — must not be seen as some form of refutation of that particular claim. *Negative evidence is no evidence.* What is found by way of archaeological excavation depends not only on whether what is being looked for had existed one day, but also on many other factors, such as whether one is searching the right site, the excavated area is large enough to yield significant findings, the site is being dug deep enough, and, above all, the sought remnants have resisted erosion in the first place. This is why the failure of archeological excavation to reveal any evidence does not, in most cases, mean anything as far as the historicity of peoples, places, and events is concerned.

The absence so far of independent, direct evidence attesting to the existence of important Biblical characters such as prophets Abraham, Isaac, Ishmael, Jacob, Joseph, and Moses should not be interpreted as indicating that these individuals never existed. Egyptologist professor Kenneth Kitchen notes that "time and again in Old Testament studies, we are told that 'history knows of no such person' as, say, Abraham or Moses, or '.... of no such events' as the battles of Genesis 14, for example." He rightly comments that such sweeping statements reflect "the ignorance not of 'history' personified but of the person making this claim." He gives a number of examples to stress the incompleteness of the current knowledge of the history of the ancient Near East, warning against rushing into premature conclusions about Biblical figures that are not yet attested in archaeological finds (Kitchen, 1977: 48).

There are many examples where historical records were treated with much suspicion for a long time because there were no archaeological findings to support them, before excavations brought to light supportive evidence. One example mentioned by Kitchen is that of the city of Ebla:

> Until 1975, Ebla was nothing more than a shadowy name: a once-prominent north-Syrian city alongside many more, such as Aleppo, Carchemish, Emanr and the rest. If anyone before 1975 had stood up and dared proclaim that Ebla had been the centre of a vast economic empire, rival to that of Akkad, under a dynasty of six kings, he or she would have been dismissed with derision. History "knew" of no such sweeping dominion, no such line of kings, no such preeminence. But since 1975, of course, the archives exhumed have changed all that. (Kitchen, 1977: 48)

This is why *absence of evidence is not evidence of absence*. In this book, no inferences will be drawn from negative findings.

In the case of Joseph and the early Israelites, there are more specific reasons as to why archaeological excavations have not yielded evidence on their presence in Egypt. As we shall see later in the chapter, many historians believe that there is strong circumstantial evidence that Joseph's story unfolded in northern Egypt during its occupation by non-Egyptian, Semitic people known as the Hyksos (ca. 1663-1555 BCE). The absence of Egyptian records referring to Joseph and the entry of the Israelites into Egypt can be attributed to the sparseness of records of the Hyksos period in general. This is why there are many unanswered questions about the history of the Hyksos. Not only the length of the reign of each of the Hyksos rulers is uncertain, but also the number of these kings. They represented the 15th Egyptian Dynasty (see Appendix B), although the 16th Dynasty was also related to them. The 3rd century BCE Egyptian priest and historian Manetho — as quoted by the 1st century CE Jewish historian Joseph ben Matthias, who is better known with his Roman name Flavius Josephus, and later Christian writers —

identified six Hyksos kings.

This absence of records is in turn attributed to two factors. **First**, the Hyksos had little influence in regions beyond the Nile Delta and northern parts of Egypt. **Second**, after the expulsion of the Hyksos, the Egyptians, who hated being under the rule of foreigners, wanted to forget this unpleasant period of their history. To erase the memory of the Hyksos, they launched a campaign that involved the obliteration and destruction of monuments erected by the Hyksos (Clayton, 1994: 94 95). This is what happened in the words of William Dever, Professor of Near Eastern archaeology at the University of Arizona:

> The end of the period [ca. 1800-1500 BCE] is marked by massive destruction levels at every site thus far excavated, undoubtedly to be correlated with the expulsion of the "Hyksos" beginning under the last king of the Seventeenth Dynasty, Kamose (about 1540 BC) and continuing under his successors of the early Eighteenth Dynasty. (Dever, 1977: 89)

Of course, it is not possible to rule out the possibility that finds that mention Joseph might be unearthed one day. The site of the Hyksos capital in Tell el-Dab'a/Avaris are today fields surrounded by villages, so a lot of archaeological evidence must have been lost.

There is another important point to stress. There are obvious inconsistencies and contradictions in the Bible (for instance, pp. 23-29, 50-68). This imperfection does not mean that the reported events are unhistorical. In such cases, one can say with certainty that two contradictory claims cannot both be true, but it is still possible, even though not necessary, that one of the accounts is true or has elements of truth in it. So, in the same way that a Biblical account does not necessarily reflect factual history, contradictory Biblical accounts of one event do not necessarily indicate that the event is unhistorical.

2.2 The Biblical Location of Israel's Entry into Egypt

The Bible states that the Israelites lived in Goshen, but this name is not found in Egyptian texts, so it cannot be associated directly with any of Egypt's known cities. But there are details in the Biblical story that link the settlement of the first Israelites in Egypt to the eastern Delta.

According to the Bible, Jacob sent his sons to Egypt to buy grain because of the famine that hit Canaan, and they later immigrated with their families to a prosperous Egypt. When asked by Pharaoh about their reason for coming to live in Egypt, Jacob's sons replied: "We have come to live as temporary residents in the land. There is no pasture for your servants' flocks because the famine is severe in the land of Canaan" (Gen. 47:4). The Bible suggests that going to Egypt in search of food was a rather frequent practice. For instance, during a severe famine in Canaan, Abraham went to Egypt (Gen. 12:10), and when another famine hit the land during the lifetime of Abraham's son Isaac, God instructed him not to go to Egypt (Gen. 26:2), which means that he would have otherwise gone to Egypt. The Bible also states that during the famine in Joseph's time "people from every country came to" Egypt (Gen. 41:57).

The significance of these statements is their harmony with the well established fact that Semitic herdsmen were often allowed entry into the eastern Delta during times of famine. One particularly useful piece of information is found in one of the Papyri Anastasi. These are named after the Swedish consul in Egypt Signor Anastasi from whom they were purchased by the British Museum in 1839. Papyrus Anastasi VI, which is thought to have come from Memphis, contains a report from an official on the eastern Egyptian frontier about the entry of Asiatic Bedouins (Shasu) from Edom to the Nile Delta escaping a drought and looking for pasturage during the reign of Pharaoh Merneptah around the end of the 13th century BCE. This text, which makes the Biblical narrative look plausible, reads as follows:

> ..... Another communication to my [lord], to [wit: We] have finished letting the Bedouin tribes of Edom pass the Fortress [of] Merneptah Hotep-hir-Maat - life, prosperity, health! - which is (in) Tjeku, to the pools of Per-Atum [of] Mer[ne]ptah Hotep-hir-Maat, which are (in) Tjeku, to keep them alive and to keep their cattle alive, through the great *ka* of Pharaoh - life, prosperity, health! - the good sun of every land, in the year 8, [intercalary] days, [the Birth of] Seth. I have had them brought in a copy of the *report* to the [place where] my lord is, *as well as* the other names of days when the Fortress of Merneptah Hotep-hir-Maat - life, prosperity, health! - which is (in) [Tj]ek[u], may be passed .... (*ANET*, 1950: 259)

Another piece of ancient Egyptian textual evidence that favors the assumption that the early Israelites dwelt in the eastern Delta is found in the Admonitions of Ipuwer: "A man of character goes in mourning because of what has happened in the land.... Foreigners have become people everywhere...." (*ANET*, 1950: 441). The Egyptians used the terms "men," "humans," and "people," as in this text, to designate themselves, in contrast to their foreign neighbors, who were not considered to be real people (Pritchard, 1950: 441). Ipuwer here condemns the Egyptianization of Semitic desert dwellers, which is again reminiscent of the settlement of Jacob and his sons in the eastern Delta. This is what a survey of such sources concludes:

> This review of epigraphic and archaeological data clearly demonstrates that Egypt was frequented by the peoples of the Levant, especially as a result of climatic problems that resulted in drought... from the end of the Old Kingdom (ca. 2190 BC) through the Second Intermediate Period (ca. 1786-1550 BC). Even during the Empire Period, there are records of hunger and thirst driving people from Canaan and Sinai to Egypt for relief. (Hoffmeier, 1999: 68)

Hoffmeier also notes that the literature of the First Intermediate Period (2181-2040 BCE) and Middle Kingdom (2040-1782 BCE) shows that the Asiatics' entry was primarily to the northeast Delta, and that archaeological evidence supports the written records (Hoffmeier, 1999: 62).

The story of Moses, which we will discuss in more detail later in the book, has also highly significant information about the Israelites in Egypt at the time of Moses. This information clearly links the entry into Egypt of the descendants of Jacob's twelve sons to the eastern Delta:

(1) The Israelites built for Pharaoh food store cities (Exo. 1:11) — something that is reminiscent of the rationing of food during the famine by Joseph, who himself lived in the Delta.

(2) Archaeologists have located these store cities in the Delta.

(3) One Qur'anic verse states that people at the court of the Pharaoh at the time of Moses had heard of Joseph (40.34).

2.3 The Biblical Dating of Israel's Entry into Egypt

The Bible is silent on the date of Joseph's entry into Egypt. But it contains details that strongly suggest that this entry into the eastern Delta happened when it was under the rule of the Hyksos. Researchers usually place the beginning of the Israelites' sojourn in Egypt in the period when the eastern Delta was under the control of the Hyksos.

Quoting Manetho's account of the Hyksos, Josephus (*Against Apion*, 1.103-105) thought that the Hyksos were the Israelites themselves. The Hyksos assumed power after the 14th Dynasty, around 1663 BCE, confining the authority of the Pharaohs to Thebes. These "Desert Princes," which is what the word "Hyksos" means, were Semites. Later Egyptian records claim that the Hyksos took control of the eastern desert and Delta regions of Egypt through a great invasion by a large number of people. However, scholars point out that there has been a continuous influx of Semitic immigrants to Egypt long before the Hyksos took control of the area. Evidence of this infiltration exists in the form of Semitic names recorded on a stela[1] from the Middle Kingdom and in lists of servants. For instance, a document from the 13th Dynasty (mid 18th century BCE) contains a list of names of eighty servants of a single Theban household, with more than forty of them stated to be Asiatic (*ANETS*, 1968: 553-554). There are also paintings from the 12th Dynasty (1991-1782 BCE) of Asiatics in the tomb of the noble Khnumhotep II at Beni Hassan in Middle Egypt (Clayton, 1994: 94). Excavations near the capital of the Hyksos in Avaris "have brought to light an assemblage of typically Palestinian material" that goes back to about 1800 BCE indicating that "the Asiatic presence in Egypt began quite early and was probably a peaceful infiltration at first" (Dever, 1977: 88). Thompson has also stressed that the influence of Semitics in the eastern Delta is visible throughout the history of Egypt and pointed out that "texts and archaeological finds from the Middle Kingdom (2040-1782 BCE) demonstrate noticeably the 'Egyptianization' of Semitic gods" (Thompson, 1977: 156).

The authority of these Semitic-speaking settlers increased gradually and late in the 18th century BCE they started to extend their rule beyond their base at Avaris (Clayton, 1994: 94). It was probably Pharaoh Seqenere Tao (ca. 1574 BCE) of the 17th Dynasty who started the military campaign to expel the Hyksos and he could well have died in one of those battles, as the terrible wounds on his embalmed skull suggest. His son and successor Kamose (1573-1570 BCE) then continued the liberation campaign of Lower Egypt. But as he ruled for three years only, the battles that finally brought the rule of the Asiatic kings to an end and expelled them from Egypt were fought by Kamose's brother and successor Ahmose I (1570-1546 BCE), the first Pharaoh of the 18th Dynasty, who ruled a re-united Egypt.

There are a number of elements in Joseph's story that favor the view that he lived under the Hyksos reign. Since these Semitics governed only in eastern delta, these details also confirm that the first Israelites' settled in that region of Egypt:

(1) The fact that the Hyksos themselves were not Egyptians but Semitics is seen as a factor that would have favored migrations of Semitics into the eastern Delta.

---

[1] An upright slab containing inscriptions and sculpture.

(2) Researchers have noted that "a non Egyptian such as Joseph could more likely have risen to prominence under the Hyksos than under 'native' rulers" (Thompson, 1977: 151). This is what the Bible says on the rising of Joseph to a high position in Egypt:

> "See here," Pharaoh said to Joseph, "I place you in authority over all the land of Egypt." Then Pharaoh took his signet ring from his own hand and put it on Joseph's. He clothed him with fine linen clothes and put a gold chain around his neck. Pharaoh had him ride in the chariot used by his second-in-command, and they cried out before him, "Kneel down!" So he placed him over all the land of Egypt. Pharaoh also said to Joseph, "I am Pharaoh, but without your permission no one will move his hand or his foot in all the land of Egypt." (Gen. 41:41-44)

(3) Another potentially significant observation is the use of the name "Jacob" by the Hyksos, as the second king of the Hyksos was called "Ya'qub-her." Researchers usually reject any correlation between the fact that the second Hyksos king was called "Ya'qub-her" and the possibility of Jacob residing in Egypt in the eastern Delta around that time (e.g. Kempinski, 1985). It should be noted that the name Jacob — like other Biblical names such as Joseph, Isaac, Ishmael, and Israel that linguists call "Amorite Imperfective" because of their construction — goes back to the 3rd millennium BCE (Kitchen, 1977: 68). However, although the name Jacob was in use long before the time of prophet Jacob, its appearance as a name for one of the Hyksos kings is highly unlikely to have been fortuitous. Interestingly, one of the kings of 16th Dynasty, who were contemporary to the Hyksos and operated by their authority, was also named after "Jacob": "Yakobaam."

If the name of the 2nd Hyksos king was indeed inspired by the name of Joseph's father, then Joseph's story must have taken place either during the reign of that king which lasted for 8 or 18 years, or probably during the rule of his predecessor and the founder of the Hyksos rulership Sheshi who may have reigned for 13 or 23 years. There is uncertainty about these figures, as is the case in general with the history of the 15th and 16th Dynasties.

(4) According to the Bible, Joseph's brothers took 20 shekels (about 200 grams) of silver for selling him as a slave to the Midianite merchants (Gen. 37:28). This is the correct average price during the first half of the second millennium BCE, which covers the Hyksos period. Inflation pushed the price up to 30 shekels in the second half of the second millennium and it reached 50 or 60 shekels by the end of the first millennium (Hoffmeier, 1999: 83-84).

(5) The Bible applies the term "saris" in its earlier meaning of "official" not its later meaning of "eunuch" to the married Potiphar who bought Joseph from the Midianite merchants (Gen. 37:36). Kitchen concludes that Joseph's career fits well into the period from the late 13th to the early 15th Dynasties (Kitchen, 1977: 74).

The Hyksos period and their capital in the eastern Delta are considered by researchers as the most likely date and place of the entry of the Israelites into Egypt.

2.4 The Qur'anic Location and Dating of Israel's Entry into Egypt

The Qur'anic account has some elements that, like the Bible, link Joseph to the Delta under the Hyksos. There are three such arguments in the Qur'an: the first confirms that Joseph lived in the Delta; the second dates the immigration of the early Israelites to the Hyksos period, which in turn confirms the Delta location, as the Hyksos occupied only that small part of Egypt; and the third confirms both the location and date of the Israelites' settlement in Egypt:

(1) Having found Joseph an honest and truthful man with paranormal abilities to interpret dreams, the king released him from prison and wanted to honor him. Joseph asked to be put in charge of the "storehouses of the land":

> The king said: "Bring him (Joseph) to me, I will choose him for myself." So when he spoke to him, he said: "Surely you are in our presence today [a man] with authority, [and who is] trustworthy" (12.54). He said: "Set me over the storehouses of the land; surely I am a good keeper, a knowledgeable one" (12.55). And thus did We give to Joseph power in the land, [that] he lives wherever he liked. We send down Our mercy on whom We please, and We do not waste the reward of the good-doers (12.56).

The reference to the "storehouses of the land" is in line with the view that Joseph lived in the Delta as this fertile land was often a sought destination at times of drought even by people from outside Egypt.

(2) The Qur'an agrees with the Bible that Joseph was promoted to a high position: "Surely you are in our presence today [a man] with authority, [and who is] trustworthy" (12.54). This promotion is more likely to have been done by the Hyksos than the native Egyptians.

(3) We come now to a piece of indirect Qur'anic evidence that Joseph lived in the eastern Delta when it was under the control of the Hyksos. This evidence comes from Moses' story. When Moses showed his first two miracles to Pharaoh, the latter accused him and his brother Aaron of intending to *drive the people out of their land*:

> We showed him (Pharaoh) all Our signs, but he rejected and refused (20.56). He said: "Have you come to us to *drive us out of our land* by your magic, O Moses" (20.57)?
>
> They said: "These are two magicians who wish to *drive you out of your land* by their magic and to take away your ideal tradition" (20.63).
>
> So he threw his staff down, and it became a manifest serpent (26.32).
>
> And he took his hand out and, lo! it was white to the beholders (26.33). [Pharaoh] said to the chiefs around him: "This is an accomplished magician (26.34) who would like to *drive you out of your land* by his magic; what is your advice" (26.35)?
>
> So he threw his staff down, and it became a manifest serpent (7.107). And he took his hand out and lo! it was white to the beholders (7.108). The chiefs of Pharaoh's people said: "This is an accomplished magician (7.109) who would like to *drive you out of your land*; what is your advice" (7.110)?

The "land" mentioned in these verses is made clear in another verse. Having seen Moses' miracles, Pharaoh accused him of practicing magic and asked him to prove the superiority of his feats by competing with the best magicians that he could gather from across Egypt. When the magicians lost the contest and witnessed what they knew for sure could not have been magic, in which they were experts, they declared their conversion to Moses' religion. This prompted Pharaoh to extend his accusation of Moses and Aaron of plotting to drive the people out of the land to the magicians as well:

> The magicians were thrown down in prostration (7.120). They said: "We believe in the Lord of all peoples (7.121), the Lord of Moses and Aaron" (7.122). Pharaoh Said: "You believe in Him before I give you permission? This is a plot that you have devised *in the city to drive its people out of it*, but you shall know" (7.123).

It is clear from verse 7.123 that the "land" referred to in the other verses above was a particular city. We know that the magicians were sought from various cities (also 7.111):

> They said: "Let him and his brother wait, and send to the *cities* summoners (26.36) who shall bring to you every skilled magician" (26.37).

So the word "city" in verse 7.123 could not have been equivalent to the whole of "the country," i.e. Upper and Lower Egypt, which consisted of a number of cities.

Now, Moses asked Pharaoh to allow him to take the Israelites and leave Egypt, so why would Pharaoh and his chiefs think of the strange accusation that Moses and Aaron, and later the magicians as well, had planned to drive the inhabitants of "the city" out of it? The answer is related to the painful memories of the Hyksos. The city that Pharaoh and his chiefs were talking about is Pi-Ramesses[2] in which Moses and Aaron met Pharaoh and where the contest with the magicians took place. This was also a city that was built on a site next to Avaris, once the capital of the Hyksos. Pharaoh did not believe Moses when he told him that he wanted to take the Israelites out of Egypt for good. He though that this was only the first step of a rerun of the disturbing episode of history when the Semitic Hyksos who came from the east took over the eastern Delta.[3] Moses, Pharaoh and his chiefs reckoned, would take the Israelites out to use them as a nucleus to build around it an army of Semitics to invade Lower Egypt to reestablish the Semitic kingdom again in the city that is now Pi-Ramesses.

But what has all this to do with Joseph and the place where he settled? Pharaoh and his chief would not have thought of this scenario had the people involved in Moses' request not been Israelites. They were well aware, of course, that these Israelites were the descendants of those forefathers who settled in the eastern Delta and had strong relations with the Hyksos. Joseph also was well known to them, which means that they knew that one of the Israelites' forefathers rose to a very prominent position in the Hyksos kingdom. This is how one of Pharaoh's people who believed in Moses addressed his people:

> Surely Joseph came to you in times gone by with clear proofs, but you ever remained in doubt about what he brought to you. When he died, you said: "Allah will not send a messenger after him" (from 40.34).

Pharaoh and his chiefs' wrong assumption about the ultimate purpose of Moses' mission represents another indication that Joseph, and the early Israelites, lived in the eastern Delta when it was under the control of the Hyksos. We will come to this point later on.

Clearly, the Qur'an agrees with the Bible in linking Joseph and the early Israelites to the Delta under the Hyksos.

---

[2] The Egyptian hieroglyphic script contains picture signs for the consonants of words but not for their vowels, hence the different spellings of Egyptian names in modern writings. This book uses the most common spellings of names.

[3] This may not necessarily indicate that the Hyksos' takeover of the eastern Delta was through invasion rather than peaceful infiltration.

There is also a significant difference between the Bible and the Qur'an that is relevant to the discussion of the location and date of the entry of the Israelites to Egypt. The Bible refers in the Book of Exodus to the monarch of Egypt as "Pharaoh" (e.g. Exo. 1:11, 19, 22) and "king" of Egypt (e.g. Exo. 1:8, 15, 17). This continues the tradition in Genesis in the story of Joseph where the monarch is sometimes called "Pharaoh" (e.g. Gen. 40:13, 14, 17) and in others "king of Egypt" (Gen. 39:20; 40:1, 5). In other words, the Bible does not differentiate between the terms "Pharaoh" and "king," using them interchangeably. This is a very significant difference between the Qur'an and the Bible.

Throughout the Qur'an, the monarch of Egypt in the story of Moses is invariably referred to as "Pharaoh." In no instance does the title "king" or "king of Egypt" replace "Pharaoh." On the other hand, significantly, the ruler of Egypt in the story of Joseph is never called "Pharaoh" but only "king" in the five verses that refer to him (12.43, 50, 54, 72, 76). The title "king" is used in the Qur'an for various monarchs, including the ruler who figures in the story of Joseph, but the title "Pharaoh" is applied exclusively to the monarch of Egypt during the lifetime of Moses.

We learned in Chapter 1 that the Qur'an states that the land to which Joseph was taken and to which his father and brothers later came is "Egypt" (12.21, 99), and that Moses also lived in "Egypt" (10.87; 43.51). Additionally, verse 40.34, in which an Egyptian believer reminds his people of Joseph, makes it totally clear that the Egypt which Joseph and his family entered was the same Egypt of the Pharaoh at the time of Moses. Why, then, does the Qur'an make this clear-cut distinction between the monarch in whose kingdom Joseph lived and the one under whose authority Moses lived, calling the former "king" and the latter "Pharaoh?"

The title "Pharaoh," which means "great house," was used to refer to the palace of the sovereign since the Old Kingdom. It was not used as an epithet for the monarch until the reign of Tuthmosis III (1504-1450 BCE) in the 18th Dynasty. So the Qur'an's use of the title "Pharaoh" to the monarch under whom Moses lived but not to the sovereign under whose rule Joseph lived is in line with the conclusion that Joseph lived during the Hyksos time when the title Pharaoh had not been applied to the monarch yet.

Significantly, the Bible also applies the title "Pharaoh" to the Egyptian monarch during whom Abraham is said to have visited Egypt (Gen. 12:15, 17, 18, 20). Abraham is believed to have lived at the beginning of the second millennium, and at the time "Pharaoh" was still being used only for the palace. The Qur'an also mentions a monarch with whom Abraham had a debate about God. Interestingly, it describes this monarch as "one whom Allah has given him kingship" (2.258), so it does not call him "Pharaoh."

2.5 What Position Did Joseph Occupy?

The Bible states that Pharaoh gave Joseph "authority over all the land of Egypt" (Gen. 41:41) made him "his second-in-command" (Gen. 41:43), and put him "in charge of all the land of Egypt" (Gen. 41:46). In another passage he is called "the ruler of the country" (Gen. 42:6), which again confirms his high status. The fact that he was second only to Pharaoh is confirmed as "all Pharaoh's officials," including "the senior courtiers of his household, all the senior officials of the land of Egypt," went with him to bury his father in Canaan (Gen. 50:7). But Joseph's unrivalled status seems to be contradicted earlier when we find him asking "Pharaoh's royal court" to get permission for him to travel to bury his father in Canaan (Gen. 50:4), but that lone statement may be ignored. Joseph's high status is also confirmed by the fact that his brothers greeted him by bowing down to him (Gen. 43:26, 28), although this does not specify his exact position.

The Qur'an tells us that the king granted Joseph his request and put him in charge of the "storehouses of the land." This would have been a high position in the administration of the fertile eastern Delta whose help with food provisions was sought by people from inside and outside of Egypt. After the seven good years and during the years of drought, in Joseph's brothers second and third visits to him, they called him "the 'Azīz." At the time they did not recognize him. They addressed him with this title first when they pleaded to him to detain one of them instead of their youngest brother whom Joseph, with the collusion of that brother, had arrested for robbery (12.78):

> They said: "O 'Azīz! He has a father who is a very old man, therefore retain one of us instead of him; surely we see you as one of the good-doers" (12.78).

The second time was when they came back to Joseph asking for further provision, hiding the real aim of their visit which was to request the release of their brother:

> So when they entered his place, they said: "O 'Azīz! Harm has afflicted us and our family, and we have brought poor goods, so give us full measure and be charitable to us; surely Allah rewards the charitable" (12.88).

Significantly, the Qur'an does not indicate that Joseph's brothers addressed him as the 'Azīz in their first visit:

> Joseph's brothers came and went in to him, and he knew them, while they did not recognize him (12.58). When he furnished them with provision, he said: "Bring to me a brother of yours from your father; do you not see that I give full measure and that I am the best of hosts (12.59)? But if you do not bring him to me, you shall have no measure from me, nor shall you come near me" (12.60). They said: "We shall ask his father regarding him, Indeed we shall do it" (12.61).

It seems that the 'Azīz was not simply the title of the keeper of the storehouses, the position that Joseph occupied immediately after leaving prison. It was rather a position of higher authority which he would have been promoted to later on and to which the office of the keeper of the storehouses was annexed. The word "'Azīz" means "invincible," "impregnable"...etc.

We also know from the Qur'an that the Egyptian dignitary who bought Joseph as a child was himself occupying the office of 'Azīz, as his wife is twice called the "'Azīz's wife":

> And women in the city said: "The wife of the 'Azīz is trying to seduce her servant; her love for him has possessed her; we surely think that she is in manifest error" (12.30).
>
> He [the king] said: "What was your matter when you tried to seduce Joseph?" They said: "Exalted is Allah! We knew of no evil on him." The wife of the 'Azīz said: "Now the truth has become manifest; I tried to seduce him, and he is surely of the truthful" (12.51).

One indication of the high status and considerable authority of the position of 'Azīz is that his wife, having falsely accused Joseph of trying to seduce her, put him in the same jail in which the king's two servants were imprisoned (21.36-45). The Old Testament also states that the king imprisoned his baker and cupbearer "in the house of the captain of the guard in the same facility where Joseph was confined" (Gen. 40:3), although the "captain of the guard" does not sound like a very high position.

Also, the fact that Joseph used the "drinking cup of the king" to implicate his brother Benjamin in a theft means that he had access to the king's belongings:

> So when he furnished them with provisions, he put the drinking cup in his brother's luggage. Then a proclaimer proclaimed: "O camel caravanners! You are certainly thieves" (12.70). They said and moved toward them: "What have you lost" (12.71)? They said: "We have lost the drinking cup of the king; and he who shall bring it shall have a camel load, and I am responsible for delivering that" (12.72).

So Joseph occupied a very high position, but was he king? There are three references in the Qur'an that have been interpreted as meaning that Joseph became king:

(1) After receiving his parents in Egypt, Joseph raised them on the "throne":

> And he raised his parents on *the throne*, and they fell down in prostration before him, and he said: "O my father! This is the interpretation of my vision of old; my Lord has indeed made it come true; and He has indeed been kind to me, as He released me from the prison and brought you from the nomad desert after Satan had sown seeds of dissent between me and my brothers; surely my Lord is subtle in making what He wants come true; surely He is the Knowing, the Wise" (12.100).

(2) Verse 12.100 is then followed by another in which Joseph thanks God for giving him "a share of kingship":

> My Lord! You have given me a *share of kingship* and taught me a share of the interpretation of talks. Originator of the heavens and the earth! You are my guardian in this world and the hereafter; make me die as a Muslim and make me join the righteous (12.101).

Note that the Qur'anic term "Muslim" does not refer to the followers of Prophet Muhammad only. It rather denotes anyone who believes in God and surrenders to His will.

(3) The third reference is found in Moses' following words to the Israelites:

> When Moses said to his people: "O my people! Remember the favor of Allah on you when He made prophets among you and *made you kings* and gave you what He has not given to any of the other peoples" (5.20).

Moses' reminder to the Israelites occurred shortly after the exodus from Egypt, which means that God made the Israelites "kings" during their sojourn in that country. But since it is highly unlikely that the Israelites attained any prominent position in Pharaonic Egypt which was always a hostile land to foreigners, this would have occurred in Lower Egypt under the rule of the Hyksos who were themselves non-Egyptians.

The understanding that Joseph became king combined with the fact that he was called the 'Azīz have made many exegetes of the Qur'an mistakenly think that the title "'Azīz" is another designation for the "king" and they have thus used them interchangeably. There is no evidence in the Qur'an that these two titles signify one and the same position. To the contrary, the contexts in which these titles are used suggest that they denote two different positions occupied by different people. Another clear evidence is found in verses 21.50-51 where the first verse mentions the "king" and the second talks about the "wife of the 'Azīz" not the "wife of the king":

And the *king* said: "Bring him [Joseph] to me." So when the messenger came to him [Joseph], he [Joseph] said: "Go back to your lord and ask him what the matter of the women who cut their hands is; certainly my Lord is aware of their guile" (12.50). He [the king] said: "What was your matter when you tried to seduce Joseph?" They said: "Exalted is Allah! We knew of no harm on him." The *wife of the 'Azīz* said: "Now the truth has become manifest; I tried to seduce him, and he is surely of the truthful (12.51).

This means that if the three Qur'anic references above really mean that Joseph was king, then he must have occupied this position later, after serving for years as the 'Azīz. In this case, Joseph must have been still occupying the position of 'Azīz as late as the time of his brothers' last visit in which he revealed to them his real identity, as in that visit they were still calling him the 'Azīz (12.88), but that thereafter and before his raising of his parents on the throne he became king.

However, it is possible to interpret the three Qur'anic references (12.100, 101; 5.20) in such a way that they do not mean that Joseph became king. These are the alternative interpretations:

(1) The throne: there are two possible meanings for "the throne." **First**, it denotes the throne of the powerful 'Azīz, as this position was next to the king. **Second**, Joseph was deputy to the king and deputized for him in his absence. This interpretation explains how Joseph was not a full king yet was at the same time sitting on the royal throne when his parents came to see him. This interpretation also explains how Joseph accused Benjamin of stealing the king's drinking cup. This would have been easy for Joseph to arrange if he had received his brothers in the king's court.

(2) The share of kingship: this also has two possible meanings. **First**, Joseph used the humble phrase "a share of kingship" instead of "kingship" to stress the limitedness of what he controlled, as he was not a "king" in the full sense of the word. **Second**, the Arabic term that is translated as "kingship" can also mean "property" or "wealth" (see, for instance, verse 4.53). In this case, the expression would mean "share of property" and would have nothing to do with kingship.

(3) Making the Israelites kings: the use of the plural might be thought to indicate that more than one Israelite, i.e. not only Joseph, became king or whatever the term here means. The use of the plural here is actually a linguistic *necessity* because it refers to the plural "Israelites." It would have been grammatically incorrect for the wording in verse 5.20 to have been "made you king" instead of "made you kings." It does not *necessarily* denote more than one king. There is no Qur'anic verse stating that any

Israelite in Egypt other than Joseph was promoted to such a high position. Moses reminded the Israelites that when God gave one or more of them "a share of kingship" then it is as if He made each and every Israelite king (see also pp. 77-78).

There is one interpretation that we can think of that would mean that making the Israelites kings did not mean that Joseph or other Israelites also became kings: the term "kings" may be used because the position that Joseph occupied was second to the king only and deputized for him.

In the absence of supportive evidence, it is not possible to rule out or in the possibility that Joseph became king, and whether any of his brothers or other Israelites also acted as kings.

3

The Exodus in the Bible

Genesis covers mainly the history of certain important and holy individuals known as the Patriarchs, concluding with the story of Jacob, who was also called Israel, and his son Joseph. The second book of the Bible, Exodus, then starts with the story of the Israelites after Joseph and then focuses on Moses' story. The latter occupies also the next three books — Leviticus, Numbers, and Deuteronomy — the last of which ends with the account of Moses' death. The first five books of the Bible are known as the "Five Books of Moses," "Pentateuch," or "Torah." In this book, we will deal mainly with the second book of the Pentateuch.

This chapter first summarizes the Biblical story of Moses before discussing problems in this account. These problems consist of discrepant passages, unrealistic claims, and statements that contradict established facts.

3.1 The Biblical Narrative

Exodus begins by telling us that Jacob's sons and their families, who migrated to Egypt to join his other sons Joseph and Benjamin, numbered 70. The Israelite population increased over the years until they became numerous. At an unidentified point in the future, a new king came to power. This must have happened a long time after Joseph for this king "did not know about Joseph" (Exo. 1:8).

Pharaoh was wary of the Israelites. He felt that they had become more numerous and stronger than the Egyptians. He shared with his people his ultimate fear: "If a war breaks out, they will ally themselves with our enemies and fight against us and leave the country" (Exo. 1:10). He set out to control the Israelite population, first by putting foremen over them and make them work hard, building store cities. As the plan proved a failure with the Israelites continuing to multiply, Pharaoh made them work even harder and turned their lives into a complete misery.

He then thought of a new plan to curb the growth of the Israelite population. He ordered their two Hebrew midwives to kill all male newborns and let only females live. But the pious midwives did not obey Pharaoh and managed to fool him into thinking that this plan was unworkable.

This prompted Pharaoh to come up with yet another plan. He commanded his people to throw in the river all boys that are born to the Israelites. It was during that time that Moses — the would-be deliverer of the Israelites — was born. Moses' mother hid him for three months, but when she realized that she could not hide him anymore she put him in a sealed papyrus basket and let it float on the Nile (Exo. 2:3).

Pharaoh's daughter and her entourage found the floating basket and pulled the baby from the water. They realized that he was a Hebrew child. At this point, Moses' sister, who was watching events closely, offered to get a Hebrew woman to nurse the child. Pharaoh's daughter agreed, so Moses' sister took him back to their mother. When Moses grew up, Pharaoh's daughter had him back and took him for a son (Exo. 2:10).

The story then recounts an important incident in the life of an adult Moses. One day he went to observe the hard labor of his people and he saw an Egyptian man attacking a fellow Hebrew man. Moses came to the rescue of the latter and killed the Egyptian. When this came to Pharaoh's knowledge, he decided to kill Moses, who had to flee to Midian (Exo. 2:15). Midian is believed to have included southern Palestine, southern Jordan, the Sinai, and western Saudi Arabia.

In Midian, he helped seven sisters water their flock. The girls' father invited Moses to his house and married him to one of his daughters, who gave birth to a son.

Moses worked as a shepherd for his father-in-law, but his life changed completely one day he was spoken to by God (Exo. 3:4). God told him that He has seen the misery of His people in Egypt and that He has decided to deliver them from their affliction and take them out of Egypt to the blessed and large land of Canaan (Exo. 3:8). He commissioned Moses to carry out his command.

God gave to Moses the authority to perform miracles to try and influence Pharaoh. Moses became able to turn his staff into a live snake and turn the color of his hand into white and then restore its original color. God also told Moses that if the Egyptians do not take notice of these miracles, then he should take water from the Nile and pour on the dry ground and it will turn into blood.

Moses told God that he was slow of speech and tongue and pleaded to Him to commission someone else. God became angry with Moses but told him that he will send his brother Aaron with him to speak to people on his behalf (Exo. 4:16).

Moses obtained the permission of his father-in-law to go back to Egypt. By this time, all the Egyptians who were seeking to kill Moses, including Pharaoh, had died (Exo. 4:19), so it was safe for Moses to go back.

In the first encounter between Moses and Aaron and Pharaoh, the two brothers tried to outwit Pharaoh by asking him to allow their people to make a three-day journey into the desert. Pharaoh rejected the request that would have meant losing the hard work of the Israelites for the duration of their absence. He forced the Hebrews to do even more work (Exo. 5:6-18). Struggling to meet Pharaoh's very harsh demands, the Israelites blamed Moses for their increasing suffering. Moses, in turn, shifted the blame onto God!

In order to convince Pharaoh that he was sent by God and that he should allow the Israelites to make their short journey to the desert, Moses showed Pharaoh the miracle of turning the staff into a snake. Pharaoh brought Egyptian magicians who replicated the miracle, but Aaron's staff swallowed up the other staffs (Exo. 7:12).

Moses and Aaron were involved in further miracles in the form of ten plagues of which Pharaoh's magicians could emulate only the first two. Moses turned the Nile into blood (Exo. 7:20); Aaron swamped the land with frogs (Exo. 8:6) and turned the dust into gnats that covered the land (Exo. 8:17); God caused a swarm of flies to invade Egypt (Exo. 8:24), and He killed all the livestock of the Egyptians (Exo. 9:6); Moses caused festering boils to break out on both people and animals (Exo. 9:10), made severe hail fall (Exo. 9:23), made locusts cover Egypt (Exo. 10:13), and covered Egypt with darkness; and finally, God killed all firstborns of the Egyptians and their cattle (Exo. 12:29).

During the first nine plagues that hit hard his country and people, Pharaoh showed various degrees of concessions but never agreed to all that Moses was asking for. After the fourth plague, when a swarm of flies invaded Egypt and destroyed the land, Pharaoh suggested that he would allow the Israelites to offer their sacrifice in Egypt rather than in the desert, but Moses rejected the offer. When Moses later threatened Pharaoh with bringing locusts that would devour the little crops that the plague of hail had left for the Egyptians and would fill their houses, Pharaoh asked Moses about who would be going to worship in the desert. Moses replied that all of the Hebrews would go and would take their sheep and cattle with them. Pharaoh had serious doubts about all the Israelites and their possessions leaving Egypt, so he offered to allow only the men to leave — another offer that Moses had to turn down.

After causing Egypt to be in total darkness for three days, Moses was summoned again by Pharaoh who came up with the better offer of allowing the Israelites to go but without their animals. This concession also did not go far enough for Moses. Finally, after the last plague, when every firstborn of the Egyptians and their cattle but not of the Israelites was killed by God, the desperate Pharaoh agreed to all of Moses' demands, allowing the Israelites and their flocks and herds to leave Egypt (Exo. 12:31-32).

Following God's commands, the Israelites plundered the Egyptians before leaving Egypt, convincing them to give them silver, gold, and clothing. Then the exodus began: "The Israelites journeyed from Rameses to Sukkoth. There were about 600,000 men on foot, plus their dependants. A mixed multitude also went up with them, and flocks and herds — a very large number of cattle" (Exo. 12:37-38). This exodus ended a 430-year sojourn of the Israelites in Egypt.

Having allowed the Israelites to leave Egypt with Moses, Pharaoh later changed his mind yet again and regretted his decision. Leading an army of chariots, horsemen, and troops, he gave chase to the Israelites until he overtook them when they were camping by the sea. When the Israelites saw the Egyptian army they were terrified and started to blame Moses for taking them out of Egypt, but Moses reminded them of God's promise, asking them not to lose faith in their Lord (Exo. 14:13-14). God instructed Moses to raise his staff and stretch out his hand over the sea to divide the water so that there would be dry ground for the Israelites to go through the sea. God then commanded Moses to extend his hand toward the sea to make the water flow back on the Egyptians, who followed the Israelites, and drown them. All the Egyptians died (Exo. 14:28).

After their exodus from Egypt, the Israelites were left in the wilderness for forty years as a punishment from God for their continuous grumbling against Him (Num. 14:26-35). Moses lived until he was 120 years old (Deu. 34:7). After his death, God spoke to his assistant, Joshua son of Nun, and ordered him to take the Israelites into the land He appointed for them. Thus, the sixth book of the Bible, which is named after Moses' successor, starts.

3.2 Problems in the Biblical Exodus

There are serious discrepancies, mistakes, and weaknesses in the Biblical story of the exodus, and these are the subject of this section.

Before discussing these problems, we should note that the imperfection of the Bible does not tell us anything about the historicity of the events concerned. Even when the Bible claims about an event is inaccurate or wrong, that still does not necessarily mean that this event is unhistorical, but obviously extra-Biblical data would then be needed to establish the historicity of the event or at least its likelihood.

Similarly, when the Bible makes two contradictory statements about an event then obviously they cannot be both true, but that also should not necessarily mean that this event was made up by the Biblical writers. Independent sources would then be needed to establish whether any of the two competing accounts is more likely to be historical. For instance, as we shall discuss shortly, it is impossible for the Israelites' sojourn in Egypt to have been as short as suggested by the Bible and for their numbers to have grown in that period as much as claimed by the same book. At least one of the two figures must be wrong. This inconsistency alone does not mean that the stay of the Israelites in Egypt or their later exodus are unhistorical, in the same way that the Biblical data alone does not allow us to conclude that any of these figures is historical. Such a conclusion requires extra-Biblical evidence. We will examine here, but more in later chapters, the Biblical account in the light of what we know from archaeology.

3.2.1 The Length of the Israelites' Sojourn in Egypt

Exodus 12:40 states that the "the length of time the Israelites lived in Egypt was 430 years." But this figure is contradicted in the Lord's following words to Abraham:

> Then the Lord said to Abram, "Know for certain that your descendants will be strangers in a foreign country. They will be enslaved and oppressed for four hundred years." (Gen. 15:13)

This Genesis passage seems to be cited by an early Christian called Stephen in his debate with Jewish leaders:

> But God spoke as follows: "Your descendants will be foreigners in a foreign country, whose citizens will enslave them and mistreat them for four hundred years." (Acts 7:6)

The 400 figure is seen by many Biblicists as a rounded figure of the more precise figure of 430 (e.g. Kitchen, 1966: 53; Noth, 1962: 100). It has been pointed out that there are instances of rounding off in the Bible. This suggestion fails to explain why there should be any rounding of as many as 30 years in a period of 430 years. This approach to reconcile the figures 400 and 430 also fails to address the apparent contradiction between the significant rounding off in Genesis 15:13 and the emphasis on the exactness of the 430 figure. In our view, the emphatic statement that the exodus occurred "at the end of the 430 years, *on the very day*" (Exo. 12:41) leaves no room for a liberal reading of the figure.

Some scholars have tried to accommodate both figures. They suggest that the 400 figure is the exact length of the sojourn whereas 430 covers the time that Israel spent in Canaan and then Egypt. They rely on versions of Exodus 12:40 that are different from the Massoretic text. The latter clearly makes the 430 years the time that the Israelites spent in Egypt. But the 430 years in Exodus 12:40 in the Septuagint covers the sojourn of Israel in "Egypt and in the land of Canaan," and the equivalent clause in the Samaritan Pentateuch[4] makes it the duration of the stay in "the land of Canaan and in the land of Egypt." It is argued that the 430 years covered the time from Jacob's return from Haran to Canaan, which is when God changed his name to Israel, according to Exodus. Subtracting the time from Jacob's return to Canaan to his entry into Egypt from 430 leaves about 400 years for the sojourn in Egypt (Riggs, 1971: 26-27).

Paul's letter to the Galatians is also said to support the 400 years sojourn view:

> Now the promises were spoken to Abraham and to his descendant. Scripture does not say, "and to the descendants," referring to many, but "and to your descendant," referring to one, who is Christ. What I am saying is this: The law that came four hundred thirty years later does not cancel a covenant previously ratified by God, so as to invalidate the promise. For if the inheritance is based on the law, it is no longer based on the promise, but God graciously gave it to Abraham through the promise. (Gal. 3:16-18)

Here the 430 is counted from the last confirmation of the covenant, which was made with Jacob in Canaan. Subtracting this period means that the sojourn lasted for about 400 years.

Support for the 400 years theory is also sought in Paul's following words in Acts:

> The God of this people Israel chose our ancestors and made the people great during their stay as foreigners in the country of Egypt, and with uplifted arm he led them out of it. For a period of about forty years he put up with them in the wilderness. After he had destroyed seven nations in the land of Canaan, he gave his people their land as an inheritance. All this took about four hundred fifty years. After this he gave them judges until the time of Samuel the prophet. (Acts 13:17-20)

---

[4] The Massoretic text is the Hebrew text of the Bible. It was copied and edited by a group of Jews called the Massoretes in the 10th century CE. The Septuagint is the Greek translation of the Bible which was done between the 3rd and 1st century BCE. Tradition has it that 72 translators were involved, hence it is also referred to as LXX, which is the nearest rounded number to 72. The Samaritans, who were shunned by the Jews after their return from the Babylonian exile, accepted only the first five books of the Old Testament or the Pentateuch. This text, which has differences with the Massoretic text, is known as the Samaritan Pentateuch.

Subtracting the 40 years spent in the wilderness after the exodus and the 7 years that the conquest of the land under Joshua took leaves 403 or about 400 years for the sojourn in Egypt.

Genesis 15:13 has a clear problem as it makes all 400 years spent in slavery. Yet Joseph was honored by the Hyksos and rose to a high position. His father and brothers also were well treated by the Hyksos. It is unlikely that the Israelites suffered slavery before the Egyptians expelled the Hyksos and took over the Delta. The Hyksos were expelled in the middle of the 16th century and the exodus took place before the end of the 13th century, so the Israelites endured slavery closer to 3 not 4 centuries.

Also relying on the Septuagint and Samaritan Bible, some scholars have concluded that the 430 years covers 215 years in each of Canaan and Egypt (Ray, 1986: 231-235; Riggs, 1971: 18-28). The Bible states that Isaac was born 25 years after Abraham's entry into Canaan (Gen. 12:4, 21:5), Jacob was born when Isaac was 60 years old (Gen. 25:26), and Jacob entered Canaan at the age of 130 (Gen. 47:9). These figures add up to 215 years and represent the time the Patriarch spent in Canaan. This leaves 215 years for the sojourn in Egypt.

One problem with this view is that "Abraham and Isaac were not 'children of Israel' but ancestors of Israel, and so their time in Canaan could not be included in the sojourn of Israel and his descendants" (Kitchen, 1966: 54). Furthermore, the Septuagint and the Samaritan Pentateuch are not considered as reliable as the Massoretic text and the different passages that such reconciliatory attempts rely on might be the result of exegetical work conducted on the original text (Ray, 1986: 234). The fact is that the 400 and 430 figures contradict each other, and the attempts to reconcile them are far from convincing.

3.2.2 The Number of Israelite Generations in Egypt

Another controversial Biblical claim is that only four Israelite generations lived in Egypt:

> Then the Lord said to Abram, "Know for certain that your descendants will be strangers in a foreign country. They will be enslaved and oppressed for four hundred years. But I will execute judgment on the nation that they will serve. Afterward they will come out with many possessions. But as for you, you will go to your ancestors in peace and be buried at a good old age. In the fourth generation your descendants will return here, for the sin of the Amorites has not yet reached its limit." (Gen. 15:13-16)

The coming out with many possessions from a foreign land in which

Abraham's descendants suffer enslavement and suppression is a clear reference to the exodus from Egypt. This is further confirmed by the 400 years figure which is close to the 430 years that Exodus 12:40-41 claim the sojourn of the Israelites in Egypt lasted. This implies that there were four generations between Abraham and Moses, but this is contradicted in other Biblical passages.

Exodus 6:14-26 state that Moses was son of Amram son of Kohath son of Levi son of Jacob. This genealogy is repeated in Numbers (26:57-60) and Chronicles (1 Chr. 6:1-3). This makes Moses the 4th generation after Jacob, who was Abraham's grandson, so it makes Moses the 6th not 4th generation after Abraham.

The Genesis passage seems to suggest four generations of 100 years each — that is 4 times the length of the modern generation. Ray (1986: 236) notes that "people in patriarchal times were recognized as living to be 100 years of age and older, as a general rule." Indeed, the Bible suggests that Levi lived 137 years, Kohath 133, Amram 137, and Moses 120. But Ray also points out that this length for a generation is not found elsewhere in the Old Testament. It may not be coincidental that the lifetimes of Levi, Kohath, and Amram add up to 407 years. If Moses took the Israelites out of Egypt when he was in his early twenties, then that would make about 430 years. As we shall see later in the chapter, there are implicit references in the Exodus that Moses was indeed a young man when he returned to Egypt, but then these are contradicted by other statements that explicitly state that he was 80 years old. Any such calculations — and one can think of many of them — are highly speculative.

The real problem with the four generation statement is that it implies that the number of the Israelites increased some 30,000-40,000 folds in such a small number of generations (e.g. Houtman, 1993: 512), as we shall see when we study the problem of the growth of the Israelite population in Egypt! The problem is actually even worse than it looks. Among those who entered Egypt with Jacob are his son Levi and Levi's three sons Gershon, Kohath, and Merari. In other words, Kohath, Moses' grandfather, was already born when the Israelites were 70. This means that the enormous increase in their number happened in 2 or 3 generations! It is worth noting one absurd yet inevitable implication of this genealogy. After the exodus, the number of the Kohathites males older than one month was 8,600 (Num. 3:28). In addition to Amram, Moses' father, Kohath had another three sons. This means that Amram and his three brothers must each have had roughly 2,150 sons and grandsons!

There has been a number of different approaches to solving the contradictions created or exacerbated by the four generations claim, focusing on interpreting the meaning of the term "generation" or the its Hebrew origin. Noth (1962: 100) considers the term "generation" in the modern sense of the word, and concludes that the 100 years that the four generations make up is a more realistic length for the sojourn of the Israelites. He rejects other irreconcilable details, such as the astronomical increase in the number of the Israelites.

Kenneth Kitchen, Professor Emeritus of Egyptology at Liverpool University, offers a different solution that reconciles the "four generations" (Gen. 15:13-16) with the 430 years that he accepts as the length of the Israelites' stay in Egypt. Kitchen, who is a staunch defender of the Bible's reliability, suggests that the Hebrew word *dôr* should not to be understood as "generation" in the modern sense. In his attempt to show that his suggestion that four *dôr* equal to 400 years is not a mere apologetic exercise, he pointed out that in Ugaritic and early Assyrian sources the word *dāru*, and hence the Hebrew word *dôr*, can mean "a 'span' or 'cycle of time' of eighty years or more" (Kitchen, 1966: 54).

There are at least four serious flaws with this assumption. **First**, even if this is a plausible definition of the term *dôr*, it does not explain why the Bible says "four" rather than "five" generations, as the latter would have been much closer to 430 — the supposedly precise number of years anyway.

Second, this attempt unjustifiably accepts one Biblical number as being precise but not another. Why would four *dôr* be equal to 400 and not 430 years, the other Biblical figure? Indeed, why would the four *dôr* be any of these figures at all? Why not 350 or 450, for instance, when Biblical numbers are imprecise and do not carry the usual meanings anyway?

Third, Kitchen's attempt suggests that the phrase "four generations" was inexplicably used to specify a period of time rather than the usual 4 levels of lineage. **Fourth**, it implies that it is merely fortuitous that the Bible repeatedly shows Moses to be the 4th generation from Jacob (Exo. 6:14-26; Num. 26:57-60; 1 Chr. 6:1-3).

Unlike Noth's suggestion that rejects the figures 400 and 430 in favor of 100 years for four generations, Kitchen's rather unconvincing theory that four *dôr* can equal 430 years does not deal with the fact that the Bible clearly makes Moses the 4th generation after Jacob. Kitchen's solution is to suggest that the Bible does not give Moses' full genealogy but "only gives the tribe (Levi), clan (Kohath), and family-group (Amram by Jochebed) to which Moses and Aaron belonged, and not their actual parents." He takes the fact that the Amramites were already numerous at the exodus to mean that "Amram must be considered to having lived much earlier" (Kitchen, 1966: 54), i.e. this Amram is not Moses' father but one of his distant ancestors.

Solutions similar to Kitchen's are advocated by Ray. This is what he has got to say about the term *dôr*:

> The Hebrews, like other ancient peoples, dated long periods of time in terms of lifetimes, or the cycle of a person's lifetime, the word *dôr* coming from a root meaning "to go in a circle." This is to be contrasted with the word *toledot* which is also translated as "generations," but in the biological sense of descendants. Therefore, *dôr* should be seen as a circle or cycle of time, rather than generations(s), as both etymology and context would suggest. (Ray, 1986: 236)

On the problem of Moses' genealogy, Ray (1986: 237) suggests that the Bible does not give the complete genealogy. Like Kitchen, citing Exodus 6:25, Ray claims that the names Levi, Kohath, and Amram represent the "the heads of the fathers' households of Levi according to their clans." He thinks that the name of Moses' father in Exodus 6:20, Amram, "may be a conflation of the name Amram who was the head of one of the third-generation families of Levi." He suggests that Moses' father was at least the grandson of the original Amram, but possibly a later descendant.

We find Kitchen's and Ray's treatments of the term *dôr* wholly unconvincing. The assumption that Moses genealogy is substantially incomplete has to be accepted as the only alternative to the totally absurd implication that Moses had 2,147 brothers and brothers' sons (Riggs, 1971: 30-31), but the reference to the four generations in Genesis 15:16 remains a problem. Also, these assumptions do not address the related problem of the astronomical growth in the Israelite population in a relatively short period of time, which we shall deal with in the next section. This is how Houtman concludes his discussion of the problems raised by the genealogy when considered with other Biblical material, including the reference to the length of the sojourn of the Israelites in Egypt:

> When one surveys the various explanations for the observed discrepancies one can only conclude that they are of a rather manufactured nature. It seems best simply to acknowledge that the manner in which the author has used material from the various sources at his disposal has led to a presentation which is not in every respect balanced and congruous. (Houtman, 1993: 514)

We agree with Houtman that the Biblical claims that the sojourn of the Israelites lasted for 400 years, 430 years, and 4 generations are impossible to reconcile. Additionally, none of these can be reconciled with the fantastic claim about the growth of the Israelite population during that relatively short period of time.

3.2.3 The Israelite Population

The Bible claims that the Israelites "were fruitful, increased greatly, multiplied, and became extremely strong, so that the land was filled with them" (Exo. 1:7). Pharaoh even feared that they would outnumber the Egyptians. More details are given later when the Bible tells us that at the time of the exodus the Israelite men numbered "about 600,000" (Exo. 12:37). This same figure is repeated in the book of Numbers in Moses' argument with God:

> Moses said, "The people around me are 600,000 on foot; but you say, 'I will give them meat, that they may eat for a whole month.' Would they have enough if the flocks and herds were slaughtered for them? If all the fish of the sea were caught for them, would they have enough?" (Num. 11:21-22)

The Bible mentions a more precise number in a census of the Israelites taken in the wilderness of Sinai and which gives more information about the age group of the males who made up that figure: "All the Israelites who were twenty years old or older, who could serve in Israel's army, were numbered according to their families. And all those numbered totaled 603,550" (Num. 1:45-46). This figure excludes the descendents of Levi, one of Jacob's sons. The total number of all Levites male over 1 month old was 22,000 according to Number 3:39 or 22,300 when computed by adding the numbers of those who descended from Levi's three sons: 7,500 (Num. 3:22), 8,600 (Num. 3:28), and 6,200 (Num. 3:34). Numbers does not specify the number of the Levite males who were old enough to fight, but if we presume that they were 50% of the counted Levites, then the Israelite army must have been around 615,000 males. This figure also excludes those who were too young, old, or weak to fight.

The 600,000 figure is at the center of a number of serious Biblical contradictions:

(1) The main problem with this figure is that it is in conflict with the combination of the following two Biblical statements: (i) the total number of the household of Jacob who settled in Egypt was 70 (Gen. 46:26-27; Exo. 1:5); (ii) the Israelites lived in Egypt at most 430 years

(Exo. 12:40-41). If we consider the reasonable assumption that there were as many Israelite females as males, the children these families had, and the elderly then the total number of the Israelites — that is all men, women, and children — who left Egypt with Moses must have been in the region of 2-3 millions. It is impossible that in 430 years only the population of the Israelites would have rocketed from less than one hundred to over 2 millions!

The Bible claims another two, shorter durations for the sojourn of the Israelites in Egypt of 400 and 215 years. These would make the increase in their Israelite population even more incredible.

Some Biblical scholars have attempted to account for the increase in population by appealing to extraordinary claims of ancient authors who suggested that Egypt's natural environment would make its inhabitants very fertile that a pregnancy could result in up to seven children! Rabbinical literature has attributed such fertility to the Israelite women in Egypt. However, Houtman (1993: 232) notes that it is not obvious from the Bible whether its writers viewed Egypt as "a land that was particularly suitable to produce a great nation in a short time" and that all that the account in Genesis allows us to conclude is that "Egypt was the land that enabled the forefathers to survive the famine, so that Israel did not prematurely perish."

Unimpressed by the impossibility of the 600,000 figure but unwilling to attribute the figure to human error, some scholars have suggested that the figure was not intended as an exact number of the Israelite men but rather as a symbolic figure that is used in the Bible to refer to an unspecified large number (Houtman, 1993: 70-71). This explanation brings in yet more problems without solving the one at hand, and there are a number of reasons to discard it. **First**, this explanation essentially confirms the unacceptable Biblical claim that the Israelites were a large nation, disputing only their exact number. **Second**, the Bible cites all kinds of numbers that are much less than 600,000, so the Biblical writers could have used any of these or closer figures if they did not mean 600,000 precisely. Particularly in the book of Numbers, whose name is derived from its coverage of various censuses and countings of the Israelites taken prior to breaking camp and leaving Sinai, there are many numbers smaller than 600,000, ranging between 22,000 (Num. 3:39) and 186,400 (Num. 2:9).

Third, the book of Numbers contains the counted numbers of the descendants of each of the twelve Israelite tribes, and the sum of these numbers, excluding the Levites', is 603,550 (Num. 1:1-46). **Fourth**, the Bible stresses in unambiguous terms that God ordered Moses to count each and every male individual: "Take a census of the entire Israelite community by their clans and families, counting the name of every individual male" (Num. 1:2). So, the Biblical writers must have really meant the large number of 600,000 which is presumably a rounding off of the more precise figure of around 615,000, as explained earlier. If this number is to be rejected as an exaggeration then all numbers that comprise it and which are listed in Numbers should similarly be discarded. In this case, we end up with a wholesale rejection of Biblical numbers, and it would not make any difference anyway as far as the historical credibility of the Bible is concerned whether we discount the figures because they are symbolic or incredibly inflated. It should also be noted that the increase in the Israelite population was regarded by the Biblical writers as a *fulfillment of God's promise to the Israelites*, so the writers of the Bible must have meant to say that the Israelites were numerous (Houtman, 1993: 232).

A number of scholars have suggested that large numbers in the Bible, not only the exodus figure, should not be taken literary. This is how one scholar put it:

> Large numbers have often been a stumbling block for accepting the Biblical accounts as legitimate records of history. If the numbers are simply reflective of a rhetorical device common in ancient Near Eastern literature, however, one may no longer question the integrity of the record by use of this argument. The large numbers are often simply figures of speech employed to magnify King Yahweh, King David, or others in a theologically-based historiographical narrative. (Fouts, 1997: 387).

Such attempts to salvage the historical reliability of the Bible contradict, as noted earlier, clear evidence that the Biblical authors meant precisely the figures they mention.

Some scholars have tried to deal with the inflated figure of six hundred thousand by suggesting that the Hebrew word for "thousand" did not mean thousand in this context, but "chief" or "captain," for example. Other attempts focused on applying a formula to the figure to reduce it substantially to a more realistic and less embarrassing figure. This is what the *New English Translation* (NET) Bible has to say, in its commentary on Numbers 1:21, about such absurd approaches:

> An army of 10,000 or 20,000 men in those days would have been a large army; an army of 600,000 (albeit a people's army, which may mean that only a portion of the males would actually fight at any time—as was true at Ai) is large even by today's standards. But the count appears to have been literal, and the

totals calculated accordingly, totals which match other passages in the text. If some formula is used to reduce the thousands in this army, then there is the problem of knowing what to do when a battle has only five thousand, or three thousand men. One can only conclude that on the basis of what we know the word should be left with the translation "thousand," no matter what difficulties this might suggest to the reader.

(2) There are a number of Biblical passages that explicitly state that the Israelites were smaller than other nations. These other peoples could not have been anywhere near the 2-3 millions that the 600,000 males figure suggests the Israelites were. These are some such statements:

> When the Lord your God brings you to the land that you are going to occupy and forces out many nations before you — Hittites, Girgashites, Amorites, Canaanites, Perizzites, Hivites, and Jebusites, seven nations more numerous and powerful than you — and he delivers them over to you and you attack them, you must utterly annihilate them. Make no treaty with them and show them no mercy! (Deu. 7:1-2)

> It is not because you were more numerous than all the other peoples that the Lord favored and chose you — for in fact you were the least numerous of all peoples. (Deu. 7:7)

> If you think, "These nations are more numerous than I — how can I dispossess them?" (Deu. 7:17)

> Listen, Israel: Today you are about to cross the Jordan so you can dispossess the nations there, people greater and stronger than you who live in large cities with extremely high fortifications. (Deu. 9:1)

> Then he will drive out all these nations ahead of you, and you will dispossess nations greater and stronger than you. (Deu. 11:23)

If there were at least seven nations in Canaan more numerous than the Israelites then there must have been at least as many as 21 million people living there!

(3) There were only two Israelite midwives, yet a nation of hundreds of thousands of women in the age of fertility would have certainly needed many more than just two midwives (Hyatt, 1971: 60). Professor Martin Noth (1962: 23) has also noted that Pharaoh's desire to prevent any growth of the Israelite population by killing their baby boys and the existence of only two Israelite midwives assume "that the Israelites lived very close together in Egypt, and had not yet grown so excessively numerous." The claim that the Israelites numbered 2-3 millions is irreconcilable with the statement that they had only two midwives.

The figure 600,000 is not only at the center of inconsistencies in the Biblical text, but its implications are also at odds with common sense and what any modern person would consider as reasonable. This is why although this huge number never bothered the Biblical writers, it started to be seen as a problem during the renaissance and this is how it is seen today (Houtman, 1993: 231-234). Cornelis Houtman, Professor of Old Testament at the Theological University in Kampen in the Netherlands, has pointed out that the historical value of the several hundred thousand figure was rejected since 1862 by J. W. Colenso, one of the fathers of modern Biblical criticism (Houtman, 1993: 70). Hayes refers to an 18th century essay by the German professor Hermann Samuel Reimarus (1694-1768) on *The passage of the Israelites through the Red Sea* which pointed out the impossibilities created by a literal interpretation of the Biblical narrative of the crossing of the sea. Noting the Biblical claim of 600,000 Israelite men crossing the sea besides other unspecified people, and estimating the numbers of women, children and animals, Reimarus concluded that the mixed multitude who crossed the sea would have consisted of, as paraphrased by Hayes (1977: 50), "about three million people, three hundred thousand oxen and cows, and six hundred thousand sheep and goats." Accordingly, "approximately five thousand wagons would have been needed to carry provisions and three hundred thousand tents would have been required to house the people at ten per tent. Had the multitude marched ten abreast, the three million would have formed a column one hundred and eighty miles long. It would have required nine days as a minimum for such a group to march through the parted sea." The precision of these calculations aside, this example shows that the 600,000 figure was vehemently attacked even by past critics.

Scholars who agree that the 600,000 figure is astronomically exaggerated have also pointed out that this figure is in conflict with established facts about the place and the time. Philip Hyatt has noted that the alleged large number of the Israelites cannot be credible given the number that could have been employed in Egypt (Hyatt, 1971: 139). Redford has sarcastically pointed out that "on the morrow of the Exodus Israel numbered approximately 2.5 million (extrapolated from Num. 1:46); yet the entire population of Egypt at the time was only 3 to 4.5 million!" (Redford, 1992: 408).

Baruch Halpern (1992: 105), Professor of Ancient History and Jewish studies at Pennsylvania State University, rejects even the much smaller figure of 80,000 given by the Egyptian priest Manetho. Frank Yurco (1997: 49) reckons that if the Israelites "initially included only the descendants of Jacob, then 6,000, or even 600, would be a more reasonable figure." Hyatt (1971: 139) has also suggested that "the correct figure is more likely to be a few thousand" and that "tradition has exaggerated the number in the years that intervened between the exodus and the earliest narrative."

Hyatt and other researcher (e.g. Dever, 1997: 72) have also noted that the desert between Egypt and Palestine could not have supported the 2-3 million people and their livestock that the Biblical version of the exodus claims. The Sinai desert could not support more than a few thousand nomads (Dever, 2003: 19). Researchers have also objected to the implications of an immigration of such a huge number of people into Canaan to which there is no evidence from archaeology.

Additionally, archaeological excavations of early Israelite sites in Palestine from the 12th century, which is when Israel entered Canaan, show smaller settlements with no support whatsoever to the astronomical Biblical figure.

Finally, what about a believer's argument that the Israelites population increased *miraculously* not naturally? This also has serious problems. **First**, this would have been an amazing miracle that lasted for centuries, so had this been the suggestion of the Bible, it would have certainly highlighted it and explicitly mentioned details of this stunning miracle. But there is nothing in the Bible suggesting that the increase in the Israelite population was miraculous. Exodus 1:7 states that the Israelites "were fruitful, increased greatly, multiplied, and became extremely strong, so that the land was filled with them." This would have been naturally followed by a confirmation that this increase was facilitated by a miracle, had this been the case, but no such statement is made. **Second**, other Biblical details about the Israelites, which we discussed in points 2 and 3 above, contradict the suggestion that they were a big nation anyway.

No matter how one looks at the figure 600,000, it cannot be taken seriously, even though the Biblical writers treated it as factual.

3.2.4 Controlling the Israelite Population by Slavery

Following from its extravagant claim about the explosion of the Israelite population, the Bible states that Pharaoh decided to enslave the Israelites and make them work hard to stop them increasing:

> So they put foremen over the Israelites to oppress them with hard labor. As a result they built Pithom and Rameses as store cities for Pharaoh. But the more the Egyptians oppressed them, the more they multiplied and spread. As a result the Egyptians loathed the Israelites, and they made the Israelites serve rigorously. They made their lives bitter by hard service with mortar and bricks and by all kinds of service in the fields. Every

kind of service the Israelites were required to give was rigorous. (Exo. 1:11-14)

There are some contradictions and weaknesses here:

(1) Pharaoh's ultimate aim of controlling the Israelite population was to prevent them from being an effective power, siding one day with his enemies and, ultimately, being able to "leave the land" (Exo. 1:10). This implies that the Israelites were already used as slaves and Pharaoh did not want to lose their services. The measures that Pharaoh took amount to enslaving people who were already slaves!

(2) The fact that the Israelites were slaves cannot be reconciled with the Biblical claim that Pharaoh wanted to control their number, because one would want to increase the number of slaves not decrease it. Also, this particular Pharaoh used to bring slaves even from abroad to cater for his obsession with erecting buildings all over Egypt (pp. 87-88).

(3) It is rather difficult to understand why Pharaoh would think that employing the Israelites as forced labor would stop them increasing.

(4) The employment of the Israelites as forced laborers had nothing to do with controlling their population. It was common practice for Pharaohs to enslave foreigners in their building projects (pp. 86-88).

(5) The Bible's suggestion that Pharaoh perceived the Israelite population as a danger could not have been true. By the time of Moses' birth, the Israelites had been dispersed throughout Egypt, as was the case with other foreign forced laborers, to cater for the needs for manpower (pp. 127-128).

3.2.5 Controlling the Israelite Population by Massacre

As birth control by slavery failed, with the Israelites further increasing, Pharaoh moved to the most extreme measure by ordering that all Israelite newborn boys, but not girls, to be killed. While the suggestion that slavery could have been used by Pharaoh to limit the Israelite population is rather absurd, it is fairly reasonable to expect a ruthless monarch to resort to massacre to control the exploding population of a people that he did not trust. However, the naive and clumsy way in which Pharaoh wanted to carry out his plan does not do lend much credibility to the Biblical story.

The Bible tells us that Pharaoh summoned the two "Hebrew" midwives and gave them the order to kill the newborn boys of their *fellow Israelites*! It is even more inconceivable that the midwives would go about killing each and every baby boy that they help with his birth — something that is supposed to take place in the midst of the babies' families and on a daily basis! Pharaoh's naivety in this plan is beyond imagination. It is obvious from Pharaoh's later questioning of the midwives about their reason for not killing the newborn boys that no Egyptian soldiers were accompanying them to carry out the killings and that the midwives were supposed to do the dirty job themselves.

If these images of an unbelievably naive Pharaoh were insufficient, the Bible adds yet another in which Pharaoh accepts the Israelite midwives' ridiculous justification of their failure to kill the innocent babies that "the Hebrew women are not like the Egyptian women — for the Hebrew women are vigorous; they give birth before the midwife gets to them" (Exo. 1:19)! The extraordinarily gullible Pharaoh did not even think of asking the obvious question about the point of the Israelites having midwives then! Professor Philip Hyatt concludes that the reply of the midwives should not be considered historical:

> The excuse offered by the midwives belongs in the realm of folklore, and is designed to show the superiority of the Hebrew women. In point of fact the Hebrew women may have been stronger and healthier than the Egyptian women of the upper classes, but they were hardly more so than all the Egyptian women. There is a touch of humour here. (Hyatt, 1971: 61)

Houtman offers a similar view:

> Taking the reply of the women seriously is the wrong approach. The narrative does not give information about the mode of delivery among Israel and in Egypt. The writer aims to tell that the king of Egypt has the wool pulled over his eye by two women who dish up a fantastic story. (Houtman, 1993: 257-258)

Let's also not forget that Pharaoh was not alone in his court and he would have been surrounded by advisors. The incredible credulity that the Bible attributes to Pharaoh must have been characteristic not only of the monarch but of his court also — an extreme example of exaggeration, to say the least.

A related indication on the historical incredibility of the Biblical account is what Houtman (1993: 188) terms as "the village atmosphere" of the story where, for instance, Pharaoh is shown to be in *direct* contact with the two Israelite midwives (see also Rogerson & Davies, 1989: 354).

Given that the Bible says that the Israelites were already numerous, hence a danger, and that Pharaoh wanted to annihilate the Israelites, Houtman also raises the reasonable question as to why Pharaoh would think of killing only the young boys and not the men as well. Killing the newborn males only would not have eliminated the danger of the already numerous Israelites.

The Biblical claims that Pharaoh ordered the murder of all Israelite newborn boys and that he enslaved the Israelites are also inconsistent with each other because the former would make the latter impossible (Houtman, 1993: 261).

Even in the highly unlikely scenario that the Israelites were living together, rather than deployed wherever they were needed like other foreign forced laborers, Pharaoh would not have thought of killing them to control their population. The obvious and far more useful solution would have been to deploy them to various building projects.

3.2.6 The Etymology of "Moses"

The Bible claims that the name that Pharaoh's daughter gave to the baby means in Hebrew "I drew him from the water" (Exo. 2:10). This claim has been rejected on two accounts. **First**, it suggests that the Egyptian princess knew Hebrew (Hyatt, 1971: 65). **Second**, the explanation given for the name depends upon similarity in sound rather than correct etymology. The name "Moses" (Hebrew: *Mōšeh*) could be an active participle of the Hebrew verb "*māšāh*," which means "draw out," whereas the Biblical explanation of the name requires a passive participle. One would expect the baby to have been called "he who is being drawn out" rather than "he who arises out of" (Houtman, 1993: 289; Noth, 1962: 26). The Biblical etymology of the name reflects a misunderstanding of the meaning of the Egyptian root from which the name Moses is derived (Thompson, 1977: 155).

Contrary to the Biblical view, scholars agree that Mōšeh is an Egyptian rather than a Hebrew name. It is a shortened form of an Egyptian name whose first element was the name of a god. Examples on such names are Ahmose, Tuthmosis, Amenmesses, and Ramesses. Such names were widely used in Egypt during the New Kingdom period (1570-1070 BCE). This is what one scholar notes:

> Ancient Israel did not know that Moses is in reality an Egyptian name, that it is a shortened form of Egyptian names like Ahmose, Tuthmosis, etc. The narrator of Exodus (2:1-10) did not know this either; otherwise he would hardly have missed the opportunity of explaining the strangeness of the name by the adoption and naming of the child by a daughter of Pharaoh. (Noth, 1962: 26)

It is interesting, however, that "Moses" is not prefixed by the name of an Egyptian God.

3.2.7 Moses' Father-in-law

The names of Moses' father-in-law in Midian are another Biblical discrepancy. He is called "Reuel" (Exo. 2:18) and "Jethro... the priest of Midian" (Exo. 3:1, 4:18, 18:1) in the Exodus; "the Kenite" (Jud. 1:16) and "Hobab" who is one of the Kenites (Jud. 4:11) in Judges; and "Hobab son of Reuel the Midianite" in Numbers (10:29). Kenites are said to be a subdivision of the Midianites or a clan with some sort of association with the Midianites, which is how the Bible's description of Moses' father-in-law as both Midianite and Kenite is explained.

Having more than one personal name, according to Kitchen (1966: 123), is due to the fact that many people in Egypt had double names. However, Moses' father-in-law definitely cannot be "Reuel" and "Hobab son of Reuel" at the same time! The Biblical account shows clear confusion. Hyatt points out that these variations are usually attributed to the fact that "the traditions concerning Moses' father-in-law gave him different names, sometimes identifying him as Midianite, sometimes as a Kenite" (Hyatt, 1971: 67).

3.2.8 The Command to Return to Egypt

This is what the Bible tells us God said to Moses at Mount Horeb:

> And now indeed the cry of the Israelites has come to me, and I have also seen how severely the Egyptians oppress them. So now go, and I will send you to Pharaoh to bring my people, the Israelites, out of Egypt." (Exo. 3:9-10)

After a rather long dialog between God and Moses, the latter returned to his family:

> So Moses went back to his father-in-law Jethro and said to him, "Let me go, so that I may return to my relatives in Egypt and see if they are still alive." Jethro said to Moses, "Go in peace." The Lord said to Moses in Midian, "Go back to Egypt, because all the men who were seeking your life are dead." Then Moses took his wife and sons and put them on a donkey and headed back to the land of Egypt, and Moses took the staff of God in his hand. (Exo. 4:18-20)

There are two problems with this passage. **First**, it is difficult to understand why Moses would not tell his father-in-law about the real purpose of his return to Egypt when his mission is anything but secret. Rather than telling him that he is going back to Egypt at the command of God to take the Israelites out of the country, Moses claims that his intention was to "see if they are still alive" (Exo. 4:18).

Second, when Moses spoke to his father-in-law, God had already commissioned him to go to Egypt to deliver his people and he had already decided to obey God and return to rescue his people. Yet the command to go to Egypt is repeated unnecessarily again: "Go back to Egypt, because all the men who were seeking your life are dead!" Hyatt (1971: 85) thinks that this must be due to the fact that Exodus 4:19 is from a different source of Biblical text.

3.2.9 Moses' Age

The Bible seems confused about Moses' age when he left Midian heading back to Egypt. Exodus (2:23) states that Moses stayed in Midian for a "long period of time." It also says that "Moses was eighty years old and Aaron was eighty-three years old" when they spoke to Pharaoh (Exo. 7:7), which means that Moses was that old when he left Midian.

This age is also implied in another combination of passages. **First**, Deuteronomy (34:7) states that "Moses was 120 years old when he died." **Second**, Joshua (1:1) claims that after Moses' death, the wandering of the Israelites in the wilderness after leaving Egypt ended and God ordered Joshua, Moses' assistant, to lead the Israelites into the *promised land*. **Third**, Numbers (14:33-34) tells us that that Israelites' stay in the wilderness lasted for 40 years. So Moses died at the age of 120 years, immediately before the end of the 40 years in the wilderness, which means he must have been 80 when he came back to Egypt.

The apocryphal book of Jubilees (47:1, 48:1) claims that Moses was 42 years old when he went to Midian and that he stayed there for 38 years (Jub. 48:2). So it also implies that he was 80 when he returned to Egypt.

Christian sources also confirm this age. The Book of Acts states that Moses was 40 years old when he left Egypt and that he stayed for 40 years in Midian, so returning to Egypt at the age of 80:

> But when he was about forty years old, it entered his mind to visit his fellow countrymen the Israelites. When he saw one of them being hurt unfairly, Moses came to his defense and avenged the person who was mistreated by striking down the Egyptian. (Acts 7:23-24)
>
> When the man said this, Moses fled and became a foreigner in the land of Midian, where he became the father of two sons. "After forty years had passed, an angel appeared to him in the desert of Mount Sinai, in the flame of a burning bush." (Acts 7:29-30)

This image of Moses being around 80 years old when coming back to Egypt is contradicted by other Biblical passages. Exodus states that Moses "had grown up" when he killed the Egyptian who was fighting with an Israelite. In the following day he tried to kill an Israelite. His flight to Midian, escaping Pharaoh's wrath, happened right after that (Exo. 2:11-

15). The Bible also says that shortly after arriving to Midian, Moses got married to Zipporah (Exo. 2:16-22). This suggests that Moses was still a very young man when he got married. Then there are two passages suggesting that Moses' sons were still young children when they left Midian with their parents heading to Egypt:

> Then Moses took his wife and sons and put them on a donkey and headed back to the land of Egypt, and Moses took the staff of God in his hand. (Exo. 4:20)

Now on the way, at a place where they stopped for the night, the Lord met Moses and sought to kill him. But Zipporah took a flint knife, cut off the foreskin of her son and touched it to Moses' feet, and said, "Surely you are a bridegroom of blood to me." (Exo. 4:24-25)[5]

Moses, therefore, would have been a young man when he arrived in the land of Midian and would have stayed there for only a few years before heading back to Egypt to rescue his people. This contradicts what other Biblical passages say.

3.2.10 Other Contradictions

There are also inconsistencies in the Exodus narrative of the miracles that God granted to Moses. For instance, after showing Moses the miracle of turning his rod into a snake, God granted Moses the miracle of changing the color of his hand to look leprous. Then He told him the following about the Egyptians: "If they do not believe you or pay attention to the former sign, then they may believe the latter sign" (Exo. 4:8). Although Pharaoh and his people rejected the first miracle, there is no mention of Moses showing them the second miracle.

Also, the claim that the Egyptian magicians were able to repeat the first two plagues of the blood (Exo. 7:22) and the frogs (Exo. 8:7) contradicts the fact that God allowed Moses to perform these miracles as paranormal feats that can be produced by the power of God only.

Another inconsistency, though of less significance, is implied in the story of Moses' birth. The beginning of the story (Exo. 2:1-2) indicates that Moses was the firstborn child of his parents, but later an older sister appears (Hyatt, 1971: 63-64; Noth, 1962: 25). A later Biblical statement (Exo. 7:7) also claims that Aaron was three years older than Moses.

---

[5] The appearance of the second passage in that particular context as well as its meaning remain a mystery.

4

The Exodus in the Qur'an

The Qur'an mentions the name of Moses in 34 Qur'anic chapters and gives more historical information about him than any other prophet. Some chapters (e.g. 19, 21, 33, 37) contain passing mentions or very brief details, whereas others give longer accounts. We have compiled in appendix A the 13 lengthiest accounts. The story of the exodus and related events occupy much of these accounts.

The Qur'an has a very different style from the Bible. The Bible addresses most issues in the context of relating history, whereas the Qur'an is not a history book. Although it contains historical stories about righteous and sinful individuals and nations, these are very limited and the emphasis is on the lessons behind them. In the case of the exodus, for instance, the Qur'an gives very little information that can be used to track the movement of the escaping Israelites.

Even when recounting history, the Qur'an has its unique style. It is eloquently succinct, and one aspect of its succinctness is bypassing details that are given prominence in traditional recounting of history. For instance, although the drowning of Pharaoh and his troops is the climax of Moses' struggle with the Egyptian monarch, this monumental ending is mentioned only very briefly. No details are given as to what exactly happened. Comparing this with the Biblical account makes the difference in style between the two books very clear.

Another aspect of the Qur'an's succinctness and limited interest in history per se is that it often does not mention the names of major characters or locations in a story. For more information on the Qur'an's unique style the reader may consult "History in the Qur'an" in our book *The Mystery of the Historical Jesus* (Fatoohi, 2007b: 513-518).

In this chapter, we will first review the Qur'anic story of Moses before discussing a number of Biblical claims that are not supported by the Qur'an. More differences between the accounts of the two books will be covered in later chapters. This chapter will also discuss a fundamental difference between the concepts of "religion" in the two scriptures.

4.1 The Qur'anic Account

After giving birth to Moses, his mother feared for his life. God inspired her to suckle the baby, put him in a coffin, and then let it float in the river. He made two promises to her: "We shall bring him back to you and make him one of the messengers" (28.7). The river drove the coffin ashore where it was picked up by Pharaoh's people. Pharaoh's wife wanted to keep baby Moses and persuaded her husband not to kill him as he may be of some use for them or even that they may adopt him. In the Biblical story, it is Pharaoh's daughter not wife who found Moses.

Having been suckled by his mother, baby Moses did not accept the milk of any wet nurse brought by the Egyptians. In the mean time, Moses' mother asked his sister to trace the young child, so she found him with Pharaoh's people. She suggested to them that she can find a nurse whose milk Moses would accept, and they agreed to the offer. The facts that Moses did not accept the milk of any nurse and that this happened because his mother suckled him are missing from the Biblical story, leaving the offer of Moses' sister difficult to understand. Baby Moses was back again in his mother's arms and the first part of God's promise to Moses' mother is already fulfilled.

Now a mature adult, Moses one day entered a city without being noticed by its people. There he was asked by one of his people for help in a fight with an enemy, who was probably an Egyptian. Moses intervened, striking the enemy fatally. The next day, the same person asked Moses again for help against another Egyptian. When Moses was about to kill the man, the Egyptian reminded him that he is behaving like a tyrant rather than a reformer. Moses restrained himself and did not hurt him. In the Bible, the second quarrel was between two Hebrews.

Then a man came from the city carrying the disturbing news of a plot by some chiefs to kill Moses. The man advised Moses to leave the city. Moses left Egypt and headed toward Midian. There he arrived at a place where some people were watering their flocks. His attention was drawn to two women who were not competing with the others for the water, so he asked them what the matter was. They told him that they could not water their flocks until the shepherds had finished watering theirs. They also told him that their father was an elderly man so they had to do the job. Moses then watered their flocks for them before resting in a shade.

Later on, one of the sisters came back to tell Moses that her father would like to invite him to reward him for helping his daughters. Moses told the girls' father his whole story. The old man then assured him that he was safe in Midian. One of the daughters suggested to her father that he should employ Moses on account of his strength and trustworthiness. The elderly man offered Moses that he marries one of his daughters and, in return, Moses would work for him for eight to ten years. Moses accepted the offer.

Having fulfilled the terms of the agreement, Moses took his pregnant wife and left Midian. It was a cold night and Moses and his wife were on the road when he noticed a fire in the distance. He asked his wife to wait while he went to bring a firebrand to use as a light and source of heat or ask the people who started the fire about the road. When he arrived at the valley where the fire was he was called by God who told him that He has chosen him to be one of His messengers. God's second promise to Moses' mother was thus also fulfilled.

God ordered Moses to throw his staff to the ground and made it turn into a running snake before returning it as it was. He then instructed Moses to enter his hand into his bosom and then pull it out turning it snow white but without harm. Having granted him these two miracles, God ordered Moses to go to Pharaoh to tell him that he must worship God and allow the Israelites to leave Egypt with him. Moses asked God to send with him his brother Aaron to help him when speaking to Pharaoh, because he had a speech impediment. God agreed to Moses' request. Moses was also concerned that the Egyptians might try to kill him for killing one of them, but God reassured him that He will protect him and his brother.

Pharaoh refused to believe Moses despite seeing the two miracles of turning the staff into a running snake and whitening his hand. Accusing Moses of being a magician, Pharaoh brought magicians from across Egypt to compete with Moses. Moses won the competition and the magicians found themselves thrown to the ground in prostration. The magicians immediately recognized that the power supporting Moses had nothing to do with magic and could only have been of divine origin, exactly as Moses claimed. They declared their belief in Moses' message, causing the frustrated Pharaoh to threaten them with torture and death.

At the command of God, Moses and Aaron settled in Egypt. Then five plagues involving flood, locusts, lice, frogs, and blood hit Pharaoh and his people. The signs from God proved that Moses is a genuine messenger of God and that they must release the Israelites and allow them to leave Egypt. After the last plague had struck, Pharaoh said to Moses that he would let the Israelites leave with him if he would ask God to put an end to the plague. Moses did what Pharaoh asked for, but the latter broke his word. God then ordered Moses to take his people and leave Egypt under the cover of the night. According to the Bible, Pharaoh allowed the Israelites to leave Egypt and changed his mind only after they had gone. The Qur'anic version is more realistic.

Pharaoh then prepared an army and went after the escapees. When the Egyptians became so close to the Israelites that both sides were able to see each other, God instructed Moses to split the sea with a strike of his staff and cross with his people to the other side through the dry path that was created. When Pharaoh and his army tried to follow the Israelites on the same dry path through the sea, the sea returned to its normal condition and they all drowned.

The Qur'an also gives details about problems that the Israelites created for Moses mainly because of their disobedience. The culmination of this was the Israelites' refusal to enter the land that God gave them because they were afraid of its inhabitants. As a result, He punished them, prohibiting them from entering that land for forty years which they had to spend wandering. The Qur'an also mentions other events involving Moses, including parts of his dialogues with God.

Appendix A contains the story of Moses in the 13 chapters that contain the lengthiest accounts of this story. Other details of the story in other chapters in the Qur'an will be cited later in the book.

4.2 Biblical Claims Unsupported by the Qur'an

In addition to contradicting details of the Biblical story of Moses and exodus, the Qur'an is also free of a number of Biblical claims. We will focus here on claims that have attracted critical attention from scholars, covering them in the order of their appearance in the Bible:

(1) The Bible claims that Pharaoh's daughter called the baby "Moses" because she thought this name meant in Hebrew "I drew him from the water" (Exo. 2:10). As already discussed in (pp. 65-65), this etymology is wrong, reflecting a misunderstanding on the part of the Biblical writers of the Egyptian root from which the name is derived. This erroneous etymology is not found in the Qur'an.

(2) Another Biblical claim that does not exist in the Qur'an is Pharaoh's commissioning of two midwives to kill the newborn males. We have discussed this story and showed that it is too absurd to have happened (pp. 63-64). Despite its absence from the Qur'an, this Biblical story has proved popular among Muslim historians and exegetes (e.g. al-Marāghī, 1946b: 108; al-Qurṭubī's commentary on verse 28.7; aṭ-Ṭabarī, undated: 199; aṭ-Ṭabarsī, 1961: 266-267). The popular tendency to integrate Biblical details into Qur'anic exegetical works can only give a confusing and inaccurate picture of the Qur'anic account. Muslim exegetical works are also often filled with details whose sources are difficult to identify. These details seem to serve the purpose of

developing accounts that are richer in detail than the Qur'an's.

(3) The Qur'an does not support all the miracles and plagues mentioned in the Bible. According to the Bible, in addition to Moses' miracle of turning his staff into a snake, Pharaoh and his people where hit by ten plagues: i) the Nile turned into blood; ii) the land was swamped with frogs; iii) dust turned into gnats and covered the land; iv) a swarm of flies invaded Egypt; v) all the livestock of the Egyptians were killed; vi) festering boils broke out on both people and animals; vii) severe hail fell; viii) locusts covered Egypt; ix) darkness covered Egypt; x) all firstborns of the Egyptians and their cattle were killed.

As well as turning of his staff into a snake, Moses is credited in the Qur'an with the miracle of turning his hand into snow white. The latter is mentioned in the Bible as one of the miracles that God allowed Moses to perform, but it does not mention that he performed it. The Qur'an says that God granted Moses nine miracles (see also 27.12) and it names five plagues that hit Egypt:

> We gave Moses nine manifest signs. Ask the Children of Israel [about] when he came to them, and Pharaoh said to him: "Moses, I think you are bewitched" (17.101). He said: "You know that none sent these down other than the Lord of the heavens and earth as proofs; I think, O Pharaoh, that you are cursed!" (17.102).
>
> We tested Pharaoh's people with droughts and shortage of crops that they may heed (7.130). When good befalls them they would say: "This is due to us," and when evil afflicts them, they would attribute it to the ill fortune of Moses and those with him; surely their ill fortune is only from Allah, but most of them do not know (7.131). They said: "Whatever sign you may bring to bewitch us, we will not believe you" (7.132). We sent on them the flood, the locusts, the lice, the frogs, and the blood as clear signs; but they behaved arrogantly and were guilty (7.133). When the plague hit them, they said: "O Moses! Pray to your Lord for us, by whatever covenant He has with you, that if you remove the plague from us we will believe you and we will send away with you the Children of Israel" (7.134).

Moses' two miracles with his staff and hand and the five plagues make up a total of seven. The unspecified torment mentioned in verse 7.134 is the eighth, and the parting of the sea is the ninth. Particularly interesting is the absence of the Biblical miracle of the killing of the firstborns of the Egyptians and their cattle.

(4) The Qur'an contains no mention of the Biblical claim that God instructed Moses to tell the Israelites to appropriate valuables from the Egyptians before leaving (also Exo. 3:21-22, 11:2 3):

> Now the Israelites had done as Moses told them — they had requested

from the Egyptians silver and gold items and clothing. The Lord gave the people favor in the sight of the Egyptians, and they gave them whatever they wanted, and so they plundered Egypt. (Exo. 12:35-36)

Many scholars have objected to the historicity of the despoliation of the Egyptians by the Israelites for a number of reasons. Leaving aside the Bible's claim that God intervened in this event, it is difficult to understand why the Egyptians would give jewelry to the Israelite slaves (Hyatt, 1971: 138), let alone the fact that these slaves were, though indirectly, behind the devastating plagues that afflicted them. Additionally, Exodus (12:33) states that "the Egyptians were urging the people on, in order to send them out of the land quickly." The Egyptians could not have agreed to the Israelites' request and given them jewelry with the full knowledge that they would never see their valuables again!

Apart from these problems, there is the moral issue of God being portrayed as instructing the Israelites to appropriate jewelry from the Egyptians. However, this is not inconsistent with other instances in the Bible where the Israelites are privileged with preferential treatment, as in the ruling that prevents the Israelites from taking interest on money they lend to each other but allows them to take interest from foreigners (Deu. 23:19-20). The issue of the despoliation of the Egyptians by the Israelites remains problematic for Biblical scholars (see, for instance, the discussion in Houtman, 1993: 382-386).

Although the Qur'an does not mention any appropriation of the Egyptians by the Israelites, exegetes of the Qur'an have incorporated this Biblical claim into their interpretations. Ibn Kathīr, for instance, reiterates in his commentary on verse 26.52 in his highly regarded exegetical work the Biblical claim that the Israelites borrowed from the Egyptians "a lot of jewelry."

(5) The Qur'an also does not support the Biblical claim that it was winds that parted the sea. It only says that the miracle was caused by a strike from Moses' staff that caused a dry path for the Israelites to cross but which disappeared when the Egyptians tried to use it (also 10.90):

> We revealed to Moses: "Strike the sea with your staff," so it split, and each part was like a huge mountain (26.63). We brought near the others (Pharaoh and his army) (26.64). We saved Moses and all those who were with him (26.65). Then We drowned the others (26.66).
>
> "Take away My servants by night, then strike for them a dry path in the sea. Do not be afraid of being overtaken or have any fear" (20.77). Pharaoh then followed them with his soldiers, so there came upon them of the sea that which came upon them (20.78).

4.3 The Bible's "Israelization" of God and Religion

The Qur'an significantly disagrees with the Bible in its account of how Moses introduced God to Pharaoh. But this disagreement underlines an even more fundamental and broader difference between the two scriptures. This important difference goes beyond the story of the exodus, which is why we are covering it in a separate section instead of annexing it to the previous one. This is the relevant Biblical account:

> Afterward Moses and Aaron went to Pharaoh and said, "Thus says the Lord, *the God of Israel*, 'Release *my people* so that they may hold a pilgrim feast to me in the desert.'" But Pharaoh said, "Who is the Lord that I should obey him by releasing Israel? I do not know the Lord, and I will not release Israel!" And they said, "*The God of the Hebrews* has met with us. Let us go a three-day journey into the desert so that we may sacrifice to the Lord our God, so that he does not strike us with plague or the sword." (Exo. 5:1-3)

The exclusive expressions "the God of Israel" and "the God of the Hebrews" are in complete contrast to how Moses described God to the Egyptian monarch in the Qur'an, calling Him the *Lord of everything and everyone and the Lord of all peoples, including Pharaoh and his people*:

> Pharaoh said: "Who is *the Lord of all peoples*" (26.23)? [Moses] said: "The *Lord of the heavens and the earth and all that is between them*, if you would be sure" (26.24). [Pharaoh] said to those around him: "Do you not hear" (26.25)? [Moses] said: "*Your Lord* and the *Lord of your forefathers*" (26.26). [Pharaoh] said: "Your messenger who has been sent to you is a madman" (26.27). [Moses] said: "*The Lord of the East and the West and what is between them*, if you would understand" (26.28).
>
> [God said:] "So go you both to him and say: 'We are two messengers of *your Lord*; therefore send the Children of Israel with us and do not torment them; we have brought to you a sign from *your Lord*; peace be upon him who follows right guidance (20.47). It has been revealed to us that the torture will come upon him who rejects and turns back'" (20.48). He (Pharaoh) said: "So who is your Lord, O Moses" (20.49)? He said: "Our Lord is He *Who created everything, then guided it* [to its course]" (20.50). He said: "Then what about the past generations" (20.51)? He said: "The knowledge of them is with my Lord, in a book; my Lord neither errs nor forgets" (20.52).
>
> Pharaoh said: "Let me kill Moses and let him call on his Lord. I fear that he will change your religion or cause corruption in the land" (40.26). Moses said: "I take refuge in *my and your Lord* from every arrogant person who does not believe in the Day of Reckoning" (40.27).
>
> We tried the people of Pharaoh before them and there came to them a noble messenger (44.17), [saying]: "Deliver to me Allah's servant; I am a trustworthy messenger to you (44.18). Do not exult yourselves above Allah; I have come to you with a manifest authority (44.19). I seek refuge

in *my and your Lord* that you do not stone me" (44.20).

Moses said: "O Pharaoh! I am a messenger from *the Lord of all peoples* (7.104). It is a duty on me to say nothing about Allah but the truth; I have come to you with clear proof from *your Lord*, therefore send with me the Children of Israel" (7.105).

Moses went out of his way to stress that his God was Pharaoh's also. This difference between the image of God in the Qur'an and the Bible is also reflected in the different objectives of Moses' mission in the two books. The Bible confines Moses' mission to taking his fellow Israelites out of Egypt. The Qur'an adds to that the attempt to convert Pharaoh, and by implication his people, and make them accept God as their Lord. The second objective is hinted to in Moses words to Pharaoh "peace be upon him who follows right guidance" (from 20.47), but it is explicitly stressed in these verses:

"Go you and your brother with My signs and do not slacken in remembering Me (20.42). Go both to Pharaoh; he has transgressed all bounds (20.43). Speak to him gentle words that *he may remember or fear*" (20.44).

Has the story of Moses reached you (79.15)? When his Lord called him in the holy valley of Ṭuwā (79.16): "Go to Pharaoh; he has transgressed (79.17). Say to him: 'Do you have the will to *purify yourself* (79.18) and to *let me guide you to your Lord so that you become pious to Him*'" (79.19)?

The exclusiveness of the God of the Old Testament as the Lord of Israel is one aspect of what may be called the "Israelization of religion." The religion of the Old Testament is tightly and inseparably linked to the Israelites' ethnic group. Israel is portrayed as God's chosen people and God is said to be exclusively theirs.

This ethnic and exclusive identification of God belongs to the realms of polytheism rather than monotheism. What the Biblical Moses said to Pharaoh is in line with the polytheistic view that each people has their own god, each city has its own deity, and so on. The polytheistic Pharaoh was not surprised to hear that the Israelites had their own God, as this was what he would expect anyway, so he was only asking for more information on this new God. The Qur'an also shows Pharaoh asking Moses about *his God* (20.49; 28.38; 40.26, 37; 43.49), but, significantly, Moses' answers correct the wrong implications of Pharaoh's question, stressing that his God is Pharaoh's and everyone else's. Being completely focused on presenting their religion and God as theirs only, the Biblical writers seem to be completely unaware of the polytheistic implications of their claims or unbothered by them.

The Qur'an confirms that God conferred special favors on the Israelites:

> O Children of Israel! Remember My favor to you and that I preferred you above all peoples (2.47).
>
> He said: "What, shall I seek a god for you other than God and He has preferred you above all peoples" (7.140)?

This preference of the Israelites over other peoples does not imply that there was anything special about the Israelites as an ethnic group, as the Bible presents it. It refers to the fact that they were privileged for a long time with being the hosts of many prophets:

> We gave the Children of Israel the Book, Wisdom, and prophethood; We provided them with good things; and we preferred them over all peoples (45.16).

The Israelites cannot claim credit for the appearance of many prophets among them for the simple reason that any prophet, including those who descended from Jacob, is not the product of his people and society but rather the making of God. This is why, for instance, the Qur'an does not praise the people of Arabia for producing Prophet Muhammad or indicate explicitly or implicitly that the Arabs or the tribe of Quraysh, to which the Prophet belonged, had any role in his being chosen as prophet. Every prophet was a revolutionary figure with values that were not accepted by the majority of his own people who, invariably, joined forces to undermine his mission. In their response to their prophets, the Israelites were no better than other peoples. This history is confirmed in both the Bible and the Qur'an. The latter states that they went as far as killing some prophets (e.g. 2.87; 5.70). Not even their deliverer from slavery, Moses, was spared their disobedience, arguing, and grumbling. The history of the Israelites even according to the Bible shows that they acted sinfully like any other nation. It may be argued that they were even worse, given that they had so many prophets sent to them.

One verse that stresses that God preferred Israel over other nations by sending more prophets to it also shows that the Israelite prophets were as outsiders to the Israelites as any prophet to his people:

> When Moses said to his people: "O my people! Remember the favor of Allah on you when He made prophets among you and made you kings and gave you what He has not given to any of the other peoples" (5.20).

The verse makes a fine but significant distinction between how the Israelite prophets related to the Israelite people and the how their kings related to them. It describes the prophets as individuals who were made to appear "among" the Israelites, whereas it makes no distinction between the Israelites and their kings, with Moses reminding the Israelites that *God made them kings*. As explained earlier (p. 45), this verse calls all the Israelites "kings" because *one* of them was a king or second to the king, but it does not call them prophets though there were a *number* of prophets among them, including Jacob, his sons, Moses, and Aaron. This distinction between prophet and king applies even when an individual combined prophethood and kingship. In his secular function as king he is one of the Israelites, but in his religious mission as prophet he is one of the nation of prophets not an Israelite. It is the overlooking of this important distinction between a prophet and his people, even if they were his offspring, that turned the name of prophet "Israel" into a name of the nation of his descendants. In contrast, the Qur'an never uses the name "Israel" for the Israelites, only calling them the "Children of Israel," in the same way it calls Adam's offspring the "Children of Adam."

It may also be argued that even if the many prophets who were sent to the Israelites were looked at primarily as prophets of God rather than Israelites, then their appearance in a relatively large number among the Israelites would still indicate the latter's special status. This is also a false argument. God confers favors on people for various reasons, foremost among which is His mercy and bounty. Whether a favor from God is deserved by its recipient or not can only be measured by that person's response to that favor. God favors many nations, groups, and individuals with wealth, power, good health...etc, but many of them abuse those favors. It would be ridiculous to suggest that the rich who spend their wealth on wrong causes or those with power who abuse it received these favors because they deserved them. Similarly, in the case of the Israelites, being the recipients of the great favor of having many prophets sent to them does not mean they were any better than other peoples until their handling of the favor is examined. The fact of the matter is that the Israelites killed many of their prophets and rejected many others, the most famous among them is Jesus, hence they have no claim to any preference over other peoples.

There is another critical point. The prophets with whom the Israelites were preferred over other peoples have long since gone. The Qur'an says that even their divine books have been lost. Later Israelite generations have no claim to the favor that God conferred on their forefathers! The Israelite generations that came after the prophets and after the loss of their teachings were not included in God's special favor to their ancestors. The fact that the later Israelites were denied being the hosts of prophets or the keepers of their heritage means that this favor was not an ethnic issue in the first place, otherwise prophets would have continued to appear among them.

Also, if the Israelites were better than other peoples in the Biblical sense of this concept, then the last prophet, Muhammad, would also have appeared among them. Contrary to the Bible, the Qur'an differentiates between people only in terms of their "faith and good works" (e.g. 2.62; 5.69; 16.97).

5

Biblical Dating of the Exodus

In this chapter, we will discuss references in the Biblical account of the exodus that can be used, with the help of archaeological findings, to date that event. As the Biblical account is not completely consistent, we will review such inconsistencies and discuss which references are more likely to be accurate.

5.1 The Silence of History on Moses

We have already explained the silence of ancient Egypt on Joseph, Jacob, and his descendants (pp. 31-33). Similarly, no Egyptian reference to the later Israelites in Egypt, Moses, or the exodus has been found. This is partly explained by the present state of the ruins of Pi-Ramesses, where the Israelites were employed as forced labor according to the Bible. This city, which has been located in modern Qantir and has been only partially dug, is now mere leveled ruins and its stonework had disappeared or had been reused in buildings elsewhere by later Pharaohs. Pointing out that the once-splendid city can now be reconstructed only from fragments and descriptions, Kitchen goes on to liken Pi-Ramesses to Solomon's Jerusalem stressing that "its golden splendours have entirely disappeared; its voluminous archives are likewise totally lost — a handful of standard wine jar dockets and a series of stamp seals alone survive." He concludes that we should not be surprised that "we have no Egyptian record of the Israelites in bondage near Pi-Ramesse; all such information, with near absolute certainty, is irrevocably lost" (Kitchen, 1977: 77).

An additional factor that should be considered is the fact that Moses' struggle with Pharaoh was a series of humiliating defeats for the latter, from the plagues that hit Egypt to the exodus that put an end to his life and his army's lives. It is natural to find no mention in the Egyptian records of pompous Pharaohs of what took place and the defeat of the Pharaoh of the time at the hand of an Israelite.

There is another critical fact to consider. The Bible presents the exodus as a pivotal event in the history of Israel, which it was. But it also presents it as a major event in the history of the time and area, which it was not. This misleading presentation of the exodus is the result of the faith driven view of the Biblical writers that history in its broad and general sense and history of the Israelites were one and the same. One expression of this misguided view is the unrealistically large scale that is given to the exodus, as in the suggestion that the Israelites were a nation of 2-3 million people when they left Egypt. One problematic ramification of this picture is that the lack of independent evidence on the exodus makes many suspect that this event never took place. However, if the exodus was a much smaller event, which is what the Qur'an says (pp. 140-142), then the lack of evidence does not become much of an issue. This is what one prominent professor had to say:

> True, the absence of any direct extra-biblical evidence, Egyptian or otherwise, need not engender undue skepticism, which, vis-à-vis the biblical tradition, has been occasionally extreme. Rather, the difference of external sources should merely indicate that the Exodus and the Conquest did not shake the foundations of the political and military scene of the day. These events proved central, however, to Israel's turbulent history. (Malamat, 1997: 16)

We discussed earlier (pp. 31-33) that the lack of any surviving mention from ancient Egypt of Joseph, Jacob, and his other sons should not be seen as evidence against the historicity of these characters. Similarly, Egypt's silence on Moses, his people, and their exodus does not represent "negative evidence" to their non-historicity.

As there is no direct Egyptian evidence to attest to the Biblical stories of Joseph and Moses, we can only search for what could be called *circumstantial* evidence. Such evidence does exist and it can lend support to major parts of the Biblical narratives.

5.2 The Pharaoh of Oppression and the Pharaoh of the Exodus

The main information in the Biblical account of the exodus that can be used to date the event is the reference to the Israelites' work as slave labor in building two named store cities:

> So they put foremen over the Israelites to oppress them with hard labor. As a result they built Pithom and Rameses as store cities for Pharaoh. (Exo. 1:11)

Pithom is now possibly identified with Tell el-Maskhuta or the nearby Tell el-Retabe in the Delta. The name occurs in the form of Per-Atum in a number of Egyptian texts from the Ramesside to the Christian period, and it is mentioned in connection with the city of Tkw, which is the Biblical Succoth (Exo. 12:37), which also existed in the Ramesside period

(Thompson, 1977: 153). One such occurrence is found in the already cited Anastasi VI about the entry of Asiatic Bedouins to the Nile Delta as they escaped a drought and looked for pasturage. The text mentions "the pools of Per-Atum [of] Mer[ne]ptah Hotep-hir-Maat, which are (in) Tjeku" (*ANET*, 1950: 259). This papyrus was written during the reign of Merneptah, the son and successor of Ramesses II.

The second city that the Bible names, Rameses, has been identified with the Egyptian city of "Pi-Ramesses" which is sited in Qantir, near Tell el-Dab'a/Avaris in the northeastern Delta (Hoffmeier, 1999: 117-119; van Seters, 1966: 127-151). Horemheb (1321-1293 BCE), the last Pharaoh of the 18th Dynasty, turned his attention to the ancient capital of the expelled Hyksos, refurbishing the temple of the local god, Seth. Later, Seti I (1293-1279 BCE), the second Pharaoh of the 19th Dynasty, built a summer palace in the city. Then his son and successor Ramesses II built Pi-Ramesses, whose full Egyptian name means "House of Ramesses Beloved of Amun, Great of Victories), with his father's palace being at the center of the new city. Ramesses II wanted his new city to be if not greater then certainly not less glorious than Memphis and Thebes, and this is what it came to be. He took Pi-Ramesses as his capital, and the city became the Delta residence of the Ramesside Pharaohs.[6] Rameses is also mentioned in Exodus 12:37 and Numbers 33:3 and 33:5 where it is identified as the city from which the Israelites started their exodus.

References in Egyptian writings to Pi-Ramesses as a store city, as described in Exodus, have survived the time. This is how one song glorifies the new city:

> His Majesty — life, prosperity, health! — has built himself a castle, the name of which is 'Great-of-Victories'. It is between Djahi[7] and Egypt, and is full of food and provisions. It is like Hermonthis,[8] and its lifetime is like (that of) Memphis. The Sun rises in its horizon, and sets within it. All men have left their towns and are settled in its territory. Its west is the House of Amon, its south the House of Seth. Astarte appears in its orient, and Uto in its north.[9] The castle which is in it is like the horizon of heaven. (*ANET*, 1950: 470)

---

[6] Out of the 18 Pharaohs of the 19th and 20th Dynasties (1293-1070), 11 were called Ramesses!

[7] The center of Djahi is the Phoenician coast but it extends down into Palestine.

[8] Hermonthis is an old cult-center south of Thebes.

[9] Amon, Seth, Astarte, and Uto are gods.

Another example comes in a letter from one scribe to his superior:

> I have reached Per-Ramses, and have found it in [very, very] good condition, a beautiful district, without its like, after the pattern of Thebes. It was [Re] himself [who founded it].
> The Residence is pleasant in life; its field is full of everything good; it is (full) of supplies and food every day, its *ponds* with fish, and its lakes with birds. Its meadows are verdant with grass; its banks bear dates; its melons are abundant on the sands.... Its granaries are (so) full of barley and emmer (that) they come near to the sky. Onions and leeks are *for food*, and lettuce of the *garden*, pomegranates, apples, and olives, figs of the orchard, sweet wine of *Ka*-of-Egypt, surpassing honey, red *wedj*-fish of the canal of the Residence City, *which* live on lotus-flowers, *bedin*-fish of the Hari-waters,....
> The Shi-Hor has salt, and the *Her* canal has natron. Its ships go out and come (back) to mooring, (so that) supplies and food are in it every day..... (*ANET*, 1950: 471)

It is obvious from these descriptions, and particularly the reference to its full "granaries," that Pi-Ramesses was very much a "store city" as described in the Bible. Yurco (1997: 54) also notes that "Ramesses II's military delta cities can be described as '"store cities,' for they were where this pharaoh's military supplies were kept in readiness for campaigns in Syria-Palestine."

Although the name of the Pharaoh is never explicitly mentioned in the Bible, the Biblical reference to the bondage of the Israelites in building Rameses implies that Ramesses II (1279-1212 BCE) is the Pharaoh who enslaved them.

The mention of "Rameses" in the Bible is not without problems. While the occurrences of this name in Exodus (1:11, 12:37) and Numbers (33:3, 5) are consistent and pose no problem, the same is not true of the appearance of this name in Genesis (47:11): "So Joseph settled his father and his brothers. He gave them territory in the land of Egypt, in the best region of the land, the land of Rameses, just as Pharaoh had commanded." The problem with this reference is that Joseph lived long before Pi-Ramesses was built! One explanation is that the use of the name Rameses in this passage was simply a mistake which was made because that text was authored long after the event it describes, and the author of the Genesis passage being different from the writers of the other passages that mention Rameses, as Exodus makes it clear that it was the Israelites during Moses time who built the city. Alternatively, this anachronistic use may have been deliberate. The later Biblical redactors may have called the Egyptian city in which Jacob and his sons lived Rameses because they settled in the same site where later generations of the Israelites lived and were enslaved to build the city.

Donald Redford (1992:260) has noted that the Bible's naming of Pi-Ramesses is problematic because it does not have the element "Pi" even though it is present in Pithom. However, other scholars have cited New Kingdom examples in which the name of the city was written without "Pi." Redford has also pointed a difference in the way the sibilants in the Egyptian "Ramesses" appear in the Hebrew name of the city. He has argued that the vocalization of the name is more in line with how the name would have been written after the 6th century BCE, in line with his theory that the Biblical account was written many centuries after the events it describes and is unhistorical. This objection was also answered by examples of similar translations of Egyptian names into Hebrew (Hoffemeier, 1999: 117-118).

For the majority of scholars who accept that the exodus was a real event, the references to Rameses places the time of the enslavement of the Israelites firmly during Ramesses II's reign.

The Bible states that the Pharaoh who enslaved the Israelites had already died when Moses was commissioned by God to return to Egypt from Midian (Exo. 2:23). This claim is reiterated without a direct reference to Pharaoh when God tells Moses: "Go back to Egypt, because all the men who were seeking your life are dead" (Exo. 4:19). Since the Pharaoh of oppression who employed the Israelites in building Ramesses was Ramesses II, his son and successor Merneptah (1212-1202 BCE) must have been the Pharaoh of exodus, i.e. the one who refused to let the Israelite leave Egypt with Moses and who pursued them with his army after they fled. Given that this Pharaoh died during the exodus of the Israelites (Exo. 14:28), we are left with the conclusion that the date of the exodus is the same date of the death of Merneptah and succession of Amenmesses in 1202 BCE.

The Bible implies that Moses and Aaron were living near to Pharaoh, as they were able to visit him on a regular, or even daily, basis. Egyptologist Frank Yurco (1997: 46) has noted that this picture makes sense only in the Ramesside era when Pharaohs' official residence was in Pi-Ramesses, which is near to where the oppressed Israelites lived. He has also emphasized that the Biblical picture of daily visits by Moses and Aaron to Pharaoh causes a problem for the scholars who think that the exodus occurred in much earlier times, for in the 18th Dynasty Pharaoh was resident in Memphis which was a three day voyage by river from the site of Pi-Ramesses.

Some researchers who reject the historicity of the exodus claim that the redactors of the Old Testament in the 7th-6th centuries BCE simply invented the account in the book of Exodus and that it has no core of truth. Yurco (1997: 46) notes that in that period which corresponds to the 26th Dynasty (664-525 BCE) the capital of Pharaoh was Sais — far to the west of Pi-Ramesses. Furthermore, he points out that in the Saite era, Jews in Egypt were not employed as forced labor in building projects, as the account in Exodus states, but were rather valued as mercenaries.

In favor of a Ramesside date for the exodus, Yurco has also drawn attention to the fact that "the Exodus contains personal names — Moses, Phineas, Hophni, Shiprah, and Puah — that are characteristic of the Ramesside era, less so in Dynasty XVIII and least of all in Dynasty XXVI. In Egyptian, the names of Moses and Phineas (Mose and Panehsy) are found frequently in Ramesside sources as personal names" (Yurco, 1997, 46-47). Additionally, given that slaves were employed at building sites throughout Egypt, it is also difficult to understand why the redactors of the Bible would have imagined their fellow Israelites of old being enslaved in building projects in Pi-Ramesses rather than Sais or another city if they were not indeed employed in the building of Pi-Ramesses.

5.3 Historical Egyptian Elements in the Biblical Narrative

In addition to the use of the Israelites to build historical store cities, there are a number of references in the Biblical story of the exodus that link it directly to ancient Egypt, thus lending further support to the historicity of the exodus account. Some of these references also confirm that the exodus occurred in the 13th century BCE:

(1) Enslavement: One significant part of the Biblical tradition with regard to dating the exodus is the *enslavement* of the Israelites in building work. There is textual evidence (*ANETS*, 1968: 553-554) that shows that since the middle of the 18th century BCE Semitic slaves were employed by the Egyptians — a practice that continued throughout the next 1,500 years. Donald Redford, Professor of Classics and Ancient Mediterranean Studies at Pennsylvania University, notes that while it is true that "the Old and Middle Kingdoms were sensitive to manpower needs, which could only be met by forcibly transplanting foreigners to the banks of the Nile, it was the empire of the New Kingdom that produced by far the largest number of captive or impressed Asiatics in Egypt" (Redford, 1997: 59).

One well-known piece of evidence from the New Kingdom comes from the tomb of Rekhmire, one of the vizers of Tuthmosis III (1504-

1450 BCE). It is a scene of laborers making bricks for a temple in Karnak and a text describing the workers as captives. There are a number of inscriptions that confirm the continuation of the practice of bringing captives from West Asia to Egypt as slaves (Hoffmeier, 1999: 112-116).

Among the Pharaohs of the New Kingdoms, it was Ramesses II who embarked on the largest scale of building projects which required large numbers of workers. In fact, he was the greatest builder among the Pharaohs of all time. The monuments that he built covered all of the land of Egypt. It is natural to conclude that Ramesses II would have resorted to forced labor more than any of his predecessors and successors. Papyri Leiden 348 and 349 from Ramesses II's reign talk about Semitics called 'Apiru, whom we will discuss in Chapter 11, transporting stones (Hoffmeier, 1999: 114). One example of the number of workers that were employed in the building projects of Ramesses II comes from inscriptions in the sandstone quarries at Gebel el-Silsila which indicate that at least 3,000 workmen were employed there in cutting stone for the Ramesseum — the giant mortuary temple that Ramesses II erected on the west bank at Thebes (Clayton, 1994: 153).

Moreover, there are writings that mention explicitly the use of forced labor for Ramesses II's huge building projects. In year 38 of his reign, Ramesses II appointed a Viceroy, Setau, who was very active in gathering forced laborers for the building projects he supervised and in raising revenues. This is a quotation from Setau's autobiographical stela at Abu Simbel (Kitchen, 1982: 138):

> My Lord again found my worth ..... So, I was appointed as Viceroy of Nubia ..... I directed serfs in thousands and ten-thousands, and Nubians in hundred-thousands, without limit. I brought all the dues of the land of Kush in double measure, I caused [peoples] to come (in submission), which no Viceroy had done since the year dot. Irem offered tribute, ... and the chief of Akuyata, with his wife, children, and all his company ....
>
> Then [I was charged to build the Temple] of Ramesses II in the Domain of Amun, it being executed in the Western Mountain in work of eternity, filled with numerous people from the captures of His Majesty, his stores being full of goods piled up [to heaven ....]. I (re)built entirely the temples of the lords of this land of Kush that had previously fallen into ruin, they being made anew in the Great Name of His Majesty, inscribed on them forever.

Kitchen also indicates that Setau's claim about enslaving captives in building Ramesses II's temple at Wadi es-Sebua is attested by the stela of the army officer Ramose (Kitchen, 1982: 138):

> Year 44:- His Majesty commanded the confidant, the Viceroy of

Nubia, Setau, together with army personnel of the company of Ramesses II, 'Amun protects (his) son', that he should take captives from the land of the Libyans, in order to build in the Temple of Ramesses II in the Domain of Amun, and (the King) also ordered the officer Ramose to raise (?) a force from the company - so, Ramose.

The Biblical claim that Pharaoh enslaved the Hebrews in building projects is consistent with how Semitics were treated in Egypt, and even more so during Ramesses II's reign.

The Bible states that when the Israelites left Egypt "a mixed multitude also went up with them" (Exo. 12:38). This is often taken to refer to other enslaved workers who joined the Israelites in their attempt to attain freedom (Hoffmeier, 1999: 114).

(2) Building with mortar and bricks: The Bible states that the Egyptians had the Hebrews doing building work using bricks and mortar:

> They made their lives bitter by hard service with mortar and bricks and by all kinds of service in the fields. Every kind of service the Israelites were required to give was rigorous. (Exo. 1:14)

The Rekhmire scene shows Semitic workers making bricks. Significantly, it shows them scooping water, making mud by mixing water with soil, forming bricks, and then taking dried bricks to the building site. The scenario described in the Bible had precedent in Egypt.

(3) Using straw for making bricks: After Moses and Aaron met Pharaoh and asked him to release their people to perform a pilgrimage in the desert, the Egyptian monarch made the lives of the Israelites even more miserable:

> That same day Pharaoh commanded the slave masters and foremen who were over the people: "You must no longer give straw to the people for making bricks as before. Let them go and collect straw for themselves. But you must require of them the same quota of bricks that they were making before. Do not reduce it, for they are slackers. That is why they are crying, 'Let us go sacrifice to our God.' Make the work harder for the men so they will keep at it and pay no attention to lying words!" So the slave masters of the people and their foremen went to the Israelites and said, "Thus says Pharaoh: 'I am not giving you straw. You go get straw for yourselves wherever you can find it, because there will be no reduction at all in your workload.'" So the people spread out through all the land of Egypt to collect stubble for straw. The slave masters were pressuring them, saying, "Complete your work for each day, just like when there was straw!" (Exo. 5:6-13)

Papyrus Anastasi V, which dates to the 13th century BCE, preserves the following interesting complaint of an official that confirms the use of straw in brick making:

> I am staying at Kenkenento, unequipped, and there are neither men to make bricks nor straw in the neighbourhood. The things which I brought as requirements have vanished (though) there are no asses (to) rob them. (*LEM*, 1954: 188).

The inclusion of straw and chaff in the clay used for making bricks came about as experience showed that this would yield a better brick (Kitchen, 1977: 77). In this period, temples were usually built of stone whereas other buildings including palaces, storehouses and residences of military and administrators were built of mudbricks (Yurco, 1997: 46). Interestingly, straw was not typically used in Canaan, where the Israelites went after leaving Egypt, for making mudbricks. This is another confirmation that the reference in the Bible reflects familiarity with Egyptian life (Yurco, 1997: 32).

(4) **Production quota system**: Exodus (5:8, 11) talks about the Hebrews being given a "quota" of bricks to make. There are indeed Egyptian writings that mention the use of production quota system. In the late 13th century BCE Papyrus Anastasi III from Memphis, an official writes proudly to his superiors about how his workers are meeting their daily target quota:

> People are making bricks in their bk [sic] and bring them to work in the house. They are making their quota of bricks daily. I am not slacking over working in the new house. (*LEM*, 1954: 106)

Kenneth Kitchen (1977: 77-78) makes the following observation:

> From Year 5 of Ramesses II (c. 1286/1275 BCE), brick accounts are recorded upon a leather scroll now in the Louvre Museum. Among other things, forty 'stablemasters' are each assigned a target quota of 2000 bricks (i.e. 80,000 all told). The successive figures added after their names and 'target' show the progress of production, the target being rarely reached.

Again, a practice mentioned in the Biblical text is confirmed by Egyptian texts from the time of Ramesses II.

(5) **Slave drivers**: Exodus (5:6, 10, 13-14) states that Pharaoh appointed Egyptian "slave masters" and Hebrew "foremen" over the Hebrew slaves. Kitchen (1977: 78) notes that these correspond to the "stablemasters" in the scroll mentioned above.

(6) **Time off for worship**: Exodus 5:1 states that Moses and Aaron told Pharaoh that "the God of Israel" has commissioned them to deliver this message to him: "Release my people so that they may hold a pilgrim feast to

me in the desert." Kitchen draws attention to the following:

> In the work rosters from the workmen's village at Deir elMedina in Western Thebes, people had days off for all sorts of reasons including 'offering to one's god' just as Moses requested 'time off' for his people to go and worship in the wilderness. (Kitchen, 1977: 78)

This is another similarity between the Biblical text and reported Egyptian practices.

(7) Escaping guarded borders: Abraham Malamat, Professor of Jewish History at the Hebrew University of Jerusalem, draws attention to another important point that further supports the Egyptian background of the exodus of the Israelites and also plausibly links it to the late 13th century BCE. The subject of this observation is the escape of the Israelites. Citing God's message, "release my people" (e.g. Exo. 5:1, 7:16), that Moses conveyed to Pharaoh, Malamat points out that this means that the Israelites could not leave the land without Pharaoh's permission. This is consistent with a number of Papyri Anastasi that show the Egyptians' tight control of their eastern frontiers. We have already seen in Papyrus Anastasi VI from the reign of Merneptah, Ramesses II's successor, Bedouins requiring the permission of officials stationed on the eastern Egyptian frontier to enter the Delta. Particularly significant is a report in Papyrus Anastasi V of an Egyptian official who was sent to capture two slaves who had run away from the royal residence at Pi-Ramesses:

> .... Another matter, to wit: I was sent forth from the broad-halls of the palace — life, prosperity, health! — in the 3rd month of the third season, day 9, at the time of evening, following after these two slaves. Now when I reached the enclosure-wall of Tjeku on the 3rd month of the third season, day 10, they told [me] they were saying to the south that they had passed by on the 3rd month of the third season, day 10. [Now] when [I] reached the fortress, they told me that the *scout* had come from the desert [saying that] they had passed the walled place north of the Migdol of Seti Merneptah — life, prosperity, health! — Beloved like Seth.
> When my letter reaches you, write to me about all that has happened to [them]. Who found their tracks? Which watch found their tracks? What people are after them? Write to me about all that has happened to them and how many people you send out after them. (*ANET*, 1950: 259)

Malamat (1997: 19-22) identifies four common features between Anastasi V and the story of the exodus: (i) the escape of slaves from Pi-Ramesses in search of freedom; (ii) the pursuit of Egyptian military officials of the escapees to return them to Egypt; (iii) the route into Sinai taken by the escaping slaves is roughly identical to that followed by the Israelites; and (iv) the occurrence of the escape under the cover of darkness.

The discussion in this section confirms the historicity of exodus and its Egyptian background. Some of the observations also place the exodus around the 13th century BCE, which is the date adopted by most scholars who accept the historicity of the exodus. Significantly, recent excavations in Palestine are increasingly pointing toward no earlier than a late 13th century BCE (e.g. Dever, 1997; Weinstein, 1997) but probably a 12th century BCE (Rendsburg, 1992) date for the settlement of the Israelites in the holy land. Taking into account that the Israelites entered the holy land 40 years after their escape, dating the exodus to Ramesses II's last year late in the 13th century BCE is completely compatible with these archaeological findings.

5.4 Contradictions in the Biblical Dating of the Exodus

We covered earlier some serious inconsistencies in the Biblical account of the exodus (pp. 50-68). The Bible contains also statements that contradict its details that date the exodus to the late 13th century BCE. We have already seen that, in particular, the reference to the enslavement of the Israelites in building Pithom and Rameses implies that Ramesses II was the Pharaoh of oppression and his son Merneptah was the Pharaoh of the exodus. However, a totally different date is implied by this Biblical passage:

> In the four hundred and eightieth year after the Israelites left Egypt, in the fourth year of Solomon's reign over Israel, during the month Ziv (the second month), he began building the Lord's temple. (1 Kings 6:1)

Scholars agree that Solomon reign was around 960-920 BCE, so this passage places the exodus in about 1437 BCE. This date is almost two and a half centuries earlier than the late 13th century BCE date concluded from other Biblical data. 1 Kings provides no data to give its 15th century BCE dating of the exodus historical credibility.

The Jewish historian Josephus gave the exodus an early date. Relying on accounts by the 3rd century BCE Egyptian priest Manetho, Josephus (*Against Apion*, 1.103-105) associated the exodus with the expulsion of the Hyksos from Egypt, which was in the 16th not 15th century BCE. Dating the exodus to the 15th century BCE remained popular until modern times when its rejection was forced by archaeological finds that date the earliest Israelite settlements in Canaan centuries later, in addition to its contradiction with the Biblical reference to the enslavement of the Israelites in building Rameses. A 15th century date is now unacceptable to most scholars.

Unsurprisingly, there have been attempts to harmonize the conflicting data of Exodus and 1 Kings. One example comes from Frank Yurco, an advocate of a 13th century date for the exodus, who has assumed that the Biblical figure 480 was intended to mean 12 generations of 40 years each. Then he suggested that if Biblical generations are refigured at 20-25 years each then the 480 years are reduced to 240-300 years. Then, working back from 958 BCE as Solomon's fourth regnal year, Yurco concludes that the exodus according to 1 Kings would have occurred sometime between 1198 and 1258 BCE with the upper limit being within the reign of Ramesses II. He (1997: 48-49) also suggests that this conclusion agrees with the dating of Exodus 15 to the 13th-12th centuries BCE.

Yurco's conclusion is totally speculative and lacking evidence. It is based on his unsupported hypothesis that the 480 years meant 12 generations, and on his equally unjustified attempt to refigure Biblical generations at 20-25 years. This is reminiscent of Kitchen's attempt to reconciles the "four generations" problem in Genesis (15:13-16) with other Biblical passages (pp. 55-56), although Kitchen ended up equating the generation to as many as 100 years. Yurco's attempt is equally speculative, unconvincing, and far-fetched.

Another discrepancy with the conclusion that Ramesses II and Merneptah were the Pharaohs of the oppression and exodus, respectively, is caused by Moses' reported age. We discussed earlier a contradiction in Jewish and Christian sources about how old Moses was when he fled Egypt to Midian (pp. 67-68). Various passages and sources suggest that he was as old as 40 years and that he stayed in Midian for another 40 years, but Exodus 2:11 only states that Moses was a grown-up man. Let's see how all possibilities are problematic.

The first claim is that Moses lived 40 years in Egypt and 40 in Midian. Even if he was brought to Pharaoh's palace in Ramesses II's first year in power, after 80 years, not only Ramesses II but also his son Merneptah would have been dead. Ramesses II ruled for 67 years (1279-1212 BCE) and his son for 10 years (1212-1202 BCE). In fact, even Merneptah's successor, Amenmesses, who ruled for 3 years only might have been dead by then!

The second claim, which suggests that Moses was a young man when he left Egypt and returned to it only after a few years, has also problems.

There is only one scenario that would be consistent with the conclusion that Ramesses II and Merneptah being the Pharaohs that Moses dealt with. If Moses was found and brought up in Ramesses II's palace later in the latter's life, then it would be possible that Pharaoh would have died while Moses in Midian and that the latter came back to confront Merneptah. But there is a serious historical problem with this scenario also. When Merneptah, Ramesses II's 13th son, succeeded his father, he was already in his sixties. As Ramesses II reigned for about 67 years, Merneptah would have been born around the time of the accession of his father. So if Moses left as a young man to Midian, Merneptah would have been in his middle age. Yet the Bible claims that God said the following to Moses when he was still in Midian: "Go back to Egypt, because all the men who were seeking your life are dead" (Exo. 4:19). But surely Merneptah, who was still alive when Moses came back, would have been one of those who wanted to kill Moses. Even if we consider the unreasonable claim that, for whatever reason, Ramesses II's son and successor was not one of those who sought Moses' life, there is still another problem. The Bible portrays the Pharaoh whom Moses encountered after returning to Egypt as someone who did not know Moses before. This, obviously, cannot be true.

5.5 Liberal consideration of the Biblical Narrative

Only those who consider the Bible to be the Word of God as a matter of faith still believe that every statement in the Bible is factual. Scientific discoveries, archeological finds, and growing knowledge of ancient history have revealed so many errors and inaccuracies in the Bible. Even scholars who accept some parts of a Biblical narrative reject others. In this section, we will discuss how some parts of the Biblical story of the exodus have been rejected to accommodate others or to "rationalize" it.

Most researchers consider the Biblical claim that the Israelites were used as slave workers to build Pithom and Rameses authentic and use it as the main piece of information for fixing the date of the exodus. But they also reject other elements of the Biblical narrative. They are particularly reluctant to associate the date of the exodus with the end of the reign of Pharaoh as the Bible claims. One factor that may have contributed to the unpopularity of this Biblical detail is the unavailability of records confirming the drowning of Pharaoh and his army. For those who believe that the Pharaoh of the exodus was Ramesses II or Merneptah, another influential factor could be the existence of the mummies of both of these Pharaohs, as one would find it unlikely for the body of a drowned Pharaoh to have been recovered from the sea and mummified. Many scholars are equally dismissive of the Biblical claim that Pharaoh died when Moses was in Midian which implies that the Pharaoh of the oppression is different from that of the exodus. This modification to the Biblical narrative allows scholars a greater freedom to pick and choose the date during the life of Pharaoh when they believe the exodus would have happened.

While rejecting these two Biblical claims, some scholars have used the Biblical account of the final plague, which is God's killing of the firstborn of the Egyptians and their cattle (Exo. 11 & 12), to pinpoint the date of the exodus. The Biblical narrative suggests that the various episodes of Moses' struggle with Pharaoh, including the ten plagues, happened over a short period of time, and that the exodus occurred immediately after the killing of the Egyptians' firstborn. Maybe researchers' rejection of the Biblical claim that the Pharaoh of the oppression died while Moses was in Midian, which would lead to the conclusion that Merneptah was the Pharaoh of the exodus, has to do with the fact that the Biblical claim about the final plague is inapplicable to Merneptah. Researchers have associated this Biblical event with the death of Ramesses II's eldest son and crown prince "Amen-hir-khopshef" who is believed to probably have been already dead by his father's 20th regnal year. Based on this correlation, Kitchen, for example, suggests that the exodus could have occurred about the 17th regnal year of Ramesses II or slightly later (Kitchen, 1982: 71, 240). Yurco prefers a date between the 20th and 30th regnal years of Ramesses II, reflecting his different estimate of the date of death of Amen-hir-khopshef (Yurco, 1997: 47-48). He has sought more evidence for this dating, as explained further below.

The irony with such attempts is that while they rely on the Bible's account of the final plague, they are based as much on rejecting the Biblical claims that Ramesses II, being the Pharaoh of the oppression, died when Moses was in Midian and that his successor drowned during his pursuit of the Israelites. It is true that this approach would reconcile Biblical claims with history, as the Biblical account of the final plague is inapplicable to Merneptah, but then there are other alternative solutions that achieve the same result. For instance, one could assume that it is the Biblical account of the killing of the Egyptians' firstborns that is false, and thus the other Biblical claim that the Pharaoh of the oppression died during Moses' residence in Midian can be accommodated. The Bible is adamant that Pharaoh was among the dead in the sea and indeed presents his death as the culmination of the punishment of God. To reject the central event and the climax of the Biblical story is a rather illogical way of accepting the Biblical narrative.

Picking the death of Ramesses II's eldest son to date the exodus implies that it is extraordinary for such an event to be mentioned in the Bible, hence is more likely to be historical than other events. But there is nothing remarkable about such an event. Death of young people in general was very common in ancient times where life expectancy was low, so there is nothing unusual in a son dying before his parent. In the case of Ramesses II in particular who lived into his 90s, the death of his eldest son before him should only be expected. Ramesses II outlived several of his 100 or so sons and daughters.

In addition to all these objections, this much relied upon event does not seem to be a certainty after all! Kitchen himself seems to indicate that there is no direct evidence to the death of the eldest son of Ramesses II but that it is indirectly concluded from the fact that by Ramesses II's 20th regnal year Amen-hir-khopshef was no more "heir apparent," as this title was enjoyed by his brother Set-hir-khopshef. It is possible that Amen-hir-khopshef was no longer heir apparent because Ramesses II passed the title to his son Set-hir-khopshef in the former's life for whatever reason. Additionally, Kitchen also states that: "By year 20, Amen-hir-khopshef was no longer Heir-Apparent (or, not by that name), and was probably dead" (Kitchen, 1982: 102). So Amen-hir-khopshef may have been still alive but no more under that name. Significantly, Amen-hir-khopshef was not the original name of Ramesses II's eldest son but one that Ramesses II chose for his son to replace his birth name Amen-hir-wonmef! Dating the exodus with reference to the alleged death of Ramesses II's eldest son is anything but safe.

One aspect of the liberal handling of the Biblical account by scholars who entertain the historicity of the exodus is the "rationalization" of the story by stripping it of its miraculous elements. For example, in order to explain the escape of the Israelites without reference to the miraculous, Malamat (1997: 17) suggests that a "punctual"[10] exodus would have occurred sometime in the period between the late 13th and the early years of the 12th centuries BCE which witnessed the breakdown of the Egyptian and Hittite empires — a development that would have given the Israelites, as well as other oppressed minorities from Anatolia to Lower Egypt, the opportunity to escape their oppressors.

The ten miraculous plagues that hit Pharaoh and his people because

---

[10] Some scholars believe that there may have been more than one exodus or that the exodus lasted for years or even centuries, as opposed to one major exodus.

of his refusal to let the Israelites leave Egypt with Moses have been obvious targets for rationalization. Efforts have focused on explaining these events naturally. Unsurprisingly, the parting of the sea has also been portrayed as a natural event rather than a miracle caused by Moses stretching out his hand over the sea. Frank Yurco (1997: 45), for example, has suggested that the present account in the Bible about the miracle of the sea is inauthentic and that the original text talked about crossing what he described as "a papyrus-filled marshy lake." This would have been particularly difficult to cross with chariots by the Egyptians.

A number of scholars have incorporated in their explanatory models another natural factor, making the most of the wind mentioned in Exodus 14:21. Hyatt has put forward the following theory: "a strong east wind, probably lasting for several days, dried the marsh sufficiently for the lightly armed Hebrews to cross; a sudden violent storm brought aid to the Hebrews so that they were able to defeat the Egyptians, who were more heavily armed, but whose chariots became bogged down in the mud. Doubtless some of the Hebrews lost their lives, but many of them made good their escape into the desert" (Hyatt, 1971: 45). Hyatt was not the first to combine a "natural wind" and a "shallow marsh" in an explanatory model. Julius Wellhausen (1844-1918) had already suggested that the Israelites forded a shallow sea which had been blown back by a high wind.

In the course of indicating that the parting of the sea was no fantasy, Kenneth Kitchen goes as far as suggesting that the wind's parting of the sea was not even a unique event, bizarrely citing the story of someone who, according to Kitchen, had an "analogous (though not fatal!) experience in his car" (Kitchen, 1977: 78-79)! Houtman (1996: 270) has noted that the question of how the Israelites could cross the sea during the heavy wind did not bother the ancient writer of the Bible. But that is understandable, because the Bible portrays this whole episode as a supernatural event. It is the position of modern scholars who accept that the sea was *naturally* parted by wind that is difficult to understand, as if their alternative explanation is more rational than a miracle!

6

The Qur'anic Identification of Pharaoh

We discussed earlier the Bible's identification of Ramesses II as the Pharaoh of oppression and his son Merneptah as the Pharaoh of the exodus. But this identification is not without problems, because of contradictions in the Bible (pp. 91-93). In this chapter, we will see how the Qur'an unambiguously identifies the Pharaoh of the exodus as Ramesses II even though it does not name him. It is the style of the Qur'an that some major characters and places, which would be named in any historical book, are left unidentified. But the Qur'an is not a book of history. The Bible also does not name the Pharaoh, but this is unusual given the Bible's interest in such historical details. The oddity of this omission has even made some suggest that the Biblical authors did not know the Pharaoh's name (Dever, 1997: 68).

There are a number of fundamental differences between the Qur'anic story of the exodus and its Biblical counterpart, and the Qur'anic identification of Pharaoh is based on one of those differences.

6.1 One Pharaoh Not Two

The Bible claims that the Pharaoh who oppressed the Israelites died when Moses was in Midian (Exo. 2:23, 4:19) and that the latter's struggle after his return from Midian was with a different Pharaoh. The Qur'an disagrees with the Bible as it speaks about *one* Pharaoh *not two*. The Pharaoh who oppressed the Israelites is the same Pharaoh who later chased them with his army after their escape from Egypt and drowned in the sea. There is not the slightest hint in the story of Moses of the accession of a new monarch in Egypt. All references in the Qur'an to "Pharaoh" are to that one particular Pharaoh.

In his popular Arabic book *The Stories of Prophets*, which was originally published early in the 20th century, 'Abd al-Wahāb an-Najjār (1986) suggested that the Qur'anic story of the exodus can be reconciled with the Biblical claim that the Pharaoh of the oppression is different from the Pharaoh of the exodus. This view was also adopted more recently by Maurice Bucaille (1995) in his bestseller *The Bible, the Qur'an and Science* which appeared in the late 70s of the last century. Some Muslim writers have also stated that the Pharaoh of the exodus is not the same Pharaoh of the oppression, but without necessarily confessing to the Biblical origin of this view (e.g. Husain, 1994: 60). This claim is difficult to understand given the clarity of the Qur'anic text which speaks about one Pharaoh only. Bucaille in particular presented in his book a detailed and convincing argument that Biblical statements cannot be assumed to be accurate and that the Bible is full of wrong information and inconsistencies. Yet he accepts uncritically and without extra-Biblical evidence the Biblical claim that Pharaoh died when Moses was in Midian.

Significantly, despite their exposure to the Bible and often influence by it, ancient exegetes of the Qur'an never understood it as referring to two Pharaohs. Some of them have in fact refuted the Biblical claim on the basis of the Qur'anic text, such as the 14th century exegete Ibn Kathīr (1985: 317) in his classical book also known as *The Stories of Prophets*. Modern exegetes who have accepted the Biblical claim of two Pharaohs have done so probably because of mistakenly thinking that the archaeological findings, of whose influence older exegetes were free, point toward this conclusion. Indeed, both an-Najjār and Bucaille put forward arguments that utilize archeological data to advocate their view that Ramesses II was the Pharaoh of the oppression and Merneptah was the Pharaoh of the exodus. The two-Pharaoh theory is not a pure interpretation of the Qur'anic text.

In addition to speaking implicitly about one Pharaoh only, the Qur'an contains other equally clear-cut pieces of evidence that the Pharaoh of the oppression and the Pharaoh of the exodus were one and the same:

(1) The first of these comes from chapter 28:

> We narrate to you [O Muḥammad!] parts of the story of Moses and Pharaoh in truth, for people who believe (28.3). Pharaoh exalted himself in the earth and made its people castes, oppressing one group of them, killing their sons and sparing their women; he was one of the corrupters (28.4). We desired to show favor to those who were oppressed in the earth, make them leaders, make them the inheritors (28.5), establish them in the earth, and show Pharaoh, Hāmān, and their soldiers from them that which they feared (28.6). We inspired Moses' mother: "Suckle him, and when you fear for him, cast him into the river and do not fear or grieve; We shall bring him back to you and make him one of the messengers" (28.7). Then the people of Pharaoh picked him up [from the river], to become for them an enemy and a sorrow; Pharaoh, Hāmān, and their soldiers were sinful (28.8). The wife of Pharaoh said: "[He will be] a delight for the eye for me and you. Do not kill him. He may be useful for us, or we may take him as a son," while they were unaware [of what was going to happen] (28.9).

Verse 28.3 states that the following verses recount the story of Moses and Pharaoh, i.e. one Pharaoh. The passage first mentions Pharaoh's evil and the atrocities that he committed against the Israelites before the birth of Moses. The Qur'an then gives details of Moses' birth and Pharaoh's permission for the child to be kept alive, follows up the story until Moses' departure to Midian, and continues the story until the exodus where it tells us that Pharaoh drowned. The text is clear that it is relating the story of Moses with one Pharaoh whose evil career extended from before the birth of Moses until he perished in the sea.

(2) A part of the dialogue between Moses after his return from Midian and Pharaoh makes it perfectly clear that this Pharaoh is the same one who took custody of Moses in his infancy:

> [Pharaoh] said [to Moses]: "Did we not rear you among us as a child, you lived a number of years among us (26.18), and then you committed what you did, being one of the ungrateful" (26.19)? He said: "I did it when I was one of those who are astray (26.20). Then I fled from you when I feared you, so my Lord granted me Wisdom and appointed me one of the messengers (26.21). Is it a favor you remind me of that you have enslaved the Children of Israel" (26.22)?

Pharaoh here reminds Moses of the time that he spent in his custody and the murder he committed and led to his flight to Midian. Moses' answer to Pharaoh's argument is even a clearer proof that this Pharaoh is the same one in whose palace he was brought up. Moses rejected Pharaoh's claim that he had done him a favor by taking custody of him. He reminded Pharaoh that the reason why he ended up in his palace in the first place was his enslavement of the Israelites, with one aspect of this bondage being Pharaoh's prevention of the Israelites from leaving Egypt and his killing of the Israelite newborn boys. The same Pharaoh who enslaved the Israelites was in power when Moses went back to Egypt.

Pharaoh's reply to Moses, "did we not rear you among us as a child, you lived a number of years among us," has been interpreted by the *modern* exegete an-Najjār (1986: 278) as a reminder from Pharaoh that they had lived together in their childhood in his father's palace. Interestingly, this same reply is interpreted by the *old* exegete Ibn Kathīr (1985: 317) as "proving that the Pharaoh he (Moses) was sent to was the same whom he had fled from. This is contrary to the account of People of the Book (the Jews) that the Pharaoh whom Moses fled from died when he was living in Midian and that the one to whom he was sent was a different Pharaoh." Ibn Kathīr had no worries whether the Pharaoh was Ramesses II, his son Merneptah, or any other Pharaoh, so he had no reason to force an arbitrary interpretation on the Qur'anic text.

(3) Another important and also unambiguous Qur'anic indication that the Pharaoh to whom Moses was sent is the same Pharaoh who was in power when he escaped to Midian comes from the first dialogue between God and Moses. This dialogue differs significantly from its Biblical counterpart. The Bible does not show Moses to have had any fears of going back to Egypt having fled from it earlier. Moses main worries were whether his fellow Israelites would believe him and the fact that he was not an eloquent speaker. It was only later that God said to Moses: "Go back to Egypt, because all the men who were seeking your life are dead" (Exo. 4:19). By portraying Moses as showing no sign of fear of returning to Egypt after what he had done, the Bible seems to be referring to its suggestion in other passages that Moses stayed in Midian for a long time (pp. 67-68), so he would have already been under the impression that Pharaoh was dead by then.

Unlike the Biblical account, the Qur'an states that when first instructed by God to go to Pharaoh, Moses voiced fears about this mission, having killed one of the people of Pharaoh and fled away years earlier:

> When your Lord [O Muhammad!] called Moses [saying]: "Go to the wrongdoing people (26.10) — the people of Pharaoh. Will they not be pious" (26.11)? He said: "My Lord! I fear that they will accuse me of telling lies (26.12), my breast will be straitened, and my tongue will not speak plainly, so call Aaron [to help me] (26.13). They also have a charge of crime against me, so I am afraid that they will kill me" (26.14). He said: "By no means. Go you both with Our signs; We shall be with you, hearing (26.15). Go to Pharaoh and say: 'We are messengers of the Lord of all peoples (26.16). Let the Children of Israel go with us'" (26.17).

> "These shall be two proofs from your Lord to Pharaoh and his chiefs; they are a rebellious people" (28.32). He said: "My Lord! I have killed a person from them and I fear that they will kill me (28.33). My brother Aaron is more eloquent than me, so make him a messenger with me — a helper to confirm me; I fear that they will accuse me of telling lies" (28.34). He said: "We will strengthen you with your brother, and We will give you both authority so that they shall not be able to reach you [for harm] on account of Our signs. You both and those who follow you will be the victorious" (28.35).

Contrary to the Biblical claim, God's answer to Moses was not to reassure him that all those who wanted him killed had died. He rather allayed his fears by telling him that He would be present with him and his brother Aaron and support them with authority that is higher than Pharaoh's.

The Qur'an leaves no doubt that it speaks about one Pharaoh who was in power in Egypt from the birth of Moses until he drowned in the sea after the exodus.

6.2 A Long-Reigning Pharaoh

When considered with other details of the Qur'anic account of the story of Moses, the fact that the Qur'an speaks about one Pharaoh who ruled Egypt from before Moses' birth to the exodus means that this Pharaoh ruled for a very long time. This significant conclusion, in turn, can help us identify this Pharaoh unambiguously.

Keeping in mind that Moses was born when Pharaoh was already in power and that the latter died during his pursuit of Moses, the length of Pharaoh's reign can approximately be calculated by adding up the following:

(1) The time that Pharaoh ruled before Moses' birth.
(2) Moses' age when he left Egypt to Midian.
(3) The time that he stayed in Midian.
(4) The length of his second sojourn in Egypt after returning from Midian.

Let's see what we can conclude from the Qur'an about each of these four periods:

(1) The Qur'an does not state in which regnal year of Pharaoh Moses was born. This means that we can only calculate the *minimum* length of the reign of this monarch.

(2) Moses' age when he left Egypt can estimated from God's following description of him before his flight to Midian:

> When he attained his full strength and settled, We gave him Wisdom and Knowledge; thus do We reward the good-doers (28.14).

Exegetes have expressed different views about the age of *attaining full strength*, with estimates ranging from the age of puberty to sixty. (See for example the many different interpretations of this verse in the classical exegeses of al-Qurṭubī, Ibn Kathīr, and al-Jalālayn.) The *attainment of full strength* is mentioned in different forms in eight verses, including the following verse which occurs twice in the Qur'an: "do not approach the property of the orphan except in the best manner until he attains his full strength" (from 6.152; from 17.34). It is possible to know the age meant in this verse by comparing it with the following verse on the same subject:

> Test the orphans; when they attain puberty see if you find them of sound judgment, [in which case] make over to them their property, and do not consume it extravagantly and hastily lest they grow up (from 4.6).

This verse specifies two conditions for handing over property to its orphan owners: reaching the age of puberty and acquiring mental maturity. So the expression "attained his full strength" in verses 6.152 and 17.34 denotes an age after that of puberty when the person becomes able to make sound and responsible decisions about his life. In other words, the age designated by the clause "attained his full strength" is not determined by physical maturity only but by mental maturity also (see also 18.82).

Prophet Joseph is described in similar terms in verse 28.14: "When he attained his full strength, We gave him Wisdom and Knowledge; and thus do We reward the good-doers" (12.22). Interestingly, after this description the story moves to talk about how his lord's wife tried to seduce him, clearly suggesting that he had become a young man.

Other verses in which variations of *attaining full strength* occur show that the age range during which the person is in full strength extends from the time of attaining physical and mental maturity to the time when the person's physical, and perhaps also mental, abilities start to deteriorate:

> O people! If you are in doubt about the Resurrection, then We created you from dust, then from a drop of seed, then from a clot, then from a lump of flesh, formed and unformed, that We may make clear to you. And We cause what We will to rest in the wombs till an appointed time, then We bring you forth as children, then that you may attain your full strength. Among you there is he who is caused to die, and among you there is he who is brought back to the most abject time of life so that, after having knowledge, he does not know anything (from 22.5).

> It is He who created you from dust, then from a drop of seed, then from a clot, then He brings you forth as a child, then that you may attain your full strength, then that you may become old — and some of you die before then — and that you may reach an appointed term, and that you may understand (40.67).

> We have enjoined on man doing good to his parents. His mother bears him unwillingly and she gives birth to him unwillingly. The bearing and weaning of him are thirty months. Until when he attains his full strength and reaches forty years, he says: "My Lord! Grant me that I may give thanks for Your favor to me and to my parents, and that I may do good that pleases You. Be gracious to me in respect of my offspring; I turn to You, and I am one of the Muslims (those who submit)" (46.15).

The exact age of *attaining full strength* thus changes from one person to another, but 16-18 years seems like a reasonable average. Comparing verses 28.14 about Moses and 12.22 about Joseph shows that in the case of Moses God mentions after Moses' attainment of full strength a stage that He refers to as *settling*. This sounds like a distinct state — probably spiritual and psychological rather than physical. It is not clear how long after the conferment of Wisdom and Knowledge on Moses he escaped from Egypt. Taking all of this into account, Moses could have been 20-22 years when he left Egypt to Midian.

(3) The length of Moses' stay in Midian is referred to explicitly in the Qur'an. After arriving to Midian, Moses met an old righteous man and married one of his daughters. Moses' father-in-law is believed to be Shu'ayb whom the Qur'an says was a prophet sent by God to the people of Midian (7.85; 11.84; 29.36). The two men agreed a dowry of 8-10 years of service that Moses would give to his father-in-law:

> He said: "I would like to marry you to one of my two daughters and in return you hire yourself to me for eight years, and it is up to you if would make it ten, for I do not want to make it hard for you; Allah willing, you will find me one of the righteous" (28.27). He said: "This is [a contract] between me and you; whichever of the two terms I fulfill, there shall be no wrongdoing on my part, and Allah is a witness on what we say" (28.28). When Moses fulfilled the term and left in the night with his family, he perceived [at a distance] a fire at the side of the mountain. He said to his family: "Stay here; I have perceived a fire that I might bring you tidings from or a firebrand that you might warm yourselves" (28.29).

The text does not specify which of the two terms Moses fulfilled. Moses' generosity and readiness to offer free help even to people he did not know, as he did with the two girls one of whom was later to become his wife, make it likely that he volunteered to work those extra two years for his father-in-law. But since we cannot be certain that Moses did not have to leave shortly after the eighth year, we will opt for the inclusive range of 8-10 years for Moses' stay in Midian.

(4) The last period of time that we need to consider is the time Moses spent in his second sojourn in Egypt. Let's first take a quick review of the Biblical version of events.

While some Biblical passages imply that Moses was a young man when he came back from Midian, others contradict this and state that he was 80 years old and 120 when he died (pp. 67-68). They also state that immediately after his death the Israelite's 40 years in the wilderness came to an end and they, under the leadership of Moses' assistant, Joshua, crossed the River Jordan into the holy land (Jos. 1:1-2). This means that Moses' second sojourn in Egypt and his struggle against the second Pharaoh lasted less than a year. Indeed, the Biblical account suggests that the various events of Moses' encounter with Pharaoh, including the ten plagues, were happening shortly after one another.

In the Qur'an, there is no explicit mention of the length of Moses' second spell in Egypt. But there are a number hints in the following set of verses that Moses stayed in Egypt for a rather lengthy period of time, measured in years:

> The chiefs of Pharaoh's people said: "Do you leave Moses and his people to cause corruption in the land and forsake you and your gods?" He said: "We will kill their sons but spare their women, and surely we will overpower them" (7.127). Moses said to his people: "Ask help from Allah and be patient; surely the land is Allah's; He gives it for inheritance to whom He wills of His servants. The [best] end is for the pious" (7.128). They said: "We were harmed before you came to us and we have been harmed since then also." He said: "May your Lord destroy your enemy and make you inheritors in the land so He sees how you act" (7.129). We tested Pharaoh's people with droughts and shortage of crops that they may heed (7.130). When good befalls them they would say: "This is due to us," and when evil afflicts them, they would attribute it to the ill fortune of Moses and those with him; surely their ill fortune is only from Allah, but most of them do not know (7.131). They said: "Whatever sign you may bring to bewitch us, we will not believe you" (7.132). We sent upon them the flood, the locusts, the lice, the frogs, and the blood as clear signs; but they behaved arrogantly and were guilty (7.133). When the plague hit them, they said: "O Moses! Pray to your Lord for us, by whatever covenant He has with you, that if you remove the plague from us we will believe you and we will send away with you the Children of Israel" (7.134). But when We removed the plague from them till a term that they must reach, they broke the promise (7.135). Therefore We took retribution on them and drowned them in the sea because they denied Our signs and were heedless of them (7.136).

First, the Israelites' complaint that they were being harmed after Moses came as they used to suffer before and Moses' advice to them to be patient suggests that these testing circumstances lasted for some time (7.127-129). **Second**, the reference to several "droughts" implies a period of a few years. **Third**, verse 7.131 further implies that the afflictions of "droughts and shortage of crops" did not happen in successive years. The people of Pharaoh were having changing spells of good and ill fortune so that they would receive any good as a deserved grace while accuse Moses and his followers of being the source of their ill fortune whenever a calamity struck.

Fourth, all this happened even before Pharaoh's people were hit by the plagues. **Fifth**, the plagues themselves must have happened over a period of time, as they were not simultaneous. A catastrophe like a flood or an attack of swarms of locusts leaves effects that can last for a few months at least. Therefore, Moses' second sojourn in Egypt can be reasonably estimated to have lasted for around 8-10 years.

There is another Qur'anic reference that implies that Moses stayed for a relatively long time in Egypt after returning from Midian. After relating details of the encounter between Moses and the magicians, the Qur'an goes on to state the following:

> But none believed in Moses except some offspring of his people while full of fear of Pharaoh and their chiefs that he would persecute them. Surely Pharaoh was lofty in the land; and surely he was one of the extravagant (10.83). Moses said: "O my people! If you believe in Allah, then rely on Him, if you are Muslims" (10.84). They said: "On Allah we rely; Our Lord! Do not make us subject to the persecution of the unjust people (10.85) and deliver us by Your mercy from the disbelieving people" (10.86). We revealed to Moses and his brother: "Take you both, for your people, houses in Egypt; make your houses *qibla*; and perform the prayer. Do give good tidings to the believers" (10.87).

The obvious implication of the divine command to Moses and Aaron to take houses to live in is that they must have stayed in Egypt for a considerable time, probably several years, before leaving with their people. (Verse 10.87 is discussed in more detail on pp. 130-133.)

Now, let's recap on our conclusions to estimate the length of Pharaoh's reign. **First**, Pharaoh had already been in power for an unknown period when Moses was born, so our estimate will be for the *minimum* time that Pharaoh reigned. **Second**, Moses was around 20-22 years old when he was still in Egypt. This was roughly his age when "Wisdom and Knowledge" were conferred on him by God. We do not know how long after that he killed that enemy and escaped to Midian. **Third**, Moses stayed in Midian for 8-10 years. **Fourth**, he stayed for about 8-10 years in Egypt after returning from Midian. Adding all these figures, Moses must have been 36-42 years old when he led the Israelites' exodus from Egypt.

This is actually a conservative underestimate. Probably Moses was not born on the same year of Pharaoh's accession, although we cannot tell how many years later. Therefore, we can safely conclude that Pharaoh reigned for at least 40 years.

This conclusion can help us identify that particular Pharaoh because throughout the history of Pharaonic Egypt only a few Pharaohs ruled for such a long time. In the second half of the second millennium BCE, which covers all possible dates of the exodus, but even possibly during the whole of the second millennium BCE, there were only two Pharaohs who reigned for more than 40 years: Tuthmosis III (1504-1450 BCE) and Ramesses II (1279-1212 BCE). The next longest reigning Pharaoh in the second half of the second millennium BCE was Amenhotep III

(1386-1349 BCE), Akhenaten's father, who ruled for 37 years.

Amenhotep III reign was probably too short for him to be the Pharaoh of the exodus. Furthermore, this Pharaoh is believed to have died late in his forties. He must have become Pharaoh when he was around 10 years old or younger. The Pharaoh that baby Moses was taken to his palace was a mature man, so it could not have been Amenhotep III.

Tuthmosis III, who ruled for 46 years, was still a young child when he succeeded to the throne of Egypt after the death of his father Tuthmosis II (1518-1504 BCE) to become the 5th Pharaoh of the 18th Dynasty. His stepmother and aunt queen Hatshepsut acted in the beginning as regent for the young Pharaoh. By the second regnal year of Tuthmosis III, Hatshepsut had been working to undermine the position of the child Pharaoh in order to usurp the throne. She strengthened her grip on power, leaving the real Pharaoh well in the shadow. It was only after Hatshepsut's death in 1483 BCE that Tuthmosis III started to act as the real and absolute monarch. This means that Tuthmosis III reigned as absolute Pharaoh for only about 33 years. He could not have been the Pharaoh that the Qur'an talks about and who was the absolute ruler for at least 40 years.

We can, thus, conclude with certainty that the Qur'an identifies the Pharaoh of the oppression and exodus as Ramesses II, who ruled for 67 years. No other Pharaoh in the period during which the exodus took place reigned long enough as the Qur'an implies that Pharaoh did. This is a very different conclusion to the one drawn from the Bible. The latter states that the Pharaoh of the oppression was different from that of the exodus, and it implies that the latter was Merneptah (pp. 82-86).

The suggestion of some modern scholars, such as an-Najjār (1986) and Bucaille (1995), that the Qur'an implies that the Pharaoh of the exodus was Merneptah is wrong. The conclusion of these writers is not based on the Qur'anic account only but on an unjustified mix of Qur'anic and Biblical narrations.

Since the Qur'an states that Pharaoh drowned during his pursuit of the fleeing Israelites, the date of the exodus must be 1212 BCE, which when Ramesses II died. This in turn means that we can now estimate the length of the sojourn of the Israelites in Egypt. Let's recall that earlier we concluded that Joseph entered Israel probably during the reign of the first Hyksos ruler, but not later than the second (pp. 37-37). In other words, Joseph entered Egypt sometime around 1660-1645 BCE, so the Israelites' sojourn in Egypt lasted around 448-433 years. The Biblical figure of 430 years is not too far off the real figure.

6.3 The Pharaoh "of the *awtād*"

The Qur'an provides another *unique* description of Pharaoh that can also be shown to be perfectly and particularly applicable to Ramesses II. Cited below are the two verses in which the unique title "of the *awtād*" is applied to Pharaoh, along with some of the surrounding verses which are needed to study the meaning of the this phrase:

> Or is it that theirs is the kingdom of the heavens and the earth and what is between them? Then let them ascend through the ways (38.10)! Defeated soldiers are the parties that are there (38.11). The people of Noah and 'Ād, and Pharaoh *of the awtād* rejected [the messengers] before them (38.12). And Thamūd, the people of Lot, and the people of the thicket; these were the parties (38.13).
>
> Have you not considered how your Lord dealt with 'Ād (89.6), the city of Iram of the lofty pillars (89.7), the like of which had never been created in the lands (89.8); Thamūd who cut the rocks in the valley (89.9); and Pharaoh *of the awtād* (89.10); who all transgressed in the lands (89.11), causing much corruption in them (89.12), so your Lord poured on them a bout of chastisement (89.13)?

Exegetes have expressed different views on the meaning of "of the *awtād*" here as the word *awtād*, which is the plural of *watad*, has a number of different meanings. Among the interpretations that have been proposed for *awtād* are "excessive power or violence," for Pharaoh was a violent tyrant, and "soldiers," for he had a large army. The opinion that has attracted more consensus is that this appellation refers to the "pegs" or "spikes" that Pharaoh used to torture or crucify people, including those who converted to Moses' religion, such as the magicians (see also 26.49):

> So the magicians were thrown down in prostration (7.120). They said: "We believe in the Lord of all peoples (7.121), the Lord of Moses and Aaron" (7.122). Pharaoh Said: "You have believed in Him before I give you permission? This is a plot that you have devised in the city to drive its people out of it, but you shall know (7.123). I will cut off your hands and legs on opposite sides, and then I will crucify you all" (7.124).
>
> So the magicians were thrown down in prostration; they said: "We believe in the Lord of Aaron and Moses" (20.70). He said: "You have believed in him before I give you permission? He must be your master who taught you magic. I shall cut off your hands and feet on opposite sides, and I will crucify you on the trunks of palm trees. You shall know who of us can give the more severe and lasting punishment" (20.71).

The Qur'an indeed *implies* that Pharaoh used "pegs" or "spikes" when torturing those who embraced Moses' religion as crucifixion would have included the use of such tools. But the word *awtād* is not used in any of these verses. Furthermore, this word appears in the Qur'an in a totally different sense. The exegetes' confusion seems to have been partly caused by the failure to notice the subtle distinction in the Qur'anic text between words *jibāl* and *rawāsī*, both of which are used to denote "mountains." This needs clarification.

There are nine Qur'anic verses (13.3; 15.19; 16.15; 21.31; 27.61; 31.10; 41.10; 50.7; 77.27) that state that God has created on the earth *rawāsī*. This is an example:

> It is He who spread out the earth and made in it *rawāsī* (mountains) and rivers (from 13.3).

Three of the nine verses (15.16; 21.31; 31.10) also tell us that these *rawāsī* or mountains function as *stabilizers* that prevent the earth from "shaking" or "trembling":

> We have made *rawāsī* (mountains) in the earth lest it might shake with them (from 21.31).

On the other hand, there is a verse in which the mountains are described as *awtād*:

> Have We not made the earth as an even expanse (78.6) and the *jibāl* (mountains) as *awtād* (78.7)?

Wrongly equating verses 78.6-7 with those verses that state that the *rawāsī* (mountains) *prevent the earth from tumbling* has misled exegetes to conclude that *awtād* means "pegs" that keep the earth stable.

Significantly, whenever mentioning the mountains' role in keeping the earth stable, the Qur'an always uses the word *rawāsī*, it never uses *jibāl* even though the latter is mentioned as many as 33 times in the book. Equally significant is the fact that the Qur'an never describes the *rawāsī* as being *awtād*. So there is no evidence that the Qur'anic statement that God has made the "*jibāl* as *awtād*" is a different way of saying that He has assigned to the mountains a stabilizing function on the earth. This misunderstanding is the result of equating totally different verses with each other. So what, then, does *awtād* mean?

The meaning of the word *awtād* in verse 78.7, where it describes the *jibāl*, can be reliably identified by examining another set of verses that also use the word *jibāl* and which have a similar function to verses 78.6-7:

> Do they not look then at the camels, how they are created (88.17)? And the heaven, how it is raised high (88.18)? And the *jibāl* (mountains), how they are hoisted (88.19)? And the earth, how it is spread out (88.20)?

Among other things, these verses are a reminder of how God built the high heaven, spread out the earth, and erected the mountains. It is this function of reminding people of the *contrasting* geographical features that God has created, and in particular the creation of an *even* earth and *high* mountains, that verses 78.6-7 also perform. Verses 88.19 and 88.20, therefore, are equivalent to verses 78.7 and 78.6, respectively, and not to the verses that describe the mountains as stabilizing the earth. In other words, *making the jibāl awtād* and *building high mountains* are two different wordings with the same meaning. We can conclude, therefore, that the word *awtād* denotes *high buildings*, in contrast to even lands.

The context of one of the two occurrences of the phrase "Pharaoh of the *awtād*" lends clear support to this interpretation of *awtād*:

> Have you not considered how your Lord dealt with 'Ād (89.6), the city of Iram of the lofty pillars (89.7), the like of which had never been created in the lands (89.8)? And Thamūd who cut the rocks in the valley (89.9)? And Pharaoh of the *awtād* (89.10)? They all transgressed in the lands (89.11), causing much corruption in them (89.12), so your Lord poured on them a bout of chastisement (89.13).

These verses give a reminder first of the people of 'Ād who used to build lofty "pillars," then of the people of Thamūd who used to cleave rocks in a valley to build houses,[11] and finally of "Pharaoh of the *awtād*." Taking the word *awtād* to mean tools used by Pharaoh to crucify people would make the phrase "Pharaoh of the *awtād*" totally out of context in these verses. On the other hand, understanding *awtād* here as denoting some kind of *high and large buildings* makes the link between all verses obvious: they all describe corrupt peoples who used to build giant, secure buildings before they were fatally punished by God.

Interestingly, in his commentary on verse 38.12 in his classical exegesis of the Qur'an, al-Qurṭubī (d. 1272 CE) starts his survey of a number of different interpretations of the word *awtād* citing Ibn 'Abbās who interpreted "of the *awtād*" as meaning "of the secure building" and then adh-Dhaḥḥāk whose comment on the phrase "Pharaoh of the *awtād*" reads as follows: "he used to build a lot; buildings are called *awtād*."

---

[11] This is also shown in the following verses in which prophet Ṣāliḥ addressed his fellow Thamūdians:

> Remember when He made you successors after 'Ād, and lodged you in the land — taking to yourselves castles of its plains and hewing its *jibāl* (mountains) into houses. Remember the benefits of Allah, and do not cause corruption on earth (7.74).
>
> Will you be left secure in this here (26.146) — in gardens, springs (26.147), sown fields, and date palms with ripe fruits (26.148), and lavishly carving of the *jibāl* (mountains) houses (26.149)?

Other exegetes, such as aṭ-Ṭabarī (840-922 CE), have cited the view of some that *awtād* means "playgrounds," which also implies *buildings*, erected to entertain Pharaoh.

Having allowed us to identify Pharaoh as Ramesses II, the Qur'an's description of Pharaoh as *of the buildings* could not have been more accurate. This Pharaoh was involved in building projects more than any other Pharaoh in the history of Egypt. He erected huge statues and built temples throughout Egypt. "As a monument builder", Clayton notes, "Ramesses II stands pre-eminent amongst the pharaohs of Egypt. Although Khufu had created the Great Pyramid, Ramesses' hand lay over the whole land." He then goes on to state the following on Ramesses II:

> His genuine building achievements are on a Herculean scale. He added to the great temples at Karnak and Luxor, completed his father Seti's mortuary temple at Gourna (Thebes) and also his Abydos temple, and built his own temple nearby at Abydos. On the west bank at Thebes he constructed a giant mortuary temple, the Ramesseum. Inscriptions in the sandstone quarries at Gebel el-Silsila record at least 3000 workmen employed there cutting stone for the Ramesseum alone. Other major mortuary temples rose in Nubia at Beit el-Wali, Gerf Hussein, Wadi es-Sebua, Derr and even as far south as Napata. (Clayton, 1994: 153)

Commenting on this Pharaoh's incredible obsession with building, Kitchen's notes that he "desired to work not merely on the grand scale — witness the Ramesseum, Luxor, Abu Simbel, and the now vanished splendours of Pi-Ramesse — but also on the widest possible front as the years passed." Kitchen stresses that "certainly in his building-works for the gods the entire length of Egypt and Nubia, Ramesses II surpassed not only the Eighteenth Dynasty but every other period in Egyptian history. In that realm, he certainly fulfilled the dynasty's aims to satiety" (Kitchen, 1982: 225). It is clear why the Qur'an calls Ramesses II "Pharaoh of the *awtād*."

The fact that the expression "Pharaoh of the *awtād*" occurs where Thamūd's practice of building houses in mountains is mentioned may suggest that this title also implicitly refers to the two temples at Abu Simbel in Nubia which were cut in the living rock of the mountainside. The first of these, the "Great Temple," is a huge building with two pairs of colossal seated figures of Ramesses II, each 18 meters high, flanking its entrance. These temples are considered to be Ramesses II's greatest building achievement.

Understanding the expression "Pharaoh of the *awtād*" as a reference to Pharaoh's preoccupation with buildings, to venerate his gods and himself and claim unparalleled glory, explains his wife's prayer in this verse:

> God has struck a similitude for the believers in the wife of Pharaoh, as she said: "My Lord, build for me a house in Paradise in Your presence, deliver me from Pharaoh and his work, and deliver me from the evildoing people" (66.11).

It is highly significant that no similar prayer is attributed to anyone else in the Qur'an. It is equally significant that Pharaoh's wife combines her prayer to God to build for her a house in Paradise with her request that He saves her from Pharaoh. By rejecting the religion of her husband she enounced, among other riches, the palaces she would have lived in and possibly the temples that he would have been built for her. Ramesses II dedicated the smaller temple in Abu Simbel of the goddess Hathor — patroness of motherhood, love, and jollity — to his wife queen Nefertari. This favorite wife of Pharaoh could not have been the one mentioned in verse 66.11 who clearly disagreed with her husband. The latter is probably the one who found baby Moses.

The Qur'an's description of the Pharaoh at the time of Moses as "Pharaoh of the *awtād*" is another clear confirmation of the Qur'an's identification of this Pharaoh. There is no better way to distinguish Ramesses II from his predecessors and successors.

6.4 A Mummified Pharaoh

The Qur'an provides another significant piece of information about Pharaoh that applies to Ramesses II, which is the preservation of his dead body.

The Bible clearly states that Pharaoh and all of his soldiers drowned in the sea when they tried to pursue Moses and the Israelites (also Exo. 15:21; Ps. 106:11, 136:13-15):

> Moses stretched out his hand toward the sea, and the Lord drove the sea apart by a strong east wind all that night, and he made the sea into dry land, and the water was divided. So the Israelites went through the middle of the sea on dry ground, the water forming a wall for them on their right and on their left. The Egyptians chased them and followed them into the middle of the sea — all the horses of Pharaoh, his chariots, and his horsemen. (Exo. 14:21-23)

> The Lord said to Moses, "Extend your hand toward the sea, so that the waters may flow back on the Egyptians, on their chariots, and on their horsemen!" So Moses extended his hand toward the sea, and the sea returned to its normal state when the sun began to rise. Now the Egyptians were fleeing before it, but the Lord overthrew the Egyptians in the middle of the sea. The water returned and covered the chariots and

the horsemen and all the army of Pharaoh that was coming after the Israelites into the sea — not so much as one of them survived! But the Israelites walked on dry ground in the middle of the sea, the water forming a wall for them on their right and on their left. So the Lord saved Israel on that day from the power of the Egyptians, and Israel saw the Egyptians dead on the shore of the sea. (Exo. 14:26-30)

Exodus 14:30 indicates that the Israelites saw the Egyptians being thrown ashore dead. But there is no reference to the body of the dead Pharaoh. The Bible would have mentioned it if Pharaoh's drowned body was seen among his soldiers'. We can safely assume that the Bible implicitly states that the body of the drowned Pharaoh was not spotted by the Israelites.

A clear confirmation that this is what the Bible implies is found in the way many Biblical scholars reacted when Merneptah's mummy was not found in his tomb in the Valley of the Kings or in the cache of royal mummies when it was discovered in 1881 near Deir al-Bahari in Thebes. They claimed that Merneptah must have been the Pharaoh of exodus who drowned in the sea so his body would have disappeared. This claim, however, had to be abandoned in 1898 when Merneptah's mummy was found in the royal mummies cache which was concealed in Amenhotep II's tomb in the Valley of the Kings along with other 15 mummies (Clayton, 1994: 158). Interestingly, the presence of a heavy encrustation of salt on the skin of Merneptah's mummy has been explained by some as a proof that he was indeed the Pharaoh of the exodus who perished in the sea. This, in fact, is the result of the embalming (Harris & Weeks, 1973: 157; Partridge, 1996: 160).

While the Qur'an agrees with the Bible that Pharaoh and his soldiers all drowned, it disagrees with it as it stress that the body of the drowned Pharaoh was saved to become a sign for people:

> We made the children of Israel to pass through the sea, then Pharaoh and his soldiers followed them in transgression and oppression; until when the drowning overtook him, he said: "I believe that there is no god but He in whom the children of Israel believe and I am one of the Muslims" (10.90). Now, having disobeyed before and having been one of the corrupters (10.91)? Today We shall save you in the body that you may be a sign to those after you. Surely many people are heedless of Our signs (10.92).

Given that Pharaoh drowned in the *sea*, and given that all those with him also drowned, one would expect Pharaoh's body to have been lost for good. It would have been extremely difficult to recover it, even if serious attempts were made, particularly if we remember the limited capabilities at the time for such a rescue operation. So the Qur'anic statement that the body of the drowned Pharaoh was saved stands completely against what one would expect to have happened.

But the Qur'an's extremely unlikely scenario is confirmed by the fact the body of Ramesses II has survived in a mummified form. Ramesses II's mummy was found in 1881 amongst 40 mummies kept in a cache near Deir el-Bahari. As the tombs of the New Kingdom Pharaohs continued to be targeted by robbers who caused damage to the mummies, concerned priests decided about 1000 BCE to gather these mummies together and conceal them in two caches — one of them contained the mummy of Ramesses II and the other contained Merneptah's. As Bucaille (1995: 239) rightly points out, nothing whatsoever was known at the time of the revelation of the Qur'an about these mummies.

There is another significant observation that we need to consider here. God mentions in the Qur'an many peoples whom He punished and made signs of for later generations. With the exception of Pharaoh, God never states that He saved the bodies of those people or made their bodies signs for others. There are many cases where the Qur'an indicates that the ruined houses and cities that these peoples left behind, which remained visible to those who lived after them, speak about God' revenge. But in none of these cases does the Qur'an state that the bodies of the perished people were still there or left for later generations to see. For instance, this is what the Qur'an says about the people of Thamūd:

> See what the end of their scheme was! We destroyed them and their whole people (27.51). Those are their houses, empty, because of what their wrongdoing (27.52).

This is also what the Qur'an says in another verse about both peoples of 'Ād and Thamūd:

> And [similarly] 'Ād and Thamūd, and it has become clear to you from their dwellings, and Satan made their work look fair to them so he turned them away from the [straight] way, though sighted they were (29.38).

This verse talks about people of old times in general:

> Is it not clear to them how many generations we destroyed before them whose dwellings they walk over! There are signs in this; do they not then hear (32.26)?

In other instances, the Qur'an indicates that the *news* itself about what happened to the people God punished for their disbelief is the sign left for later generations to ponder on. In these cases also He never states that He preserved the bodies of those people as a sign. Remarkably, this applies even when God states that He made a sign for later generations of a people that He destroyed by drowning them, i.e. as He did to Pharaoh and his soldiers. He never says that the bodies of the drowned people are the sign, implying that it is the *news* about what happened to them that represents the sign:

> When the people of Noah rejected the messengers we drowned them and made them a sign for people. And we have prepared for the wrongdoers a painful chastisement (25.37).

Another fact worth noting is that the Qur'an states that God rescued Pharaoh's body in order to make of him a sign for those *after him* and did not confine this statement to the people of Egypt and/or to those who lived at the time. Since its discovery, Ramesses II's mummy has been seen by people from everywhere. It is currently one of the major tourist attractions in the Egyptian Museum in Cairo.

6.5 Miscellaneous Notes

There are a number of secondary points that are still worth noting in passing:

(1) Pharaoh knew Joseph: While the Bible claims that the Pharaoh of oppression did not know Joseph (Exo. 1:8), the Qur'an makes it clear that Joseph was known to Pharaoh, as seen in the following words of an Egyptian believer to the monarch and his council:

> Surely Joseph came to you in times gone by with clear proofs, but you ever remained in doubt about what he brought to you. When he died, you said: "Allah will not send a messenger after him." Thus does Allah cause to err him who is an extravagant doubter (40.34).

That Pharaoh and his people knew of Joseph is a far more reasonable suggestion than the Bible's opposite claim. Both books agree that Joseph rose to a high position and both imply that this was under the rule of the Hyksos. Both scriptures also imply that the Pharaoh in question is Ramesses II who we know lived in the same area of Egypt where Joseph lived a few centuries before. The claim that Ramesses II had not heard of that high-ranking Israelite is unrealistic. It was Pharaoh's knowledge of the history of the Israelites and their past relationship with the Hyksos that made him think that Moses might have been thinking of leading his people to *drive the Egyptians out of their land* (pp. 38-40).

(2) Adoption of Moses as a son: After finding Moses, Pharaoh's wife appealed to her husband not to kill the baby, mentioning the possibility that they may adopt him:

> The wife of Pharaoh said: "[He will be] a delight for the eye for me and you. Do not kill him. He may be useful for us, or we may take him as a son," while they were unaware [of what was going to happen] (28.9).

Some exegetes, such as al-Qurṭubī and Ibn Kathīr in their respective comments on verse 28.9, believe that this indicates that Pharaoh's wife had no children. In his commentary on the same verse, aṭ-Ṭabaṭabāʾī claims that Pharaoh and his wife did not have a son. Exegetes, such as al-Jalālayn and Ibn Kathīr in their respective comments on 12.21, have drawn a similar conclusion from a similar verse claiming that the person who bought Joseph in Egypt had no children:

> The man who bought him from Egypt said to his wife: "Give him an honorable abode; he may prove useful to us, or we may adopt him as a son" (from 12.21).

The conclusions about those who considered adopting Joseph and Moses are both unnecessary. In each case one finds in the Qur'an a possible reason, other than the deprivation of children, as to why a wish of adoption was expressed as a second possibility besides taking the child as a slave. In Joseph's case, it was his exceptional beauty (12.31), and in Moses' it was the love that God conferred on him: "I threw over you love from Me" (from 20.39). Shaikh 'Abd al-Qadir al-Jilani notes that "it has been said that anyone who would look him in the eye would love him" (al-Jilani, 2008: 69).

There is another argument to make. Had the couple who bought Joseph or Pharaoh and his wife been without children and interested in adopting one, they would have done that earlier and would not have waited for the odd chance that a child would suddenly turn up in strange circumstances as happened with Joseph and Moses.

(3) Day of the encounter between Moses and the magicians: When Pharaoh challenged Moses to choose a time to compete with the magicians he was going to bring, Moses chose the day of *zīna*:

> He said: "Have you come to us to drive us out of our land by your magic, O Moses (20.57)? We too shall produce to you magic like it. Set an appointment between us and you, which neither we nor you shall break, in a place where both shall have even chances" (20.58). He said: "Your appointment shall be the day of *zīna* (decoration), and let the people be gathered together in the early afternoon" (20.59).

The Arabic word *zīna* means "adornment" or "decoration," so this must have been a festive day. It seems to denote a festival in which people dress up smartly, the city itself is adorned or, probably, both take place. During Ramesses II's reign, the Egyptians celebrated many festivals all over Egypt and throughout the year. The festival specified by

Moses must have been celebrated in Pi-Ramesses, though not necessarily exclusively.

It is appropriate here to talk briefly about the fundamental difference that the Qur'an makes between Moses' miracles and the magicians' feats. Magicians are usually experts in particular tricks, so Pharaoh must have chosen magicians who were particularly trained in producing feats similar to Moses' ability to turn the staff into a snake. But what the magicians did was trickery, even though very impressive. In one verse, the Qur'an says: "Their cords and staffs *looked* to him, because of their magic, as if they were moving" (from 20.66). The verb "*looked*" stresses that the magicians' cords and staffs were not in reality moving. A second verse describes the magicians' feats as follows: "So when they threw, they *deceived peoples' eyes*, frightened them, and they produced a mighty feat of magic" (from 7.116). The phrase "*deceived peoples' eyes*" confirms that what the magicians did was an illusion.

On the contrary, Moses' paranormal feat with his staff was real: a miracle. When God first spoke to him he made his staff turn into a snake:

> So he threw it down; and behold! it became a crawling serpent (20.20).
>
> "Throw down your staff." When he saw it moving like a snake he fled without tracing his steps (from 27.10).
>
> "Throw down your staff." When he saw it moving like a snake he fled without tracing his steps (from 28.31).

When Moses went to see Pharaoh he performed this miracle, and the Qur'an confirms that that staff became a snake:

> So he threw his staff down, and it became a manifest serpent (7.107; 26.32).

Another confirmation that the transformation of Moses' staff into a snake was real comes from the fact that it swallowed the magicians' cords and staffs during the contest:

> We revealed to Moses: "Throw your staff"; then lo! it devoured what they faked (7.117).
>
> "Throw down what is in your right hand, and it shall devour what they have worked; that which they have made is a magician's work, and the magician shall not be successful wherever he may go" (20.69).
>
> Then Moses threw down his staff, and it swallowed that which they falsely showed (26.45).

Notice also how verse 7.117 describes what the magicians' feats as "fake."

(4) Ramesses II's magician son: One of Ramesses II's prominent sons, Khaemwaset, who is believed to have died in about the 55th regnal year of his father, became later known by the title of "the magician." There is a papyrus that is said to have been found in Thebes and which is dated to the Ptolemaic Period, around the 3rd century BCE, which relates a story that shows the interest that Khaemwaset had in magic, calling him "a good scribe," i.e. "a magician" (Lewis, 1948: 67-68). The story may have something to do with memories of the competition between Moses and the magicians whom Khaemwaset's father gathered.

7

Who Was Hāmān?

One of the significant differences between the Qur'anic account of Moses' encounter with Pharaoh and its Biblical counterpart is the presence in the former of someone called Hāmān. This figure in Pharaoh's court looks to have been instrumental in the opposition to Moses' mission.

We will study this Egyptian figure first and then examine a Persian Hāmān mentioned by the Bible. We will show that the Qur'anic Hāmān is historical whereas the unhistorical Biblical Hāmān was probably created by changing the original story of the Egyptian Hāmān during the centuries-long editorial work that gave the Bible its final shape.

7.1 The Qur'anic Egyptian Hāmān

Hāmān is mentioned six times in the Qur'an. One verse mentions him in passing, stressing that he drowned with Pharaoh. It belongs to a set of verses that name a number of individuals and peoples whom God destroyed:

> And [similarly] Korah, Pharaoh, and Hāmān. Moses came to them with clear signs, but they behaved proudly in the earth, although they could not outstrip Us (29.39). We seized each one of them on account of his sin. We sent a violent storm on some, we destroyed some by the cry, we made the earth to swallow some, and we drowned others. Allah would not have wronged them, but they wronged themselves (29.40).

Korah was not an Egyptian courtier but a wealthy Israelite (28.76-82). His story in the Bible is recounted in Numbers 16.

Hāmān's close association with Pharaoh is confirmed in verses that state that Moses was sent to Hāmān also:

> We sent Moses with our signs and clear authority (40.23) to Pharaoh, Hāmān, and Korah, but they said: "A lying magician!" (40.24).

Hāmān's prominence is further confirmed in verses that talk about "Pharaoh, Hāmān, and *their* soldiers" (28.6, 8):

> We narrate to you [O Muhammad!] parts of the story of Moses and Pharaoh in truth, for people who believe (28.3). Pharaoh exalted himself in the earth and made its people castes, oppressing one group of them, killing their sons and sparing their women; he was one of the corrupters

(28.4). We desired to show favor to those who were oppressed in the earth, make them leaders, make them the inheritors (28.5), establish them in the earth, and show Pharaoh, Hāmān, and *their* soldiers from them that which they feared (28.6). We inspired Moses' mother: "Suckle him, and when you fear for him, cast him into the river and do not fear or grieve; We shall bring him back to you and make him one of the messengers" (28.7). Then the people of Pharaoh picked him up [from the river], to become for them an enemy and a sorrow; Pharaoh, Hāmān, and *their* soldiers were sinful (28.8).

Attributing the soldiers to Hāmān also means that he was probably Pharaoh's second-in-command or the army chief. Note that, as expected, Korah is not mentioned in these verses.

Verses 28.6 and 28.8 refer to future events which were to follow the commissioning of Moses. They do not imply that Hāmān who advised Pharaoh on his confrontation with Moses was present at the time of Moses' birth. His absence at that time can be concluded from two observations. **First**, when mentioning the massacre of the Israelite male infants, verse 28.4 names Pharaoh only as the culprit. Had Hāmān had a hand in that massacre the Qur'an would have mentioned him with Pharaoh because it does mention him immediately after that in the other two verses that mention Pharaoh (28.6, 8).

Second, Hāmān's mention with Pharaoh is associated in both cases with a mention of "their soldiers." The soldiers are clearly those who drowned in the sea and could not have been Pharaoh's soldiers at the time of Moses' birth. The final showdown between Moses and Pharaoh and his army was at least four decades after Moses' birth (pp. 101-105). By then, most if not all of the soldiers at the time of Moses' birth were no longer in service.

The verses above mention the destruction of Pharaoh, Hāmān, and their soldiers after mentioning the killing of the Israelite boys to emphasize that the massacre did not prevent God from inflicting revenge in the future at the hand of someone whom Pharaoh wanted to kill while an infant. So verses 28.6 and 28.8 speak about a Hāmān during Moses' second sojourn in Egypt. This observation is important for determining Hāmān's identity, because it implies that he was in that influential position from at least Moses' return to Egypt until the exodus — a period of several years (pp. 103-105).

This conclusion may prompt the following doubtful question: If Hāmān and the soldiers were those of a future time even though they are mentioned in the middle of verses on Moses' birth, why would the same not apply to Pharaoh? Why would one not assume that the Pharaoh of the exodus was different from the one who was in power when Moses was born? The answer is that the Qur'an explicitly states in verse 28.3 that the Pharaoh who features in verses 28.6 and 28.8 is the same one who killed the Israelite baby boys and who is mentioned in verse 28.4 (pp. 98-100).

Further conclusions about Hāmān's identity can be made by examining the etymology of his name. It looks has to have a clear link to the name of the Egyptian god Amun. Based on this observation, Syed (1984) has proposed that "Hāmān" in the Qur'an is a *title* not a *name*. He reckoned that as "Pharaoh" was a title and not a proper personal name, the same is true of "Hāmān." Syed suggests that the title "Hāmān" referred to "the high priest of Amun." In support of this analysis, Syed's quotes the following:

> The dispersion of the worship of Amen is noted as pointing to its coming through the Oases and there seems no reason to question that the primitive Oasis worship of Ammon or Hammon, was the origin on the one hand of the Egyptian Amen or Amun, and on the other of the Carthaginian Baal Haman. (Petrie, 1924: 21)

Citing the fact that Egyptian priests used to personate the gods, Syed (1984: 87) suggests that "Amon or Hāmān was the generic title of the high priests when personating the god Amon." With respect to the influence of the position of "Hāmān" or "the high priest of Amun" in Egypt, Syed provides another quote:

> Thus the 'first Prophet' or the high priest of Amon, was at the same time the 'Great Superintendent of Works,' and in this capacity was required to take under his charge the extensive building operations connected with the temple, and to provide splendour in his sanctuary. As 'General of the Troops of the God' he commanded the military forces of the temple, like a mediaeval archbishop and as 'Prefect of the Treasury' had under his control the by-no-means simple administration of the finance. Nor did his authority extend only over the Amon temple and its priesthood. He was also 'Prefect of the Prophets of the Gods of Thebes' and 'Prefect of the Prophets of all Gods of the South and the North.' This can mean nothing else than that all the priests of the country were subordinate to him and that he was the supreme spiritual authority of the realm. (Steindorff, 1905: 96-97)

Syed's identification of Hāmān as "the high priest of Amun" is plausible. Although the gods Re and Ptah were also both honored during Ramesses II's reign, Amun was given supremacy over other gods. The primacy of Amun would have rendered the high priest of this god a very prominent position in Egypt — something that is in line with the Qur'an's portrayal of Hāmān as someone with very high authority in the

Pharaonic court.

According to Kitchen, the positions next to Pharaoh in power were those of the southern and northern viziers, usually of Thebes and Memphis, respectively. The position of high priest of a god was not held by someone who was a priest by training, but was often offered to a vizier or another distinguished personage at the time of retirement to honor him, though sometimes a royal prince would take the job (Kitchen, 1982: 158). If this picture applied to the late years of Ramesses II's reign then the high priest of any god, including Amun, would not have *necessarily* been the most influential figure after Ramesses II, though would still have immense power. The role played by Hāmān in Pharaoh's concerted efforts to foil Moses' mission shows Hāmān as having high authority but does not portray him *necessarily* as the highest ranking person in the court of Pharaoh.

Hāmān might well have been particularly prominent in the conflict with Moses because of its very nature, i.e. being a religious confrontation. As the high priest of the main god of the empire, the high priest of Amun had to be consulted on the threat that the new religion posed and his advice would have been far more important than that of any other official in Pharaoh's court, including the southern and northern viziers. In support of this it should be stressed that Moses' mission did not represent an *immediate military* danger to Pharaoh but mainly a *religious* threat.

Pharaoh was anxious not to let the Israelites leave to Canaan fearing that they would join forces with ambitious Semitics and return to Egypt to militarily claim Pi-Ramesses, the ancient capital of the Hyksos (pp. 38-40). But this danger was easy to avert by simply preventing the Israelites from leaving Egypt, which Ramesses II did. Yet the longer Moses stayed in Egypt — and he was not going to leave Egypt without his people — the greater the danger he posed to Egypt's religion. The immediate problem that Pharaoh had to deal with was the religious threat, hence the presence of Hāmān as his main advisor. The Israelites had probably kept their own religion, although they had also been influenced by the Egyptians (pp. 143-149), but they were never a threat to Egypt's religion. It was Moses, who was supported by astonishing miracles, that represented a real threat. Killing Moses was not an option, as he was enjoying divine protection that matched his stunning miracles (pp. 130-131).

A crucial factor in the perception of Pharaoh and his court of Moses' mission as a serious threat to their religion was its timing, coming only 120-130 years after the persecution of the god Amun at the hands of

Amenhotep IV (1350-1334 BCE). This Pharaoh, who changed his name to Akhenaten or "Servant of *the Aten*," proscribed the worship of Amun and closed its temples, replacing it with the sun disc: the Aten. This radical Pharaoh even moved to a new capital which he called Akhetaten and which, unlike other older cities, had not been dedicated to any god previously. But Akhenaten's successor started the efforts to restore Amun as god of the empire. Moses' mission would have brought back all those memories and prompted him to seek the advice of the high priest of Amun:

> Pharaoh said: "Let me kill Moses and let him call on his Lord. I fear that he will change your religion or cause corruption in the land" (40.26).
>
> They said: "These are two magicians who wish to drive you out of your land by their magic and to take away your ideal tradition" (20.63).

Syed's plausible identification of Hāmān as the high priest of Amun is consistent with the Qur'anic account and, at the same time, does not contradict what is known about Ramesses II's Egypt. But this general identification cannot be described as definite until supportive evidence is found.

Further significant information is revealed in the Qur'an's following mentions of Hāmān:

> Pharaoh said: "O chiefs! I know no god for you other than me, so kindle for me [a fire], O Hāmān, to bake the mud, and set up for me a lofty tower that I may look at Moses' god; I believe he is one of the liars" (28.38).
>
> Pharaoh said: "'Hāmān, build for me a tower that I may be able reach the ways (40.36) — the ways of heavens to look at Moses' god. I believe he is a liar." So Pharaoh's evil work was made to look fair to him and he was turned away from the straight path. Pharaoh's scheming is bound to fail (40.37).

There are a number of interesting observations. **First**, we have an explicit reference to the use of baked mud in building (28.38) — something that is well-attested in Egyptian literature. **Second**, the use of mudbricks to build the tower is expected, as only temples were usually built of stone. **Third**, Hāmān is portrayed as someone in charge of building projects. **Fourth**, the Pharaonic building command is a reaction very much in consonance with what would be expected of a Pharaoh who was immensely obsessed with building. **Fifth**, Pharaoh's concept of checking the truthfulness of Moses' claims about God by ascending to the heaven via a tower is in line with the Egyptian concept of "the ladder leading to the sky (which) was originally an element of the solar faith," as stated by Breasted (1912: 153) and cited by Syed (1984). Syed also quotes

Petrie's assertion of the prevalence of "the religious notion of the desire to ascend to the gods in the sky" (Petrie, 1924: 84).

In sum, what the Qur'an says about Hāmān is congruent with our knowledge of Ramesses II's Egypt, although currently there is no historical information that would allow us to identify this character.

7.2 The Biblical Persian Hāmān

The Bible does not know of such an influential figure in Pharaoh's court whether under the name of Hāmān or any other name. Apart from Pharaoh himself, there is no prominent Egyptian character in the Biblical account of the exodus. However, an important Hāmān does figure in the Book of Esther whose story is supposed to have taken place in Persia centuries after the exodus.

In Esther we see the Jews after the Babylonian exile being under the rule of Ahasuerus, king of the Persians and the Medes. At some point the king promotes a certain Hāmān to the office of prime minister. Mordecai, a Jewish courtier, refuses for untold reasons to bow before the new prime minister, enraging Hāmān who seeks revenge by planning the destruction of the Jews in the Persian empire. With the help of Esther, Mordecai's cousin and Ahasuerus' wife, the plot fails and Mordecai and his fellow Jews prevail over Hāmān who ends impaled on the stake. This is a very brief summary of the story of Esther.

Starting from the popular yet misguided assumption that the Qur'an contains freely edited content from the Bible, a number of scholars have suggested that the appearance of Hāmān in the Qur'anic story of Moses has resulted from a misreading of the Bible that moved Hāmān from the court of the Persian king Ahasuerus to the Egyptian court. For instance, the entry for "Hāmān" in *The Encyclopedia of Islam* reads as follows: "name of a person whom the Kur'an associates with Pharaoh, because of a still unexplained confusion with the minister of Ahasuerus in the Biblical book of Esther" (Vajda, 1971: 110). This is a reiteration of that source's claim that the Qur'anic account of Pharaoh and Moses is a modification of the narrative of Exodus with "misplaced recollections of both the book of Esther and the story of the tower of Babel." The furthest that *The Encyclopedia of Islam* goes to acknowledge some independence of the Qur'anic account of the Bible is to only concede that "in the fragmentary accounts given in the Kur'an, certain non-biblical elements may be detected!"

The view that the Qur'anic Hāmān is the same Hāmān of Esther but having been misplaced by the confused author of the Qur'an in the story of Moses has a number of fundamental problems. **First**, there is no evidence that the Qur'an's Hāmān is a reproduction of the Biblical Hāmān. **Second**, it unjustifiably ignores the possibility that there was someone called Hāmān in Pharaoh's court. **Third**, it implies, also without justification, that either Hāmān is an unhistorical figure that never existed outside the Bible, so the Qur'an could have learned about it only from the Bible, or that if he was historical then he would have to be the prime minister of the Persian king Ahasuerus, as depicted in the book of Esther. Both implications are false.

Researchers have suggested that "Ahasuerus" might have been how the Persian name that the Greeks rendered as Xerxes (486-465 BCE) was heard by Hebrew speakers. But there has been no possible historical identification of Hāmān or other personnel in Esther, including the Jewess after whom the book is named. The story in Esther also contains information that is known to be wrong, such as the suggestion that Persia was divided into as many as 127 satrapies or provinces. The equivalent numbers given in other historical sources do not exceed 30. It is agreed that Esther has enormous historical problems and that describing it as a historical book cannot be further from the truth. The book is so unhistorical that one recent study has concluded that it is "best seen as a historical novella set within the Persian empire" (Levenson, 1997: 25). This view is accepted by most scholars. The book is so distant from history proper that Levenson goes on to state that "it is misleading to translate Ahasuerus's name as 'Xerxes',[12] since that implies some correlation with the figure known from the Greek sources. Instead, it would seem that the author borrowed Xerxes' name but little else about him in order to create the novella" (Levenson, 1997: 25).

Furthermore, the Bible is known to have anachronous problems — placing characters in the wrong historical periods and places. For instance, Pharaoh Shabtaka (ca. 697-690 BCE) appears in the Table of Nations (Gen. 10:7) as a Nubian tribe (Redford, 1992: 258). So why not think that the Hāmān of Esther rather than the Hāmān of the Qur'an is a case of a misplaced character? The Bible is full of instances of what we have called "contextual displacement" in our book *The Mystery of the Historical Jesus: The Messiah in the Qur'an, the Bible, and Historical Sources*. Contextual displacement denotes a special kind of "textual

---

[12] Bible translations that misleadingly use "Xerxes" for "Ahasuerus" include the *New Century Version*, *New International Version*, *New Living Translation*, and *Contemporary English Version*.

corruption" where "a character, event, or statement appears in one context in the Qur'an and in a different context in other sources." They are often claimed to be proofs that the Qur'an has copied inaccurately from Jewish and Christian sources. The Qur'an argues that it reports the true contexts, and that any different contexts in other sources have resulted from changes made to the original accounts. So contextual displacements are the result of "the Bible's editors moving figures, events, and statements from their correct, original contexts" (Fatoohi, 2007b: 39).

There are good reasons to believe that Hāmān has been the subject of a contextual displacement with a Biblical writer moving him at some point from Pharaonic Egypt to Persia:

(1) The Qur'an's descriptions of Hāmān are fully in line what it is known of Egypt at the time.

(2) The name Hāmān sounds very much like an Egyptian rather than Persian name, being derived from the name of the god Amun.

(3) The Book of Esther is known to be unhistorical.

(4) The unhistorical Hāmān of the fable of Esther is portrayed as the prime minister, i.e. the second figure in Persia after the king. This is the role of the historical Hāmān in Ramesses II's confrontation with Moses.

(5) The plot of the unhistorical Hāmān to annihilate the Jews in the Persian empire was in retaliation to Mordecai's refusal to bow to him because he was a Jew. This plot is suspiciously reminiscent of the role of the Egyptian Hāmān in suggesting and executing the second massacre of the Israelite newborn males to demoralize the Israelites and discourage them from following Moses (pp. 169-172):

> And We sent Moses with our signs and clear authority (40.23) to Pharaoh, Hāmān, and Korah, but they said: "A lying magician" (40.24). When the truth from Us came to them they said: "Kill the sons of those who are with him but spare their women." The scheming of the disbelievers is bound to fail (40.25).

So we can conclude with confidence that there was a Hāmān with Ramesses II but the Hāmān of the Bible is unhistorical.

8

Leaving Egypt

This chapter looks into how Moses prepared the Israelites for the exodus, how they escaped Egypt, and how many of them took part in the flight. The chapter shows that, unlike the contradictory Biblical narrative, the consistent Qur'anic account is in line with historical data.

8.1 Dispersed Enslaved Israel

The Bible implies that the Israelites continued to live together in the eastern Delta of Egypt where their forefathers Jacob and his twelve sons lived. While stressing that the Israelites had become numerous, the contradictory Biblical statement that only two midwives were needed to serve the women of the whole community suggests that the Israelites had not grown in number (Noth, 1962: 23). The Biblical claim that Pharaoh tried to use the two midwives to control the population of the Israelites confirms that. The existence of only two midwives also implies that the Israelites were living together, something that is in line with the Bible's claim that all the Israelites were used as slaves in building the two store cities of Pharaoh. This is the picture that the Bible draws of the Israelites in Egypt: an oppressed foreign people living together on their own in a separate settlement. As put by one scholar, "the picture resembles that of a canton contiguous to Egypt rather than a dispersed ethnic labor force within the country" (Redford, 1997: 62).

This picture is at odds with what is known of how foreigners were treated in Egypt, particularly in the New Kingdom. As far as the Egyptians' treatment of the servile Asiatic labor force is concerned, Redford stresses, "there is little evidence that communal groups were kept together in one part of the country, the whole purpose of the exercise being to meet the need for laborers all over Egypt." He goes on to point out that the fact that certain groups who functioned as units "were momentarily quartered in one part of the country did not imply permanent domicile there. And nowhere during the New Kingdom is there any evidence that any part of this servile population attempted over time to retain its mores and preserve itself as a distinct ethnic entity" (Redford, 1997: 59-60).

It is perfectly reasonable to suggest that throughout the rule of the

Hyksos the Israelites were more or less living together as a community in that particular part of Egypt. Given the high position that Joseph attained, the Israelites probably continued to receive some form of special treatment by the Hyksos even after Joseph's death when they had no one in a position of high authority. At least, they were not persecuted. But this must have changed after the expulsion of the Hyksos from Egypt. The Egyptian authorities had an unrivaled notoriety for mistreating foreigners on their soil. They had no reason to be exceptionally nice to the foreign Israelites and let them continue to live peacefully and comfortably. Successive Pharaohs were always in need for slave laborers for their endless buildings projects; the Israelites could not have escaped this fate.

It has been argued by some that the Israelites must have started to suffer slavery at some point under the Hyksos, otherwise they would have left with them when the Egyptians expelled them from Egypt (Rea, 1961: 5). The suggestion that the Hyksos started enslaving the Israelites is possible, but the fact that the Israelites did not leave with them is not enough evidence to make this assumption plausible. The Israelites were a different ethnic group and they could have chosen to stay in the Delta or were unable to leave for whatever reason. They surely knew that the Egyptians would be worse than any other masters anyway, which suggests that leaving Egypt was probably not an option for them.

Even in the unlikely case that the servitude of the Israelites started under the Hyksos, the expulsion of the latter meant that the Israelites were no longer living in one part of Egypt as a distinct community. They were deployed to various parts of Egypt as the needs for labor force dictated. Interestingly, an Egyptian captain of a Nile vessel called Ahmose stated in his biographical record that as a consequence of his bravery during the conquest of Avaris, the capital of the Hyksos, he was awarded one man and three women as slaves whom he carried off as spoil from the city (*ANET*, 1950: 233). The Israelites were certainly treated similarly and ended up being taken away as slaves individually and in groups. They could not have been singled out for a better treatment than other unfortunate fellow foreigners in other parts of Egypt. Furthermore, the Egyptians had every reason to be particularly nasty to those who not only befriended the expelled Hyksos enemies but even shared some power with them for some time.

The Bible states that the suffering of the Israelites began when "a new king, who did not know about Joseph, came to power over Egypt" (Exo. 1:8) and that this was the same Pharaoh who enslaved and employed them in building Pithom and Rameses (Exo. 1:11), i.e. Ramesses II. Historically, this claim can only be false. By the time they were engaged in servile work at Pi-Ramesses, the Israelites had already lived almost 300 years under the rule of some 15 Egyptian Pharaohs each of whom would have detested to death the memories of the Hyksos and hated those foreigners who built friendly relations with the usurpers of Egyptian land. One can only conclude that the Israelites' servitude started right away after coming under the rule of an Egyptian Pharaoh — probably Ahmose I who expelled the Hyksos — and that their living circumstances turned upside down since then.

Pierre Montet (1974: 171) must have felt the obvious weakness in the Biblical text so he suggested that the Pharaohs of the 18th Dynasty "did not trouble about these nomads (the Israelites)" until the time when Ramesses II decided to build his new capital at ancient Avaris, near to where the Israelites were living. Being peaceful nomads did not mean that the Israelites could not make good slaves, and living in the eastern Delta would not have made them unusable or put them out of the reach of Pharaohs who were in the habit of bringing captives even from outside Egypt. In addition, Montet overlooks the crucial fact that those "nomads" had close relations with the Pharaohs' sworn enemies, the Hyksos — something that no Pharaoh could have ignored.

It might well be the case that many Israelites were gathered from various parts of Egypt and employed in building Pi-Ramesses. But both Biblical implications that *all* the Israelites were employed in the sites of Pithom and Pi-Ramesses and that the servile labor consisted of Israelites only fly in the face of historical facts. The massive size of the building work in the new capital would have required mobilizing many slaves, including Israelites, from various parts of Egypt. Supposing that the unrelenting enslavement of the Israelites had turned them over the centuries into exceptionally skilled building workers, they would have been particularly targeted for employment at the site of the new capital. Even allowing for this, it does not make any sense to suggest that Ramesses II who built nationwide would not have moved at least some of those skilled builders to work at other projects elsewhere.

Even after the new capital was completed in the early regal years of Ramesses II, some slaves would have been kept there to do various jobs in the city or continue some ongoing building work. Some of those slaves were Israelites, and among them was Moses' family. However, in the half a century or so between the completion of the city and Moses' return to Egypt, the majority of those Israelite and non-Israelite slaves were redeployed to various parts of the country where Ramesses II's ambitious building projects required their services.

Let's remember that the need for slave labor was at times such that it prompted the Egyptians to launch military campaigns to import captives, as in the campaign to the "land of the Libyans" in Ramesses II's 44th regnal year (p. 87). The participation of even so many Israelites in building Pi-Ramesses did not help them gather together. By the time Moses returned to Egypt they were still spread throughout the country, though there was a group of them employed permanently in Pi-Ramesses.

8.2 Gathering Israel for the Exodus

While the Biblical narrative contradicts the historical picture of what happened to the Israelites in Pharaonic Egypt, the Qur'an's account is in line with what history says:

> When the magicians came, Moses said to them: "Cast down what you have to cast" (10.80). So when they cast, Moses said: "What you have performed is magic; Allah will make it vain; Allah does not allow the work of corrupters to thrive (10.81). Allah will show the truth to be the truth by His words however much the guilty may hate it" (10.82). But none believed in Moses except some offspring of his people while full of fear of Pharaoh and their chiefs that he would persecute them. Surely Pharaoh was lofty in the land; and surely he was one of the extravagant (10.83). Moses said: "O my people! If you believe in Allah, then rely on Him, if you are Muslims" (10.84). They said: "On Allah we rely; Our Lord! Do not make us subject to the persecution of the unjust people (10.85) and deliver us by Your mercy from the disbelieving people" (10.86). We revealed to Moses and his brother: "Take you both, for your people, houses in Egypt; make your houses *qibla*; and perform the prayer. Do give good tidings to the believers" (10.87).

The fact that only "some" of Moses' people believed in him is in line with what happened to every prophet whose following among their people increased only gradually and remained confined to a small minority, at least in the early stages of his missions. But the belief of only a minority of the Israelites has probably another reason also.

This was not because they feared the revenge of their masters, because verse 10.83 tells us that the believers kept this faith secret, so the rest could have done so as well. Moses was not only a prophet for the Israelites but he also came to deliver them from their misery and give them hope, so why didn't all the Israelites believe in him? Additionally, the Qur'anic statement that only "some" of Moses' people believed in him comes after his victory over the magicians and their conversion to his religion — a miracle that was performed in public.

There is also another miracle that those Israelites were aware of.

Moses enjoyed impunity from God that protected him from Pharaoh. When Moses told God that he was afraid to go back to Egypt because he had killed an Egyptian, God reassured him:

> He said: "My Lord! I fear that they will accuse me of telling lies (26.12), my breast will be straitened, and my tongue will not speak plainly, so call Aaron [to help me] (26.13). They also have a charge of crime against me, so I am afraid that they will kill me" (26.14). He said: "By no means. Go you both with Our signs; We shall be with you, hearing" (26.15).

> He said: "We will strengthen you with your brother, and We will give you both authority so that they shall not be able to reach you [for harm] on account of Our signs. You both and those who follow you will be the victorious" (28.35).

> "Go you and your brother with My signs and do not slacken in remembering Me (20.42). Go both to Pharaoh; he has transgressed (20.43). Speak to him gentle words that he may remember or fear" (20.44). They said: "O our Lord! We fear that he may hasten to do evil to us or that he may play the tyrant" (20.45). He said: "Do not fear; I am with you, hearing and seeing" (20.46).

Indeed, the following verse makes it clear that Pharaoh considered killing Moses:

> Pharaoh said: "Let me kill Moses and let him call on his Lord. I fear that he will change your religion or cause corruption in the land" (40.26).

Throughout the story, there is the obvious implication that Pharaoh was unable to harm Moses. This is why he had to direct his hostilities towards the Israelites:

> The chiefs of Pharaoh's people said: "Do you leave Moses and his people to cause corruption in the land and forsake you and your gods?" He said: "We will kill their sons but spare their women, and surely we will overpower them" (7.127).

This situation was not the result of Pharaoh's powerlessness but rather Moses' impunity. This was purely a divine gift, in the same way that the wonders of his staff were divinely facilitated. Miracles are not amenable to rational explanation.

So given that the Israelites were well aware of Moses' miracles and that he brought with him the hope of freedom, why would only a minority of them believe in him? We are inclined to believe that the reason is that only some Israelites where living at the time in Pi-Ramesses where Moses settled. Those who were living elsewhere may have heard of Moses, but they were not close to witness his miracles.

Some may still argue that verse 10.83 refers to the experience of almost every prophet whereby only a small number of his people believed in his message. But if that verse is open to this interpretation, verse 10.87 can only be understood in terms of the presence of only a small group of the Israelites in Pi-Ramesses when Moses returned to Egypt.

The first part of verse 10.87, "take you both, for your people, houses in Egypt," commands Moses and Aaron to take for the Israelites houses in Egypt. But were the Israelites not already in Egypt? After all, Moses returned to Egypt to deliver the Israelites from their slavery there! Answering this question, and indeed gaining an insight into the divine plan for the Israelites in Egypt under Moses' leadership, requires a proper understanding of the use of the term "Egypt" in the Qur'an. This term occurs in three Qur'anic verses in addition to 10.87. Let's look first at the following two verses:

> The man who bought him from Egypt said to his wife: "Give him an honorable abode; he may prove useful to us, or we may adopt him as a son." And thus did We establish Joseph in the land, and so We could teach him a share of the interpretation of talks; and Allah has full control over His affair, but most people do not know (12.21).
>
> Then when they entered Joseph's place, he admitted his parents to his private place and said: "Enter into Egypt, Allah willing, secure" (12.99).

These two verses make it clear that the term "Egypt" designates the land where the forefathers of the Israelites settled, i.e. Lower Egypt, or more precisely the eastern Delta, which was then under the control of the Hyksos. The term "Egypt" in these verses could not have referred to Upper Egypt as well because it was under the rule of native Egyptian Pharaohs. The divine command to Moses and Aaron to take houses for their people in "Egypt" means that they and their people should settle in the eastern Delta, perhaps somewhere near to where their forefathers lived. Pharaoh was resident in Pi-Ramesses. This interpretation means that, contrary to what the Bible claims, the Israelites were not all already living together as a distinct community near Pi-Ramesses.

If all the Israelites were already living together then it would have been meaningless to ask Moses and Aaron to take houses for their people in Egypt. It would be also difficult to understand why God ordered Moses and Aaron to take residence in "Egypt" if there was one Israelite settlement, which would have certainly been their default and natural place of living. The Qur'an's implication that the Israelites were scattered throughout Egypt rather than living together as a separate community is in agreement with our knowledge of the treatment of the Pharaohs of foreigners in Egypt.

This interpretation of the first part of verse 10.87 is further supported by its second part which orders Moses and Aaron to make their and their people's houses a *qibla*. The Arabic word *qibla* generally means "direction." In one specific religious context in the Qur'an it is used to mean the direction that Muslims face when praying. Thus, *al-Masjid al-Ḥarām* in Makkah which embraces the Kaʻba is called the *qibla* of prayer. Another related meaning for *qibla* is "destination." For instance, it is not uncommon to use *qibla* in modern Arabic in expressions such as "so and so place is the *qibla* of, say, scholars" meaning that this particular place is where scholars go to gain knowledge. It is in this particular sense that the word *qibla* is used in verse 10.78.

The overall meaning of the divine order to Moses and Aaron in this verse is that they should take houses for themselves and for their people in the eastern Delta and that those houses should become a nucleus around which the Israelites, most of whom by that time had been scattered throughout Egypt, should come together. God was subtly positioning the Israelites for their preordained exodus from Egypt.

This interpretation of the referent of "Egypt" and the order given to Moses and Aaron makes the context of the third occurrence of "Egypt" in the Qur'an, which comes from Moses' story this time, quite clear:

> Pharaoh proclaimed among his people: "O my people! Do I not possess the kingdom of Egypt, and these rivers flow beneath me? Do you not see (43.51)? Am I not better than this fellow (Moses) who is contemptible and can hardly speak clearly" (43.52)?

This argument of an enraged Pharaoh occurs after he and his people had suffered the plagues, i.e. late in Moses' sojourn in Egypt and shortly before the exodus. During those 8-10 years that Moses' stay lasted, the Israelites, or at least most of them, migrated gradually from all parts of Egypt and gathered where Moses, Aaron, and the original small Israelite community at Pi-Ramesses were living. Pharaoh's complaint that *the eastern Delta* is his is related to the fact that the Israelites had gathered in a part of that area part of which was increasingly looking to be more under Moses' than his control. This explains Pharaoh's angry assertion that "Egypt" is his.

There are other verses that, like the verses above, can only support the picture of the Israelites moving from all parts of Egypt to gather in the eastern Delta:

> We gave Moses nine manifest signs. Ask the Children of Israel [about] when he came to them, and Pharaoh said to him: "Moses, I think you are bewitched" (17.101). He said: "You know that none sent these down other than the Lord of the heavens and earth as proofs; I think, O Pharaoh, that you are cursed!" (17.102). So he sought to *drive them out of the land* but We drowned him and all those who were with him

(17.103).

The core dispute between Moses and Pharaoh was the refusal of the latter to let the Israelites leave Egypt with Moses. So it would make no sense to suggest — as some Muslim exegetes, such al-Qurṭubī and al-Jalālayn in their comments on 17.103 — that Pharaoh's attempt to *drive the Israelites out of the land* meant that he wanted to force them out of Egypt. Pharaoh's attempt to *drive the Israelites out of the land* occurred *after* most of the Israelites had gathered where Moses and Aaron lived. The only logical interpretation of verse 17.103 is that Pharaoh wanted to remove the Israelites from the eastern Delta and disperse them again throughout Egypt.

We know now why the exodus of the Israelites from Egypt had to happen several years after Moses' return. The Israelites were scattered throughout Egypt, so to escape together from Egypt, aided by divine power, they had to gather together in a place near to their future departure point. This process took that much time. The exodus took place at its specific time because of Pharaoh's decision not to tolerate the expanding settlement of the Israelites any longer and his intention to move to forcefully disperse them again. God ordered the unexpected escape of the Israelites to preempt Pharaoh's plan and foil it.

But does this mean that *all* the Israelites gathered where Moses lived and later left with him? There is nothing in the Qur'an to confirm this. In fact, one particular description by Pharaoh of the escaping Israelites which we will discuss later suggests that probably only some of them went out with Moses (p. 141). This could be because they did not believe Moses or found his call to gather where he lived and then escape with him too risky.

There is one last question to consider about our interpretation that the Israelites gathered in Pi-Ramesses. Given that the Israelites were oppressed slaves, how could they manage to relocate from various places in Egypt to where Moses lived? Why did the Egyptians allow this internal migration of slaves? Regardless of how many Israelites made the journey, how far they came from, and what their specific circumstances were, such a migration must have been facilitated *miraculously* by God.

It is difficult to tell exactly what forms this miraculous intervention took, but it may have included letting the Israelites escape to Pi-Ramesses undetected and having them helped by Egyptian converts. Of course, this is not the only divine, paranormal intervention in the story of the Exodus. Baby Moses' escape of Pharaoh's massacre that claimed the lives of many Israelite children and bringing up him in the palace of that Pharaoh were the first of many miracles. His second sojourn in Egypt saw him perform a number of miracles. God also intervened to protect him and Aaron from any harm that Pharaoh may have tried to cause them. Splitting the sea was the last miracle that Moses performed before leading his people to complete freedom, but his miracles continued after the exodus also, as we will discuss in more detail later (pp. 159-161).

8.3 A Night Escape

Another difference between the Qur'anic account of the exodus and its Biblical counterpart is Pharaoh's position on the departure of the Israelites. The Bible states that after the death of the firstborns of the Egyptians and their cattle, Pharaoh conceded to Moses' demand and gave him the permission to take the Israelites out of Egypt to worship the Lord:

> It happened at midnight — the Lord attacked all the firstborn in the land of Egypt, from the firstborn of Pharaoh who sat on his throne to the firstborn of the captive who was in the prison, and all the firstborn of the cattle. Pharaoh got up in the night, along with all his servants and all Egypt, and there was a great cry in Egypt, for there was no house in which there was not someone dead. Pharaoh summoned Moses and Aaron in the night and said, "Get up, get out from among my people, both you and the Israelites! Go, serve the Lord as you have requested! Also, take your flocks and your herds, just as you have requested, and leave. But bless me also." (Exo. 12:29-32)

Pharaoh then regretted his decision and decided to give chase to the Israelites — something that is seen by some critics not as much a change of heart by Pharaoh as a contradiction in the Biblical narrative (Hyatt, 1971: 44):

> When it was reported to the king of Egypt that the people had fled, the heart of Pharaoh and his servants was turned against the people, and the king and his servants said, "What in the world have we done? For we have released the people of Israel from serving us!" Then he prepared his chariots and took his army with him. (Exo. 14:5-6)

Contrary to the Bible, the Qur'an states that Moses always made it clear to Pharaoh that he intended to take the Israelites out of Egypt for good. He never tried to hide that fact by claiming, as stated in the Bible, that he only wanted to accompany the Israelites on a "three-day journey into the desert" to sacrifice to their God (Exo. 5:3) or making any other misleading claim. A more significant difference between the Qur'an and Bible is the former's assertion that Pharaoh *did not* consent to the Israelites' departure from Egypt:

> They said: "Whatever sign you may bring to bewitch us, we will not believe you" (7.132). We sent on them the flood, the locusts, the lice, the frogs, and the blood as clear signs; but they behaved arrogantly and were guilty (7.133). When the plague hit them, they said: "O Moses! Pray to your Lord for us, by whatever covenant He has with you, that if you remove the plague from us we will believe you and we will send away with you the Children of Israel" (7.134). But when We removed the plague from them till a term that they were to reach, they broke the promise (7.135). Therefore We took vengeance on them and drowned them in the sea because they denied Our signs and were heedless of them (7.136).
>
> We also sent Moses with Our signs to Pharaoh and his chiefs, and he said: "I am the messenger of the Lord of all peoples" (43.46). But when he came to them with Our signs, they laughed at them (43.47). We did not show them a sign but it was greater than its fellow. We seized them with the torment that they may return (43.48). They said: "O you magician! Pray to your Lord for us, by whatever covenant He has with you, and we shall be guided" (43.49). But when We removed the torment from them they broke the promise (43.50). Pharaoh proclaimed among his people: "O my people! Do I not possess the kingdom of Egypt, and these rivers flow beneath me? Do you not see (43.51)? Am I not better than this fellow (Moses) who is contemptible and can hardly speak clearly (43.52)? Why then have bracelets of gold not been cast on him or angels not come with him conjoined" (43.53)? He fooled his people so they obeyed him. They were ungodly people (43.54). When they angered Us, We took revenge on them and drowned them all (43.55).

The fact that the Israelites left Egypt without Pharaoh's permission explains God's instruction to Moses to leave with his people in the darkness of the night:

> We revealed to Moses: "Take away My servants by night, then strike for them a dry path in the sea. Do not be afraid of being overtaken or have any fear" (20.77).
>
> We revealed to Moses: "Take away My servants by night; you will be pursued" (26.52).
>
> "Take away My servants by night. You will be followed" (44.23).

We saw earlier in the chapter that the Israelites' escape on a particular date, which was ordered by God, was to preempt and avert a new hostile action by Pharaoh who was planning to scatter them throughout Egypt. Having ordered Moses and Aaron to establish that Israelite settlement to allow the Israelites to leave together, God was not going to allow Pharaoh to carry out his plan. Moses received the divine command to leave Egypt with his people and they escaped in the night.

Angered by the unexpected escape of Moses and his followers, Pharaoh led an army in pursuit of them. When the Egyptians caught up with the escapees, God instructed Moses to strike the sea with his staff, parting it and creating a dry path that the Israelites followed. When Pharaoh and his soldiers took the same path the sea returned to its normal state and Pharaoh and his army drowned:

> We made the children of Israel to pass through the sea, then Pharaoh and his soldiers followed them in transgression and oppression. When the drowning overtook him, he said: "I believe that there is no god but He in whom the children of Israel believe and I am one of the Muslims" (10.90).
>
> We revealed to Moses: "Take away My servants by night, then strike for them a dry path in the sea. Do not be afraid of being overtaken or have any fear" (20.77). Pharaoh then followed them with his soldiers, so there came upon them of the sea that which came upon them (20.78).
>
> "Take away My servants by night. You will be followed (44.23). Leave the sea dry; they are a host to be drowned" (44.24).

8.4 Going East

The following verses provide further information about the exodus:

> We revealed to Moses: "Take away My servants by night; you will be pursued" (26.52). Then Pharaoh sent into the cities summoners (26.53). [Saying] that: "These are a small isolated group (26.54), they are offending us (26.55), and we are apprehensive of a coalition" (26.56). So We removed them from gardens, springs (26.57), treasures, and a fair abode (26.58); and We caused the Children of Israel to inherit them (26.59). Then they pursued them *mushriqīn* (eastward) (26.60). When the two gatherings became close enough to see each other, those who were with Moses said: "We will be caught" (26.61). He said: "No way! My Lord is with me; He will show me a way out" (26.62). We revealed to Moses: "Strike the sea with your staff," so it split, and each part was like a huge mountain (26.63). We brought near the others (Pharaoh and his army) (26.64). We saved Moses and all those who were with him (26.65). Then We drowned the others (26.66).

Many commentators — such as al-Qurṭubī, aṭ-Ṭabaṭabāʾī, and al-Jalālayn — have understood the Arabic word "*mushriqīn*" in verse 26.60 as meaning "at sunrise." This is indeed one meaning of this word in the Qur'an, as one verse states that the people of Lot were set to be destroyed "*muṣbiḥīn* (in the morning)" (15.66) and another later confirms that they were punished "*mushriqīn*" or "at sunrise" (15.73). Taking the word "*muṣbiḥīn*" in 26.60 also to mean the same, the picture of the exodus given by most exegetes is that of the Israelites escaping in the night and Pharaoh and his army setting out to chase them early in the morning. The significance of identifying the start of the chase to be in the morning must be to indicate that it happened *a few hours* after the escape of the Israelites.

Had this not been the case, there would have been no particular purpose for identifying the time of day when the pursuit started. But the suggestion that Pharaoh and his army started chasing the Israelites *a few hours* after their escape, and thus understanding "*mushriqīn*" as meaning "at sunrise," contradicts verse 26.53.

This verse states that after the escape of the Israelites, Pharaoh sent messengers to other cities to gather an army to pursue them. This would have taken many days — probably a few weeks. Pharaoh and his army could not have pursued the Israelites in the morning that followed the night of their departure. Ibn Kathīr has suggested that it was the *arrival* of the Egyptians to the place of the Israelites rather than their *departure* in pursuit of the escapees that occurred "at sunrise." This reconciliatory interpretation still contradicts verse 26.60 which clearly states that the Egyptians "pursued" not *reached* the Israelites "*mushriqīn*."

Also, Pharaoh and his army caught up with the Israelites when the latter had arrived at the sea. Regardless of which water that sea was (see below), it was not close to Pi-Ramesses, so the pedestrian Israelites must have travelled for days before the much more mobile Egyptian army, with its chariots and horses, caught up with them. The Egyptians must have started their pursuit of the escapees many days after the escape. Had they started the chase within hours after the exodus of the Israelites, they would have needed even less time to catch the escapees.

Taking "*mushriqīn*" this word to mean "at sunrise" not only contradicts what the Qur'an says, but it also conceals an important piece of information about the exodus that this word reveals.

In addition to "at sunrise," the word "*mushriqīn*" also means "eastward," which is how it is used in 26.60. This verse tells us that the Israelites escaped eastward and that Pharaoh and his army followed them in that direction. While most exegetes have understood "*mushriqīn*" as "at sunrise," some have suggested that it should be interpreted as "eastward." In his commentary on 26.60, al-Qurṭubī mentions some scholars who have preferred this interpretation. We should note that, according to the Qur'an, Moses was frank with Pharaoh about his mission to take the Israelites out of Egypt, so he must have also told him where he wanted to take them. Pharaoh knew well the direction of the escapees.

The Qur'an uses the combination of the words "*mashriq*" and "*maghrib*," which mean "east" and "west," respectively, to cover all directions:

> The east and the west are Allah's, so wherever you turn there is the face of Allah. Allah is all-embracing, all-knowing (2.115).

The word "east" includes all the directions in the eastern half-circle from the north to the south, which includes the north-east and south-east, as well as the east. "West" denotes all the directions in the western half-circle from the north to the south, which includes the north-west and south-west, in addition to the west. This is confirmed in the following verse that takes about "*mashāriq* (easts) and "*maghārib* (wests)":

> I swear by the Lord of the easts and the wests that We are able (70.40).

This use of the words "*mashāriq* (easts)" and "*maghārib* (wests)" is related to the change of the positions of sunrise and sunset throughout the year. The literal meanings of "*mashāriq*" and "*maghārib*" are "the locations of sunrise" and "the locations of sunset," respectively.

Other than saying that the Egyptians pursued the Israelites eastward, the Qur'an does not give details about the route of the exodus. The Bible states that Israel's first station after the escape was Sukkoth (Exo. 12:37) and then "Etham, on the edge of the desert" (Exo. 13:20). The escapees next camped "before Pi-hahiroth, between Migdol and the sea... by the sea before Baal Zephon opposite it" (Exo. 14:2). These details are confirmed and more information about the route is given in Numbers:

> The Israelites traveled from Rameses and camped in Succoth. They traveled from Succoth, and camped in Etham, which is on the edge of the wilderness. They traveled from Etham, and turned again to Pi-hahiroth, which is before Baal-Zephon; and they camped before Migdal. They traveled from Pi-hahiroth, and passed through the middle of the sea into the wilderness, and went three days' journey in the wilderness of Etham, and camped in Marah. They traveled from Marah and came to Elim; in Elim there are twelve fountains of water and seventy palm trees, so they camped there. They traveled from Elim, and camped by the Red Sea. They traveled from the Red Sea and camped in the wilderness of Zin. They traveled from the wilderness of Zin and camped in Dophkah. And they traveled from Dophkah, and camped in Alush. They traveled from Alush and camped at Rephidim, where there was no water for the people to drink. They traveled from Rephidim and camped in the wilderness of Sinai. (Num. 33:5-15)

There is no evidence to support the Bible's route and these specific stops or even the general picture of the escapees going southeast first, during which the encounter with the Egyptian army took place, and then northeast. But we know that the ultimate destination of journey and where they ended up — modern day Palestine — was "eastward." The Biblical route, as traditionally interpreted, which suggests that the Israelites went southeast, can still be described as "eastward" by the Qur'an, as explained above. But, of course, it is equally possible that the escapees headed "east" not "southeast."

What makes forming a view on the route of the exodus more complex is that the exact location of the sea that Israel successfully crossed and the Egyptians drowned in is unclear. The name of the sea in Hebrew is *Yam Sūf*. The word *Sūf* means "reeds," "rushes," or "water plant," which is taken by some scholars — in particular those who prefer a natural interpretation of the miracle of crossing the sea — to denote shallow lakes or marches. But in many places in the Greek translation of the Old Testament, the Septuagint, *Yam Sūf* is translated as the "Red Sea." The Latin translation of the Old Testament, the Vulgate, followed suit. This resulted in most English translations also identifying the sea as the Red Sea (Hoffmeier, 1999: 200). The Red Sea is salt water so it does not have any reeds and so would not have been called the Reed Sea. One popular choice for *Yam Sūf* is any of the marshy lakes in the Isthmus of Suez between the Gulf of Suez and the Mediterranean. A more specific form of this interpretation identifies the Bitter Lakes, the southernmost chain of lakes in the Isthmus of Suez, as *Yam Sūf*. The unproven view that these lakes, which are currently 18 kilometers north of the Gulf of Suez, may have been connected to the Gulf of Suez in ancient times explains for some how the Hebrew term was translated as the Red Sea.

The final liberation of the Israelites came with the very danger of the approaching Pharaonic army. When they became so near that the two groups could see each other, most Israelites doubted that they would be saved (26.61). God then instructed Moses to split the sea, and he crossed it with his people. For the Egyptians, this miracle was even greater than the ones Moses had already shown them. They had one last chance to believe in Moses, but they missed it. They tried to give chase to the Israelites, but they all drowned.

8.5 A Small Isolated Group

As we have already seen, the Bible's claim that 600,000 Israelite men left Egypt with their families and cattle as well as an unspecified number of other people is simply impossible. Almost all scholars reject the historicity of an exodus of 2-3 million Israelites from Egypt to Canaan. Lowering this number considerably makes the exodus possible to have occurred even in the eyes of many researchers who reject the Biblical version of the exodus. An exodus of a relatively small number of people could have occurred without causing a major disturbance in the area, explaining the inexistence of supportive archaeological evidence:

> There are hints here and there to indicate that something like an

exodus could have happened, though on a vastly smaller scale, but there is not a word in a text or an archaeological artifact that lends credence to the Biblical narrative as it now stands. (Ward, 1997: 105)

Stressing the absence of extra-Biblical evidence on "the Biblical account of the sojourn in Egypt or a large-scale migration by the Children of Israel out of that country," One scholar concludes that "if there was an historical exodus, it probably consisted of a small number of Semites migrating out of Egypt in the late 13th or early 12th century BCE" (Weinstein, 1997: 87, 98). Those who entertain the possibility of a historical exodus agree that the number of the escaping Israelites would have been small — much smaller than the impossible 2-3 millions figure. This is indeed in agreement with what the Qur'an said 14 centuries ago.

Contrary to the exaggerated Biblical claim but in line with what archaeological and historical research shows, the Qur'an states that the Israelites who left Egypt with Moses were a small group. The Qur'anic reference to this small number comes in Pharaoh's description of the Israelites as "*shirthimatun qalīlūn*" or a "small isolated group":

> We revealed to Moses: "Take away My servants by night; you will be pursued" (26.52). Then Pharaoh sent into the cities summoners (26.53) [saying] that: "These are a *small isolated group* (26.54), they have angered us (26.55), and we are apprehensive of a coalition" (26.56).

Pharaoh ordered his people to pursue the Israelites, reminding them that the latter were only a small group — probably several thousands — in comparison with his large army. The Arabic term "*qalīlūn*" means "small in number" or "few."

The Arabic term "*shirthimatun*," which we have translated as "isolated group," is also used to refer to small groups. A group of tens of thousands would not be called "*shirthimatun*." This word carries also a sense of deprivation of allies. Pharaoh told his people that the Israelites were a small group and had no allies to reckon with.

"*Shirthimatun*" also means "leftovers," "cutoffs," "remnants," or what is left from a larger group. This further supports the plausibility of the view that not all the Israelites in Egypt escaped with Moses. Some might not have believed Moses and others could have found his plan too dangerous. Furthermore, Pharaoh massacred some of the Israelites (pp. 169-172), so this can also explain why the escapees were a remnant group.

Pharaoh's description of the fleeing Israelites as "small isolated group" is further evidence on the kind of danger he saw in their departure which he long vehemently resisted (pp. 38-40). Here, he reminds his people that they must destroy the *small and isolated* Israelites before they join forces with other Semitics and become *many* and *with allies*. Pharaoh's concern is made even clearer when he follows up his description of the Israelites as a "small isolated group" with the statement: "we are apprehensive of a coalition." Pharaoh never doubted his belief that Moses wanted to take the Israelites out of Egypt to form an alliance with other Semitics and get back to drive the Egyptians out of Pi-Ramesses and re-establish a Semitic kingdom.

One example of the heavy influence of Muslim exegetes by Jewish sources is their reiteration of the Biblical claim that the Israelites numbered 600,000 when they left Egypt. For instance, the well-known 13th century exegete al-Qurṭubī attributes this claim, in his commentary on verse 10.83, to the highly regarded 7th century scholar Ibn 'Abbās; and so does the equally popular work of the 14th century exegete Ibn Kathīr in its commentary on 12.100, claiming that the highly respected 7th century scholar 'Abdullah bin Mas'ūd has stated that the Israelites were 670,000 when they escaped. Another classical exegetical work, by the 10th century exegete aṭ-Ṭabarī, mentions the figure 600,000 in several places, including its commentaries on verses 2.50, 7.128, and 10.90. Obviously, these commentators are directly quoting this figure from Jewish sources. One telling illustration of the great influence of Muslim exegetes by Jewish sources is that the Biblical astronomical figure or its claim that Israelites were numerous are at times quoted at the same place where the term "*shirthimatun*" is explained as meaning a "small group" (see, for instance, al-Qurṭubī in his commentary on 26.53-54 and aṭ-Ṭabarī in his commentary on 2.50, 12.100, and 26.53-54).

Although an old man in his nineties, Ramesses II took part in the pursuit of the Israelites because the confrontation with Moses had become such a personal matter to him. He wanted to be an eye witness to the destruction of the Israelites and, probably more so, Moses and his brother who humiliated him without him being able to harm them. The small number of the Israelites would have also encouraged him to be involved personally in that military action. The aged Pharaoh did not think that he was going to conduct a major military campaign. This was a relatively small scale action against a small number of unarmed former slaves and their leader. The frail Ramesses II was not expecting as much a battle as a complete surrender to slaughter by the Israelites. The outcome, however, was rather different. It was a complete and extremely unwelcome surprise.

9

Post Exodus

The Biblical narrative of the Israelites' invasion of Canaan, from chapter 13 of Numbers to and including Joshua, describes a relatively swift, complete, and systematic conquest of Canaan by a unified Israel under the leadership of Moses and Joshua. This is significantly contradicted by the descriptions in another Biblical book. Judges depicts the conquest as a more gradual process conducted by Israelite tribes acting individually and not always succeeding in their first attempts (Miller, 1977). Also, archaeological excavations in sites mentioned in the Biblical tradition of the conquest of Canaan have revealed massive historical problems in the Biblical account (Dever, 1992). Scholars who retain faith in the historical value of the Biblical text suggest that Joshua should not be read literally and that the reader must be aware that it contains "hyperbole" that is characteristic of the writings of the time (Hoffmeier, 1999: 38-42). One clear problem with this approach is that when the alleged hyperbole engulfs the whole story or most of it, the difference between declaring it as unhistorical and qualifying its historicity by calling it hyperbolic can become rather negligible.

Unlike the Bible, the Qur'an gives very limited historical information about the Israelites immediately after the exodus. Almost all of the reported events seem to belong to the early period after the exodus and before the entry into the holy land. Unsurprisingly, it does not contain anything that supports the Biblical narrative of the conquest of Canaan. But the two books paint a similar picture of the Israelites as a people who, despite the miracles they witnessed, persistently failed to behave properly in a number of different situations. They were impatient, grumpy, lacking firm belief, and continuously questioning Moses' judgments and instructions.

In this chapter, we will cover the small amount of information in the Qur'an about Moses and the Israelites after the exodus and compare it with what the Bible says. We will also examine the earliest mention of Israel in an ancient record and its ramifications for the exodus.

9.1 Polytheistic Behaviors

We have pointed out that Moses' identification of God in his dialog with Pharaoh as being specifically of the Israelites is one aspect of the Bible's wider approach of defining its religion ethnically (pp. 75-76). We have also noted that this portrayal of God and religion is closer to polytheism than monotheism. The Qur'an reports a number of events after the exodus that show how much the Israelites had become influenced by Egypt's polytheistic religion and lost touch with the monotheistic religion of their ancestors Jacob and his sons.

The event described in the following verses looks like the earliest from the post-exodus history of the Israelites that the Qur'an reports:

> We made the Children of Israel cross the sea. They came upon a people who worshipped idols they have created. They said: "Moses, create for us a god as they have gods." He said: "You are ignorant people (7.138). What they are engaged in shall be destroyed and what they are doing is in vain" (7.139). He said: "What, shall I seek for you a god other than Allah when He has preferred you above all peoples" (7.140)?

This, probably peaceful, encounter with an idol worshipping people shows that the centuries of living in polytheistic Egypt have greatly influenced the Israelites. When later Moses left his people for an appointment with God they easily relapsed into the idolatrous worship of a calf despite the presence of Aaron among them. The most detailed account of this event is given in these verses:

> O Children of Israel! We have rescued you from your enemy, appointed a meeting for you on the right side of the mountain, and sent down on you the manna and the quails (20.80), [saying]: "Eat of the good things We have given you, but do not transgress in them, otherwise My wrath would fall on you. Whoever My wrath falls on he would perish (20.81). I am forgiving to the person who repents, believes, does good works, and is guided" (20.82). [We said]: "What have made you rush away from your people, O Moses" (20.83)? He said: "They are hard on my footsteps, but I have rushed to you, My Lord, that You might be pleased" (20.84). He said: "We have tempted your people after you and the Sāmirī has misled them" (20.85). Moses went back angry and sad to his people and said: "O my people! Has your Lord not promised you a good promise? Has the time been too long for you, or did you want wrath from your Lord to fall on you so you broke my appointment" (20.86)? They said: "We did not break your appointment of our volition, but we were made to carry loads of people's ornaments, and we threw them, and so did the Sāmirī" (20.87). He (the Sāmirī) produced for them a calf — a body that lowed, and said: "This is your god and Moses' god," and he forgot (20.88). Could they not see that it did not return any speech and could not help or harm them (20.89)? Aaron had told them before: "O my people! You have been tempted by it and your Lord is Allah, so follow me and obey my commands" (20.90). They said: "We will not cease our devotion to it until Moses comes back to us" (20.91). He (Moses) said: "O Aaron! What prevented you, when you saw that they have gone astray (20.92), from

following me? Have you disobeyed my command" (20.93)? He said: "O son of my mother! Do not seize me by the beard or head. I feared that you may say 'you have divided the Children of Israel and have not observed my word'" (20.94). He (Moses) said: "What is the matter with you, O Sāmirī" (20.95)? He said: "I saw what they did not see, so I grasped a handful from the messenger's track and cast it; so did my soul suggest to me" (20.96). He said: "Go then, you are doomed in this life to say 'do not touch me,' and you will have an appointment that you will not miss. Look to your god which you remained devoted to, we shall burn it and scatter its ashes into the sea" (20.97).

It looks like the Israelites were supposed to follow Moses to where he was commanded to go to meet God. They, however, stayed behind, having been tempted by someone to worship a calf. The verses suggested that the calf, which was made of ornaments, was made to low like a living animal by the Sāmirī, thus encouraging the Israelites to worship it. It is not clear whether what the Sāmirī did was a form of magic. The number of the Israelites who worshipped the calf must have been large enough for Aaron to fear that his insistence on stopping their idolatrous behavior might cause a major division in the community — something that Moses had ordered him to avoid. The meaning and role of the "messenger's track" are unclear.

The Qur'an considers associating deities with God the biggest sin (4.48, 116). The Israelites' worship of the calf is mentioned a number of times in the book (2.51-54, 93; 4.153; 7.148-153). But it also states that God forgave the sinners except those who insisted on it.

This incident is recorded also in the Bible but with significant differences with the Qur'anic account:

> When the people saw that Moses delayed in coming down from the mountain, they gathered around Aaron and said to him, "Get up, make us gods that will go before us. As for this fellow Moses, the man who brought us up from the land of Egypt, we do not know what has become of him!" So Aaron said to them, "Break off the gold earrings that are on the ears of your wives, your sons, and your daughters, and bring them to me." So all the people broke off the gold earrings that were on their ears and brought them to Aaron. He accepted the gold from them, fashioned it with an engraving tool, and made a molten calf. Then they said, "These are your gods, O Israel, who brought you up out of Egypt." When Aaron saw this, he built an altar before it, and Aaron made a proclamation and said, "Tomorrow will be a feast to the Lord." (Exo. 32:1-5)

God then told Moses about what his people had done and commanded him to return to them. He destroyed the calf in a fire and rebuked Aaron for his role in what happened.

One major difference between the story in the Qur'an and the Bible is that the former does not suggest that Aaron was involved in what happened. He told the Israelites that worshiping other than God was wrong (20.90), but he could not stop what they were doing and was even threatened with death if he tried to stop them. He also felt that his insistence on confronting the idol worshippers could split the community:

> When Moses returned to his people angry and grieved he said: "Evil is what you have done after me. Would you hasten your Lord's matter?" He threw down the Tablets and seized his brother by the head, dragging him. He said: "O son of my mother! The people weakened me and almost killed me. Do not make my enemies gloat over me and do not consider me with the wrongdoing people" (7.150). He said: "My Lord! Forgive me and my brother and admit us into Your mercy; You are the most merciful of the merciful" (7.151).

Some of those who believe that the Qur'an is derived from the Bible claim that the Qur'anic story appropriates and confuses two Biblical stories, the one above and another one reported in 1 Kings. After the death of Solomon, the Israelites who were living in the northern part of his kingdom revolted against his son and successor Rehoboam. They chose a new king called Jeroboam, and Rehoboam had to escape to the south were he continued as king. So Solomon's kingdom split into the northern kingdom of Israel whose capital was Samaria and the southern kingdom of Judea with Jerusalem as its capital. Concerned that if his subjects go to the temple in Jerusalem to offer sacrifices their loyalty to the Davidic king of Judea may return and they may then overthrow him, Jeroboam created two gold calves and suggested to his people that they should worship them instead of traveling to Jerusalem (1 Kings 12:1-32).

This story does not look to have any common feature with the Qur'anic story which has a lot of similarity with the story of Exodus 32. It is alleged, however, that the account in 1 Kings 12 is another source of the Qur'an for two reasons. **First**, some translate the term "Sāmirī" as "Samaritan," i.e. from the city of Samaria. In modern Arabic, Sāmirī refers to someone from Samaria. But at the time of Moses Samaria had not been established, so it is concluded that the reference to the Sāmirī must have come from Jeroboam's story and that the Qur'an used the term anachronistically. **Second**, adherents of this view liken the Qur'an's statement that the Sāmirī was doomed to say "do not touch me" in this world with the Jews' belief that the Samaritans were impure or *untouchable* because they worshiped idols. This point is seen as confirming that the Qur'an's term "Sāmirī" means "Samaritan" and, thus, its anachronistic error. There are a number of serious problems with this view:

(1) The similarities between the Qur'an's story and the story of Exodus 32 leave no doubt that the Qur'an recounts that particular event which happened at the time of Moses. The alleged contribution of the story in 1 King 12 depends only on linking the term "Sāmirī" to the town of "Samaria" and the fact that this story involves the worship of 2 gold calves. There is hardly anything else that the story in 1 Kings 12 shares with the Qur'anic account, whereas the latter shares a lot of details with the story of Exodus 32. Linking the Qur'an's story to 1 Kings 12 is no doubt prejudicially motivated by the view that the Qur'an has copied Biblical stories and confused them.

(2) While "Sāmirī" is clearly a title, as it is preceded by the definite article and has an ending suggestive of attribution, the Qur'an gives no reason whatsoever to suggest it is derived from the name of the city of Samaria or indeed any other city. The Qur'an does not give any hint about the origin of the title. Again, linking the title to Samaria is an assumption rather than a conclusion. Some Muslim exegetes have suggested that "Sāmirī" means "from Samaria," but the same sources have also derived the title from a "tribe" or even linked it to a different place altogether. For instance, in his commentary on verses 20.97-98, aṭ-Ṭabarī cites the view that the Sāmirī was from a tribe called "Samira" but in his commentary on 2.51 he quotes the view that this person was from a place called "Bajirma" and that he was from a people who worshiped cows, implying that "Sāmirī" is not derived from "Samaria." Al-Qurṭubī also quotes the contradictory views that the Sāmirī was from a tribe in Syria known as "Samira," he was Coptic and left Egypt with Moses, he was from a place called "Karmān," and he came from a town called "Samira." While linking the titles to the town called "Samira" was only one of the views expressed, it might have also been created by suggestions from Biblicists.

(3) The Samaritans, as a religious group, derive their name not from "Samaria" but from a Hebrew word meaning "keeper" or "observer" of the law.

(4) The term "Sāmirī" is applied in the Qur'an to one person only. Suggesting that this individual represented one member of a group each of whom is a "Sāmirī," regardless of what this title meant, is speculative.

(5) There is a fundamental problem with the general accusation to Prophet Muhammad of copying inaccurately, deliberately, or unwittingly from the Bible which we discussed in more detail elsewhere:

> The problem with this popular approach is that, on the one hand,

it claims that Muhammad had access to and detailed knowledge of the Bible and other Jewish and Christian writings, which is reflected in various details in the Qur'an, yet, on the other, he is supposed to have made some clearly wild errors. (Fatoohi, 2007b: 167)

The story of the Sāmirī is the Qur'anic version of the story in Exodus 32 and has nothing to do with 1 Kings 12 and conclusions drawn from this alleged link are baseless.

The Israelites' inclination to worship a deity other than God manifested itself again on another occasion:

> Moses said to his people: "Allah commands you to slaughter a cow." They said: "Are you making fun of us?" He said: "I take refuge with Allah from being one of the ignorant" (2.67). They said: "Pray to your Lord for us to clarify to us what she is." He said: "He says she is neither old nor a heifer but middle-aged between the two, so do what you are commanded" (2.68). They said: "Pray to your Lord for us to clarify to us her color." He said: "He says she is a yellow cow, bright is her color, and she is pleasing to the beholders" (2.69). They said: "Pray to your Lord for us to clarify to us what she is, for the cows look the same to us; Allah willing, we shall be guided" (2.70). He said: "He says that she is a cow that is not used to plough the land or water the field. She is sound, blemishless." They said: "Now you have brought the truth." They slaughtered her, but they nearly did not do (2.71).

Some of Moses' people had been treating a particular cow differently. The divine command to have this cow slaughter aimed at eradicating this other instance of polytheism, although it is not clear how far those people had gone in terms of turning this cow into a subject of worship. It is also interesting to note that incident of the Sāmirī also involved a calf.

This event is also found in the Bible but, again, in a very different account:

> The Lord spoke to Moses and Aaron: "This is the ordinance of the law which the Lord has commanded: 'Instruct the Israelites to bring you a red heifer without blemish, which has no defect and has never carried a yoke. You must give it to Eleazar the priest so that he can take it outside the camp, and it must be slaughtered before him. Eleazar the priest is to take some of its blood with his finger, and sprinkle some of the blood seven times directly in front of the tent of meeting. Then the heifer must be burned in his sight — its skin, its flesh, its blood, and its offal is to be burned.
> And the priest must take cedar wood, hyssop, and scarlet wool and throw them into the midst of the fire where the heifer is burning. Then the priest must wash his clothes and bathe himself in water, and afterward he may come into the camp, but the priest will be ceremonially unclean until evening. The one who burns it must wash his clothes in

water and bathe himself in water. He will be ceremonially unclean until evening."

'Then a man who is ceremonially clean must gather up the ashes of the red heifer and put them in a ceremonially clean place outside the camp. They must be kept for the community of the Israelites for use in the water of purification — it is a purification for sin. The one who gathers the ashes of the heifer must wash his clothes and be ceremonially unclean until evening. This will be a permanent ordinance both for the Israelites and the resident foreigner who lives among them. (Num. 19:1-10)

Such differences between the Biblical and Qur'anic accounts are instances of "contextual displacement" (p. 125).

9.2 Inscription of the Tablets

The Bible states that Moses was on the mountain for forty days and that God wrote for him the Tablets:

> The Lord said to Moses, "Come up to me to the mountain and remain there, and I will give you the stone tablets with the law and the commandments that I have written, so that you may teach them." So Moses set out with Joshua his attendant, and Moses went up the mountain of God. He told the elders, "Wait for us in this place until we return to you. Here are Aaron and Hur with you. Whoever has any matters of dispute can approach them." Moses went up the mountain, and the cloud covered the mountain. The glory of the Lord resided on Mount Sinai, and the cloud covered it for six days. On the seventh day he called to Moses from within the cloud. Now the appearance of the glory of the Lord was like a devouring fire on the top of the mountain in plain view of the people. Moses went into the cloud when he went up the mountain, and Moses was on the mountain forty days and forty nights. (Exo. 24:12-18)

> He gave Moses two tablets of testimony when he had finished speaking with him on Mount Sinai, tablets of stone written by the finger of God. (Exo. 31:18)

According to the Qur'an, the appointment that God made for Moses was originally for 30 days but was later extended by another 10 days. The meeting place was the top of a mountain. In that meeting, Moses was given the Tablets of the Torah:

> We appointed for Moses thirty nights and then completed them with another ten, so the appointed time of his Lord was completed to forty nights. Moses said to his brother Aaron: "Take my place among my people, act rightly, and do not follow the path of the corrupting ones" (7.142). When Moses came to our appointment and was spoken to by his Lord he said: "My Lord, enable me to see You." He said: "You shall not

see Me, but look at the mountain; if it remains steady, you shall see Me." When his Lord manifested Himself to the mountain He turned it into dust, and Moses fell down in a swoon. When he regained consciousness he said: "Glory be to You! I repent to You, and I am the first of the believers" (7.143). He said: "O Moses! I have chosen you over people for My messages and words, so take what I have given you and be among the thankful" (7.144). We wrote for him on the Tablets an admonition concerning everything and a detailing of everything. [We said to him:] "Take them firmly and command your people to observe their most excellent teachings. I will show you the abode of the ungodly (7.145). I will turn away from My signs those who unjustly behave with arrogance in the earth so if they see any sign they do not believe it, if they see the path of righteousness they do not take it for a path, and if they see the path of transgression they take it for a path. This is so because they have rejected Our signs and have been heedless of them (7.146). The works of those who rejected Our signs and the encounter of the hereafter will be in vain. Shall they be rewarded other than for what they have done" (7.147)? The people of Moses took to themselves [as a god] after him a lowing corporeal calf made of their ornaments. Did they not see that it did not speak to them and did not guide them in the path? They took it and were wrongdoers (7.148). When they realized what they have done and saw that they have sinned they said: "If our Lord does not show mercy to us and forgive us we will be among the losers" (7.149). When Moses returned to his people angry and grieved he said: "Evil is what you have done after me. Would you hasten your Lord's matter?" He threw down the Tablets and seized his brother by the head, dragging him. He said: "O son of my mother! The people weakened me and almost killed me. Do not make my enemies gloat over me and do not consider me with the wrongdoing people" (7.150). He said: "My Lord! Forgive me and my brother and admit us into Your mercy; You are the most merciful of the merciful" (7.151). Those who took the calf [as a god] shall have wrath from their Lord and humiliation in the life of this world, and so do We reward the forgers (7.152). As for those who commit evil things then repent after that and believe, Your Lord will be to them, after that, forgiving, merciful (7.153). When Moses' anger calmed down, he took the Tablets, in the inscription of which there are guidance and mercy for those who fear their Lord (7.154).

It is not clear whether this mountain is the same one at which Moses was called by God when He made him a prophet and commissioned him to go to Egypt (19.52; 28.29-30, 46). The fact that the Qur'an mentions one specific mountain that it calls "*Ṭūri Sīnīn*" or "Mount Sinai" (95.2) may suggest that it was the same mountain. There is also a reference to a special tree, although not much information given:

[I swear] by the figs, olives (95.1), and Mount Sinai (95.2).

And a tree growing out of Mount Sinai which produces oil and a condiment for those who eat (23.20).

The Qur'an reminds the Israelites several times of the fact that God *raised over them* the mountain (2.63, 93; 4.154). The mention of the Israelites means that this reference is to what happened on the mountain when Moses received the Tablets and the fact that He gave that book to them through Moses, not to Moses' first call by God when he left Midian with his family. This is further supported by the fact that the mention of the raising of the mountain over the Israelites is often accompanied by a reminder that they were given the book:

> When We took a covenant with you and raised the mountain above you [saying]: "Take firmly what We have given you and remember what is in it that you may become pious" (2.63).

> When We raised the mountain over them as if it were a covering, and they thought it was going to fall over on them, [and We said]: "Take firmly what We have given you and remember what is in it that you may become pious" (7.171).

The Qur'an also links the raising of the mountain, and accordingly the revelation of the Torah, with a covenant that God had with the Israelites:

> When We took a covenant with you and raised the mountain over you [saying]: "Take firmly what We have given you and listen." They said: "We hear but we disobey." Their hearts became filled with adoration for the calf because of their disbelief. Say: "Evil is what your faith commands you, if you are believers" (2.93).

> We raised the mountain over them on account of their covenant (from 4.154).

9.3 The Holy Land

The Bible claims that the objective of the exodus was to take the Israelites out of Egypt and ultimately into the holy land, as in the Lord's following words which He communicated to the Israelites through Moses:

> I will bring you to the land I swore to give to Abraham, to Isaac, and to Jacob — and I will give it to you as a possession. I am the Lord (Exo. 6:8).

While making it clear that Moses tried also to convert Pharaoh, the Qur'an agrees that the main goal of Moses' mission to Egypt was to take the Israelites out of it. A reference to the fact that this escape was planned to ultimately lead them to the "holy land" is found in Moses' following appeal to his people:

> O my people! Enter the *holy land* which Allah has decreed for you and do not turn back, otherwise you would turn about losers (5.21).

God's following words to the Israelites are one passage that defines the "holy land" in the Bible, but more details are given in Number 34:

> I have promised that I will bring you up out of the affliction of Egypt to the land of the Canaanites, Hittites, Amorites, Perizzites, Hivites, and Jebusites, to a land flowing with milk and honey. (Exo. 3:17)

In line with its style of naming characters and towns, the Qur'an does not give a direct definition of the term "holy land." However, there are three verses that shed some light on the location of this land. The first verse indicates that the holy land is where Abraham immigrated to with his relative prophet Lot:

> We delivered him (Abraham) and Lot to the land that *We have blessed* for all people (21.71).

The second verse suggests that the holy land is where Solomon ruled:

> We subjected to Solomon the wind blowing stormily — running at his command to the land that *We have blessed*. We know everything (21.81).

Finally, this verse confirms that the Israelites at the end took over the holy land:

> We made the people who used to be oppressed to inherit the eastern and western parts of the land that *We have blessed*. The good word of your Lord was fulfilled for the Children of Israel because of their patience, and We destroyed what Pharaoh and his people wrought and what they built (7.137).

These verses do not justify equating the "holy land" with "Canaan/Palestine," but they show the former as part of the latter, as Abraham, the Israelites who escaped from Egypt, and later Solomon all lived in Palestine. Verse 7.137 seems to imply that the holy land was large enough to merit a mention of its "eastern and western parts."

Some exegetes, such as al-Qurṭubī, have mistakenly suggested that the land mentioned in verse 7.137 includes Egypt as well. This erroneous view was facilitated by the failure to correlate the phrase "that We have blessed" in 7.137 with the term "holy land" in verse 5.21 and, particularly, with the same phrase in verses 21.71 and 21.81 and. These scholars misunderstood the clause "that We have blessed" as meaning that the land was blessed with "fields, fruits, and rivers." Al-Jalālayn also suggested that the blessing of the land had to do with "water and trees" but they still understood the land to be Canaan. The blessedness mentioned in these verses is spiritual, which is why that land is called the "holy land" in 5.21.

9.4 The Failure to Enter the Holy Land

According to the Bible, God ordered Moses to send 12 spies, one from each of the tribes of Israel, to check and see whether Canaan was conquerable by Israel. Ten of the spies argued that Israel could not take over the land because "the inhabitants are strong, and the cities are fortified and very large" (Num. 13:28). They also claimed that the land was inhabited by giants (Num. 13:33). The other two spies, Caleb and Joshua, insisted that their people could conquer Canaan (Num. 13:30, 14:6-9). The majority won the argument.

The Israelites' failure to obey God's command angered Him to the point of deciding to annihilate the whole nation, but Moses' prayer succeeded in making God forgive the rebels. God still punished the Israelites by declaring that all of them, apart from Caleb and Joshua, would die in the wilderness and never enter the holy land, as He condemned them to forty year in the wilderness (Num. 14:11-38). Moses also was destined to die outside the promised land (Deu. 34:5). Joshua son of Nun, Moses' assistant and one of the two spies who were spared God's punishment, then led the Israelites into the holy land. The accounts of these military campaigns contain contradictions and historically wrong information, as we have already pointed out.

The Qur'an's account of the failure of the Israelites to enter the holy land is confined to this passage:

> When Moses said to his people: "O my people! Remember the favor of Allah on you when He made prophets among you and made you kings and gave you what He has not given to any of the other peoples (5.20). O my people! Enter the holy land which Allah has decreed for you and do not turn back, otherwise you would turn about losers" (5.21). They said: "O Moses! There is a mighty people in it; we will not enter it until they go out of it. If they go out, we will enter it" (5.22). Then two men who fear [God] whom Allah has given favor to said: "Enter on them by the gate. Once you have entered you will be victorious. Put your trust in Allah if you are believers" (5.23). They said: "O Moses! We will never enter it as long as they are in it. Go you and your Lord and fight. We will sit here" (5.24). He said: "My Lord! I do not control other than myself and my brother, so separate between us and the rebellious people" (5.25). He said: "It shall then be forbidden for them for forty years in which they shall wander in the earth, so do not grieve for the rebellious people" (5.26).

The Qur'an agrees with the Bible that the Israelites did not enter the holy land because they were frightened of its inhabitants, two Israelite men tried to persuade their people to obey God's command, and they were punished by God by preventing them from entering the holy land

and living as wanderers for 40 years.

There are other interesting observations in the Qur'anic passage. **First**, the Israelites' argument against fighting their way into the holy land implies that they were not a powerful nation. Significantly, the two believers did not try to convince the Israelites to enter the holy land on the grounds that they were a powerful nation but by reminding them that victory would come from God. This is consistent with the Qur'anic description of the Israelites who escaped from Egypt as a small nation (pp. 140-142) and disagrees with the Biblical claim that the Israelite men were as many as 600,000 when they left Egypt (pp. 57-62).

Second, the Israelites' use of the phrase "your Lord" when addressing Moses further confirms their polytheistic inclinations, which we discussed earlier in the chapter. **Third**, God's punishment was clearly targeted at the Israelites not Moses, as He forbade the holy land "for them." Aaron was also exempted, as Moses' prayer clearly shows that he did not err like the rest. **Fourth**, the chastisement was to make Israel "wander in the earth." The Arabic word translated "earth" is the same one for "land." What the verse meant is that the Israelites would not have a permanent living place, probably moving around like nomads. The Qur'an does not use an equivalent of the term Biblical "wilderness."

There is another incident reported in the Qur'an that may look to some to be connected to the Israelites' failure to enter the holy land. It is their rejection to enter a particular town to live there:

> When it was said to them: "Live in this town and eat from wherever you like. Say '*ḥiṭṭatun*' and enter the gate prostrating so that We forgive your sins and give increase to the good-doers" (7.161). The wrongdoers among them then changed what had been said to them with another saying, so We sent down on them a punishment from heaven because of their wrongdoing (7.162).
>
> When We said: "Enter this town and eat from wherever you like as much as you like. Enter the gate prostrating and say '*ḥiṭṭatun*' so that We forgive your sins and give increase to the good-doers" (2.58). The wrongdoers then changed what had been said to them with another saying, so We sent down on those who did wrong a punishment from heaven because of their rebellion (2.59).
>
> We raised the mountain over them on account of their covenant and said to them: "Enter the gate prostrating." And We said to them: "Do not exceed the limits of the Sabbath," and We took from them a firm covenant (4.154).

It may be suggested that this town was in the holy land, and this link may be seen supported by the use of the term "gate" which is also used in verse 5.23 which discusses the entry into the holy land. We do not believe this connection is likely and we think that the command to enter this town is completely separate from the command to enter the holy land. The term "*ḥiṭṭatun*" has vexed exegetes who have suggested a number of different meanings, including being the name of one of the gates of the temple, but the most popular view is that it means asking for forgiveness.

The Israelites' grumbling and impatience later led them to a go to a certain town:

> When you said: "O Moses! We cannot endure one kind of food. Pray to your Lord to produce for us of what the earth grows — its beans, cucumbers, garlic, lentils, and onions." He said: "Would you exchange that which is better for that which is meaner? Go down to some town and you shall have what you asked for." Humiliation and abasement were stamped on them and they incurred wrath from Allah, because they used to deny Allah's signs and unjustly kill prophets. That is because they disobeyed and transgressed (2.61).

Assuming that the Israelites' refusal to enter the holy land and the subsequent punishment of wandering outside it for 40 years occurred shortly after their departure from Egypt, the event above would have then taken place sometime during the 40 years. The impatient Israelites would not have waited for years to voice their displeasure with the food of manna and quails. This even must have taken place early in the 40 years of punishment.

The verse does not name the town where Israel went to live, but the implication is that it was outside the holy land. However, as noted earlier, the holy land is situated in Canaan, and while the Israelites were banned from entering the holy land, they could have still lived in other parts of Canaan.

9.5 Entering the Holy Land

The imposing of the 40-year *wandering in the earth* implies that the Israelites ultimately entered the holy land. This is recounted in detail in the Bible in Joshua, but the Qur'an refers to it only in passing. For instance, it is implied in God's promise to make the Israelites overcome their Egyptian slave masters:

> We desired to show favor to those who were oppressed in the earth, and to make them leaders and make them the inheritors (28.5).

But there are also direct references to the Israelites' ultimate success:

> Therefore We took vengeance on them and drowned them in the sea because they denied Our signs and were heedless of them (7.136). We made the people who used to be oppressed to inherit the eastern and

western parts of the land that We have blessed. The good word of your Lord was fulfilled for the Children of Israel because of their patience, and We destroyed what Pharaoh and his people wrought and what they built (7.137).

So We removed them (Pharaoh and his people) from gardens, springs (26.57), treasures, and a fair abode (26.58); and We caused the Children of Israel to inherit them (26.59).

They (Pharaoh and his army) left behind many gardens (44.25), crops, a noble dwelling (44.26), and favors in which they enjoyed themselves (44.27). Thus, We made another people inherit them (44.28). The heaven and the earth did not weep for them, and they were not respited (44.29).

Significantly, all four sets of verses describe Israel's ultimate victory as an act of *inheriting* the Egyptians. Parts of the holy land were originally under the control of Egyptian vassals hence the fall of that land into the hands of the Israelites is described as an inheritance by the Israelites of their Egyptian enemies. The ending of verse 7.137 refers to Pharaoh and his people's buildings in the holy land not Egypt. Obviously, Israel's takeover of the holy land resulted in the destruction of the buildings of Pharaoh and his people there, not in Egypt. This destruction might refer to militant conquests of parts of the holy land.

The mention of Israel's inheritance after recounting the death of Pharaoh and his army does not mean that the Israelites took over the land immediately after their victory over Pharaoh. This happened 40 years later. These references only underline the ultimate result of defeating Pharaoh and which was the main goal of the exodus. Readers interested in more details about the Qur'an's characteristic style in relating history may consult "History in the Qur'an" in our book *The Mystery of the Historical Jesus* (Fatoohi, 2007b: 513-518).

Israel's entry into the holy land is also confirmed in verse 17.104:

So he sought to drive them out of the land but We drowned him and all those who were with him (17.103). We said to the Children of Israel after him: "Dwell in the land. When the last promise comes to pass, We will bring you in a mixed crowd" (17.104).

The "land" in verse 17.103 denotes the eastern Delta where the Israelites had gathered (pp. 130-133). But the reference in 17.104 is to the holy land. Some exegetes, such as al-Qurṭubī and Ibn Kathīr, have mistakenly thought that the "land" in 17.104 includes Egypt also. The mention of the *first promise* implies that there is another one. The following verses shed light on the two promises:

We decreed to the Children of Israel in the Book: "You will cause corruption in the earth twice and you will show great loftiness (17.4). When the first of the two promises comes to pass, We will send against you servants of Ours with great might who will invade your dwellings; this promise is certain to be fulfilled (17.5). Then We will make it your turn to prevail over them and supply you with a lot of wealth and children and make you more enormous (17.6). If you do good work you do so for your own souls, and if you commit evil you do so to your own detriment. When the second promise comes to pass, they will make your faces full of grief, enter the mosque as they did the first time, and destroy what they control" (17.7).

There is a common misunderstanding of the two promises. They do not denote *two occupations* of the holy land by the Israelites but *two divine punishments* for the corruption they cause in the holy land. The "first of the two promises" involves sending invaders. Verse 17.7 also implies that the invading army would enter the temple. The phrase "this promise is certain to be fulfilled" confirms that this punishment is what is meant by the first promise. Similarly, the "second promise" is the second divine punishment that responds to the second causing of corruption by Israel. The invaders would make the Israelites grieve, enter the mosque as they did the first time around, and destroy what they conquer. While the Qur'an describes the holy land as a place that God had *decreed for the Israelites* (5.21), it has no description of the holy land as the *promised land* to Israel.

The first Israelite occupation of the holy land took place 40 years after the exodus, and the first promise of punishment was fulfilled early in the 6th century BCE. In 597 BCE, the Babylonian king Nebuchadnezzar captured Jerusalem and took its prominent people captive to Babylon. In a second campaign in 586 BCE he destroyed Judea and the temple. The Biblical Book of Jeremiah (52:28-30) claims that Nebuchadnezzar took Jewish captives to Babylon three times, corresponding to 597, 586, and 582 BCE. Although verse 17.7 talks about the invading troops only *entering* the mosque, its *destruction* may be implied by the phrase "destroy what they control," which might apply to the first promise also. The first promise can be pinpointed to the Babylonian invasion of 586 BCE when the temple was first destroyed.

After defeating the Babylonians in 539 BCE, the Persian king Cyrus allowed the exiled Jews to return to Palestine, and they rebuilt what is known as the second temple. But the temple was destroyed again in 70 CE when the Roman commander Titus entered and destroyed Jerusalem, ending a Jewish revolt. This is a potential identification of the second promise, as it shares two descriptions given to both promises: the invasion of troops of the holy land and their entry into the temple.

This identification of the second promise looks doubtful in the light of verse 17.104. This verse seems to suggest that God would *bring* the Jews to the holy land *shortly before* the second promise is fulfilled. When Titus destroyed Jerusalem, the Jews had been living there for 6 centuries — which looks too long for the implication of the verse. Furthermore, the verse states that God would bring the Israelites "*lafīfā*" or "in a mixed crowd." This description applies perfectly to the present day Israelite inhabitants of the holy land who gathered there from almost every part of the world.

The fact that the Israelites entered the holy land forty years after the exodus, which occurred in 1212 BCE, means that we can date their entry into the holy land to exactly 1172 BCE. But to avoid any inaccuracy in dating the death of Ramesses II to exactly 1212 BCE, the date of the entry of the Israelites to the holy land may be expressed in Pharaonic regnal years. This places the entry in the 11th regnal year of the 2nd Pharaoh of the 20th Dynasty, Ramesses III (1182-1151 BCE). Interestingly, Ramesses III was busy in his 11th regnal year with a major military action in which he crushed invaders to the Delta. Was this invasion a distraction for Ramesses III that facilitated the Israelites with an undisturbed entry into the holy land? This seems plausible.

Significantly, this dating fits well with the archaeological discovery of the "proliferation of small sites in the highlands regions" of Palestine in the 12th century. Scholars almost unanimously agree that "this wave of settlement is to be association *in some sense* with Israel's arrival or emergence in Canaan" (Bimson, 1991: 4). Bimson not only stresses that the settlement in the hill country could not have been a 13th-century but a 12th-century phenomenon, he goes further to state that "it is quite probable that it did not begin until the second quarter of the century" (Bimson, 1991: 13). This matches perfectly well our dating of the entry of the Israelite to the holy land to 40 years after Ramesses II's death!

Would one expect the entry of the Israelites to the holy land to have been mentioned, directly or indirectly, in Egyptian records? If this entry was anything close to the major invasion depicted in the Bible, then the answer must be positive. The fact that those cities were run by vassals of Pharaoh would have certainly made those local chieftains report the advances of the Israelites to their lord in Egypt, as in the case of the cuneiform Amarna letters from the 14th century BCE which contain complaints of local rulers in Canaan to Pharaoh of threats they were facing from enemies of Egypt. The availability of such records today, however, is a totally different matter, as explained earlier (pp. 31-33, 81-82). On the other hand, if the Israelites' entry was not a major event as far as the Egyptians were concerned, then we should not be surprised if it went unnoticed or unrecorded.

9.6 Miracles

The Qur'an mentions a number of miracles that happened to the Israelites after the exodus:

(1) God sent down on them the manna and quails to eat (also 2.57; 7.160):

> O Children of Israel! We have rescued you from your enemy, appointed a meeting for you on the right side of the mountain, and sent down on you the manna and the quails (20.80), [saying]: "Eat of the good things We have given you, but do not transgress in them, otherwise My wrath would fall on you. Whoever My wrath falls on he would perish" (20.81).

This miracle is mentioned in the Bible also. After hearing the murmuring of the Israelites against Moses and Aaron for bringing them out of Egypt to a desert where there was no meat or bread, God performed the following miracles:

> In the evening the quail came up and covered the camp, and in the morning a layer of dew was all around the camp. When the layer of dew had evaporated, there on the surface of the desert was a thin flaky substance, thin like frost on the earth. When the Israelites saw it, they said to one another, "What is it?" because they did not know what it was. Moses said to them, "It is the bread that the Lord has given you for food. (Exo. 16:13-15)
>
> The house of Israel called its name "manna." It was like coriander seed and was white, and it tasted like wafers with honey. (Exo. 16:31)

The Bible states that the Israelites ate manna for forty years (Exo. 16:35), but this is not confirmed in the Qur'an.

(2) Although not much information is given about God's overshadowing of the Israelites with clouds, the context in which this event is mentioned suggests that it was a miracle rather than natural happening:

> We overshadowed you with the clouds and sent down on you the manna and the quails, [saying]: "Eat of the good things We have given you." They did not wrong Us but they were wronging themselves (2.57).

The Biblical equivalent of this miracle might be this rather different event which occurred in the evening in which the quails first appeared:

> As Aaron spoke to the whole community of the Israelites and they looked toward the desert, there the glory of the Lord appeared in the cloud. (Exo. 16:10)

(3) One day the Israelites had no water to drink and asked Moses for help. God inspired Moses to perform a miracle with his staff:

We divided them into twelve tribes — nations. We inspired Moses when his people asked him for drink: "Strike the rock with your staff," so twelve springs burst forth. Every people knew their drinking place. We overshadowed them with the clouds and sent down on them the manna and the quails, [saying]: "Eat of the good things We have given you." They did not wrong Us but they were wronging themselves (7.160).

When Moses asked for drink for his people We said: "Strike the rock with your staff," so twelve springs burst forth. Every people knew their drinking place. [We said]: "Eat and drink of what Allah has provided and do not cause corruption on the earth" (2.60).

The Bible says that when the Israelites murmured against Moses complaining that they were thirsty and had no access to water, Moses said to God that his people are on the verge of killing him so God intervened:

> The Lord said to Moses, "Go over before the people; take with you some of the elders of Israel and take in your hand your staff with which you struck the Nile and go. I will be standing before you there on the rock in Horeb, and you will strike the rock, and water will come out of it so that the people may drink." And Moses did so in plain view of the elders of Israel. (Exo. 17:5-6)

(4) At some point the Israelites asked Moses to show them God, otherwise they would not believe him. In addition to reflecting continued doubts about Moses, imagining God to be visible to the eye is also influenced by the Israelites' sojourn in Egypt whose many gods could be represented in various physical forms. God commanded Moses to bring a group of them to put them through an experience that would teach them that God is invisible and that asking to see Him in order to believe in Him was a sin. Those who were involved died as a result of the experience, but God then resurrected them:

> When you said: "O Moses! We will not believe you until we see Allah plainly," so the thunderbolt caught you while you were looking on (2.55). Then We resurrected you after your death that you may give thanks (2.56).
>
> The People of the Book asked you to cause a book to come down on them from heaven. They asked of Moses a greater thing, saying: "Show us Allah openly." So the thunderbolt caught them because of their wrongdoing. They then took the calf [for a god] after the proofs had come to them, but we forgave that. We gave Moses a manifest authority (4.153).
>
> Moses chose from his people seventy for our appointment. When the earthquake overtook them he said: "My Lord! Had you willed, you could have killed them and me before. Would You kill us for what the fools among us have done? This is not but Your trial with which You send

astray whom You will and guide whom You will. You are our guardian, so forgive us and show mercy to us, and You are the best of forgivers (7.155). Write down for us good in this world and in the hereafter. We have repented to You." He said: "I will strike with My torment whom I will, and My mercy embraces everything, so I shall write it down for those who are pious, give alms, and believe in Our signs" (7.156).

This incident is different from another that involved Moses only. In the latter, which happened during Moses' 40-day solitude with God, Moses asked God to allow him to see Him:

> When Moses came to our appointment and was spoken to by his Lord he said: "My Lord, enable me to see You." He said: "You shall not see Me, but look at the mountain; if it remains steady, you shall see Me." When his Lord manifested Himself to the mountain He turned it into dust, and Moses fell down in a swoon. When he regained consciousness he said: "Glory be to You! I repent to You, and I am the first of the believers" (7.143).

Moses did not have doubts about God as the Israelites did, but he genuinely wanted to see God, whose voice he used to hear. Another difference between this case and the one involving the seventy Israelites is that God did not cause Moses to die but by having him to watch the mountain turn into dust as God manifested Himself to it, He taught him that He is invisible. Moses realized that asking to see God was wrong, so he asked for forgiveness. The expression "glory be to You" recognizes the subtle and invisible nature of God.

The equivalent account of Moses' experience in the Bible may be this:

> And Moses said, "Show me your glory." And the Lord said, "I will make all my goodness pass before your face, and I will proclaim the Lord by name before you; I will be gracious to whom I will be gracious, I will show mercy to whom I will show mercy." But he added, "You cannot see my face, for no one can see me and live." The Lord said, "Here is a place by me; you will station yourself on a rock. When my glory passes by, I will put you in a cleft in the rock and will cover you with my hand while I pass by. Then I will take away my hand, and you will see my back, but my face must not be seen." (Exo. 33:18-23)

There are very significant differences between this passage and the Qur'anic account, so it may or may not refer to the same event.

9.7 Merneptah's "Israel Stela"

In 1896, Flinders Petrie discovered in the ruins of Merneptah's mortuary temple in western Thebes a 2.25-meter-high black granite stela containing a poetic hymn that commemorates Merneptah's victory over the invading Libyans in their six-hour battle in the spring of his 5th regnal year in 1207 BCE. This 28-line stela, which has also survived in a fragmentary duplicate in the Temple of Karnak, concludes with a brief mention of a victorious military campaign for Merneptah in Canaan sometime during his first five years as Pharaoh. The stela records Pharaoh's submission of Ashkelon and Gezer in the south of Canaan and Yanoam, probably, in the north.

The exceptional excitement that the discovery of this stela generated was not for preserving this information but for containing the only known mention of "Israel" in ancient Egyptian inscriptions and the oldest outside the Bible.[13] This is how the poetic hymn of the "Israel Stela" concludes:

> The princes are prostrate, saying: "Mercy!"
>   Not one raises his head among the Nine Bows.
> Desolation is for Tehenu; Hatti is pacified;
>   Plundered is the Canaan with every evil;
> Carried off is Ashkelon; seized upon is Gezer;
>   Yanoam is made as that which does not exist;
> Israel is laid waste, his seed is not;
>   Hurru[14] is become a widow for Egypt!
> All lands together, they are pacified;
>   Everyone who was restless, he has been bound
> by the King of Upper and Lower Egypt;
> Ba-en-Re Meri-Amon; the Son of Re:
> Merneptah Hotep-hir-Maat,[15]

---

[13] The next oldest extra-Biblical mention of "Israel" occurs in the stela of Mesha, king of Moab, which is dated to after 849 BCE and in which we read of "Israel" the kingdom (*ANET*, 1950: 320). The oldest extra-Biblical mention of "Israelite" comes from inscriptions of the Assyrian king Shalmaneser III (858-824 BCE) with a reference to "Ahab the Israelite" (*ANET*, 1950: 279). It is notable that after the mention of Israel in Merneptah's stela, the ancient world, as we know it from texts and artifacts that have been recovered by archaeological excavation, is dead silent for three and a half centuries on the Israelites who developed a large and prosperous kingdom during that time! This is a vivid example on how the absence of textual or artifactual evidence should not be construed as "negative evidence." Obviously, the farther we go back in history the more meaningless its silence as read from archaeology.

[14] The "Nine Bows" were the nine traditional enemies of Egypt. "Tehenu" was a name for Libyans. "Hurru" was the land of Biblical Horites, or Greater Palestine (Pritchard, 1950: 376-378). Hatti was the land of the Hittites with whom Merneptah's predecessor, Ramesses II, had established a peace treaty in his 21st regnal year after the battle of Qadesh. Merneptah honored that treaty.

[15] These are various names of Merneptah.

given life like Re every day. (*ANET*, 1950: 378)

Hieroglyphic writing has unpronounced signs called "determinatives" that specify the kind of word to which they are attached. For instance, the determinative attached to Canaan in the above inscription is that for a foreign land. Predictably, the determinative used with Ashkelon, Gezer, and Yanoam indicates that they are cities, but the determinative attached to Israel is that for a people not a place. Researchers have also noted that while the names of foreign countries and cities were considered as syntactically feminine in Egyptian, the writer's use of a masculine pronoun with Israel indicates his awareness of the fact that Israel was a name of an eponymous ancestor (Bimson, 1991: 14).

Noting the poetic nature of the text of the Israel Stela and the absence of independent documentary evidence, some scholars have suggested that the recorded campaign into Canaan never took place in reality and that the claim is nothing but typical Pharaonic exaggeration. However, Kitchen has indicated that there is independent evidence that Merneptah "*did* conduct at least one small campaign in Palestine," and this evidence is in the form of an inscription at the temple of Amanda in Nubia in which Merneptah's epithet "Binder of Gezer" figures as prominent as the title "Seizer of Libya" which refers to Merneptah's well known war with the Libyans (Kitchen, 1966: 60).

Frank Yurco has discovered battle reliefs carved on the western outer wall of the court at the Karnak temple which he identified as a pictorial representation of Merneptah's Canaanite campaign. He based his identification on similarities between the battle reliefs and the text on the Israel Stela. **First**, the reliefs show four battle scenes — the same number of battles mentioned in the Israel Stela. **Second**, three of the battle scenes are against fortified city-states while the fourth, though it has lost its upper portion, clearly depicts a battle in a hilly country against a Canaanite enemy that had no fortified city. This corresponds to the reference in the Israel Stela to three battles against cities and a fourth against a people, the Israelites, who are not identified with a city.

Third, one of the fortified cities in the battle reliefs is named Ashkelon, which is one of the cities mentioned in the Merneptah Stela. **Four**, Yurco notes that no other war by Merneptah in Canaan is attested in any of his monuments, concluding that the battle reliefs and the Israel Stela must be recording one and the same campaign into Canaan (Yurco, 1997).

If Yurco's identification of the fourth battle scenes with Merneptah's attack on the Israelites is correct, then it means that they were a people without a fortified city in as late as the reign of Merneptah. This is an insurmountable hurdle for the theory that dates the exodus to immediately after the supposed death of Ramesses II's eldest son which, ironically, Yurco himself advocates (p. 94). This theory places Israel's departure from Egypt around the 17th of Ramesses II's 67 regnal years, meaning that at least 50 years after their exodus the Israelites were still a people without a city over. No scholar would consider this view credible.

Whether or not these battle reliefs depict Merneptah's Canaanite campaign is not of much relevance to the question of the historicity of the exodus. In fact, even if Merneptah's Canaanite campaign never took place and that it is mere Pharaonic hyperbole, as a minority of scholars think, the Israel Stela would retain its significance of revealing the Egyptians' knowledge of the presence of a people called Israel outside Egypt, somewhere in Canaan, by the 5th regnal year of Ramesses II's successor. Bimson (1991: 24) takes the argument even further to state that "if Israel had become well known to Egyptian scribes *without* an encounter on the battlefield to make it the object of their attention" then "it is all the more striking as evidence of Israel's importance in [Merneptah's] day." Having said that, Kitchen's observation of the existence of an independent inscription that calls Merneptah the "Binder of Gezer" in addition to "Seizer of Libya" is a strong piece of evidence that this Pharaoh's campaign into Canaan did indeed take place.

The fact that the Israelites were in Canaan by Merneptah's 5th year is in line with the Qur'anic dating of the exodus to the end of Ramesses II's reign. Interestingly, Merneptah's Canaanite campaign is thought to have taken place probably before the end of his 3rd and possibly during his 1st regnal year (Bimson, 1991: 10). Here we have the plausible assumption that Merneptah campaigned into Canaan to quell rebellions that took place in some cities after the news of the dramatic defeat and death of Ramesses II and his army reached the areas around Egypt. The much feared Pharaoh who ruled single-handedly for 67 years was no more and some of his army disappeared with him. This could have sounded to some local rulers in Palestine an opportunity too good to miss to try their luck with the new monarch.

As Merneptah's campaign occurred no later than 5 years after the exodus, any encounter that his army had with the Israelites must have been outside the holy land, which is part of Canaan. If those portrayed in the Karnak battle reliefs as a people with no fortified city were indeed the Israelites, then Merneptah's Canaanite campaign would have occurred prior to Israel's entry into the town mentioned in the following verse:

> When you said: "O Moses! We cannot endure one kind of food. Pray to your Lord to produce for us of what the earth grows — its beans,

cucumbers, garlic, lentils, and onions." He said: "Would you exchange that which is better for that which is meaner? Go down to some town and you shall have what you asked for." Humiliation and abasement were stamped on them and they incurred wrath from Allah, because they used to deny Allah's signs and unjustly kill prophets. That is because they disobeyed and transgressed (2.61).

But if the fourth scene of the battle reliefs only means that the Israelites were not living in a *fortified* city then there is no reason to reject the possibility that the assault could have occurred after their entry into the unnamed town. In this case, it would be also possible to correlate Merneptah's attack on the Israelites with the link the verse makes between the Israelites' entrance into the unnamed town and their subjection to "humiliation and abasement." Another possibility is that Merneptah's army might have met Israel not necessarily in Canaan but en route to it. After all, there is no name of a city given.

But there is a more likely scenario. While the majority of scholars believe that Merneptah's Canaanite campaign did take place, there is no reason to presume all the details mentioned in his Stela must be true. To be more specific, the fact that Merneptah raided and overran Ashkelon, Gezer, and Yanoam does not necessarily guarantee the verity of account of the encounter with Israel. There is one particularly significant difference between the account of the three cities and that of Israel. Ashkelon, Gezer, and Yanoam are cities of well-known locations, so Merneptah could have left Egypt targeting them specifically. He would not have gone to Canaan had he not had prior knowledge of something wrong going on there anyway. So unless Merneptah had got wind that Israel had settled in a specific city one cannot presume that he and his army marched on in Canaan until they came across the Israelite wanderers and slaughtered them! Yet if Merneptah attacked the Israelites in a city then the Stela would have named that city. This remains a problem unless one assumes that the Israelites were living in one of the three Canaanite cities that the Stela names. The other solution is that, being a small nation, the Israelites were living in a small city that is not worth mentioning. But this then takes us back full circle to the unanswered question of how Merneptah could have known of their presence there in the first place.

While suggesting that the exodus and settlement in Palestine took place in the 11th century BCE, Rendsburg (1992: 517) has made the interesting observation that while "the biblical writers did not shy away from including material about Israel's defeats," there is no mention of this supposed attack by Merneptah in the Bible. Another point that can be raised to support the argument that Merneptah never met the

Israelites in Canaan is the Stela's clear exaggeration that Israel was obliterated — something that is obviously not factual. Pritchard (1950: 378) has noted that the claim that the offspring of Israel has been exterminated is a typical brag of power at that period, but it could also be completely made up. The wording used to describe Israel's defeat in particular may have sprung from Merneptah's will to take revenge on those who defeated and caused the death of his father. Merneptah had a strong reason to claim that he wiped out Israel. The conclusion that seems more likely to us is that while Merneptah campaigned in Canaan, he never met the Israelites. Interestingly, Merneptah's claim of a battle with the Israelites is without independent evidence. In the unlikely situation that the Canaanite campaign never took place, the case would be even stronger for the view that the mention of the Israelites was a Don Quixote kind of revenge by a bitter Merneptah on those who caused the humiliating death of his father.

The Israel Stela represents a considerable problem for those who claim that Merneptah was the Pharaoh of the exodus and that he died at the exodus. Bucaille, for one, attempted to explain away the Israel Stela's incompatibility with his theory by suggesting that the Israelites were not only living in Egypt and that Merneptah's declaration of exterminating the Israelites referred only to those Israelites whom he fought in Canaan. But one problem with this explanatory attempt is that unlike the Stela's treatment of the first three victories where cities are named, it describes Israel as a people not a city. In other words, according to Bucaille's theory, the Stela should have mentioned a fourth city where the Israelites were presumably living. Additionally, exterminating a people cannot mean but rooting out each and every individual. Merneptah could not have made this claim if Israelites were not only still living in Egypt but were being the cause of many problems there, including the plagues!

10

Pharaonic Massacres

Both the Qur'an and the Bible agree that Pharaoh massacred Israelite newborn boys, but there are significant differences between the two scriptures. They disagree on the reason for the massacre at the time of Moses' birth. The Qur'an also mentions a similar massacre when Moses returned to take the Israelites out of Egypt. This massacre is not mentioned in the Bible.

In this chapter we will examine both scriptural accounts. We will then critique a misleading approach that reduces many historical stories, scriptural and non-scriptural, to motif works.

10.1 The Motive of Pharaoh's First Massacre

The Bible claims that Pharaoh feared that the growing Israelite population might one day side with one of his enemies (p. 47). He first tried to overwork them, but that did not work, so he asked the Hebrew midwives to kill all newborn males. When this plan also failed he turned to his people to carry out this massacre: "All sons that are born you must throw into the river, but all daughters you may let live" (Exo. 1:22).

The suggestion that Pharaoh considered Israel a danger cannot be true. Contrary to what the Bible claims, the Israelites were not dangerously numerous. Furthermore, the expulsion of the Hyksos resulted in the dispersion of the Israelites throughout Egypt where they were employed as forced labor in various construction sites (pp. 127-128). Ramesses II's massive building projects all over Egypt would have scattered the Israelites even more during his reign. The alleged threat posed by the large number of the Israelites, which the Bible claims Ramesses II wanted to eliminate, could not have existed in the first place.

The Biblical claim that Pharaoh killed the newborn males to control the Israelites population could not be accepted even in the context of the Biblical narrative. Even if the Israelites were living together, which is the unhistorical implication of the Bible, Pharaoh and his advisers would have simply deployed them to his building sites throughout Egypt. Ramesses II's great need for slave laborers was such that he had to send military expeditions to neighboring lands to gather people (pp. 87-88).

The Biblical accounts of the growth of the Israelite population in

Egypt (pp. 57-62) and using slavery (pp. 62-63) and massacre (pp. 63-65) to control it are full of internal contradictions as well conflicts with established historical facts. There must have been a different objective for massacring the Israelite male babies from the one found in the Bible.

The Qur'an agrees with the Bible that Pharaoh launched a vicious campaign to kill all Israelite baby boys. It differs in stating that the method of killing was *slaying not drowning* in the Nile. Throwing baby Moses in the river was the emergency plan that God inspired his mother to carry out once she sensed an imminent danger to the life of the child. He commanded her to put the baby in a *coffin, not a papyrus basket* as the Bible states, and cast it in the river. He promised her that He would return her child to her and would also make him one of His messengers:

> We narrate to you [O Muhammad!] parts of the story of Moses and Pharaoh in truth, for people who believe (28.3). Pharaoh exalted himself in the earth and made its people castes, oppressing one group of them, killing their sons and sparing their women; he was one of the corrupters (28.4). We desired to show favor to those who were oppressed in the earth, make them leaders, make them the inheritors (28.5), establish them in the earth, and show Pharaoh, Hāmān, and their soldiers from them that which they feared (28.6). We inspired Moses' mother: "Suckle him, and when you fear for him, cast him into the river and do not fear or grieve; We shall bring him back to you and make him one of the messengers" (28.7). Then the people of Pharaoh picked him up [from the river], to become for them an enemy and a sorrow; Pharaoh, Hāmān, and their soldiers were sinful (28.8). The wife of Pharaoh said: "[He will be] a delight for the eye for me and you. Do not kill him. He may be useful for us, or we may take him as a son," while they were unaware [of what was going to happen] (28.9).
>
> "We have thus conferred favor on you again (20.37). [The first was] when We revealed to your mother that which is revealed (20.38), saying: 'Put him in a coffin, then throw him down in the river. The river shall throw him onshore; there shall take him up one who is an enemy to Me and an enemy to him.' And I threw over you love from Me, and that you should be brought up according to My will" (20.39).

One implication of the Qur'an's assertion that the escaping Israelites were a small group (pp. 140-142) is that, contrary to the Biblical claim, Pharaoh's massacre of the newborn males of Israel could not have targeted controlling the Israelite population. The Qur'an never confirms the Biblical claim that the killing was intended to control the Israelites' number.

The Qur'an does not state explicitly the purpose of Pharaoh's bloody campaign. But there is a consensus among Muslim scholars that it was triggered by learning of the imminent birth of an Israelite boy who would cause his downfall. There seems to be an implicit reference in the Qur'an to this. Verse 28.4, which mentions the massacre of the Israelite newborn boys, is followed immediately by the story of Moses' birth and the fact that he was going to be the cause of Pharaoh's downfall.

Muslim exegetes and historians have expressed a number of different views about how Pharaoh came to know about the danger that awaited him from an Israelite newborn boy. Some have suggested that Pharaoh had a dream which was interpreted for him by some priests, others have thought that some priests and astrologers conveyed to Pharaoh the disturbing news about the imminent birth, whereas others have pointed to prophecies of past prophets that specified the place and time of Moses' birth (Ibn al-Athīr, 1929: 96; Hijāzī, 1954, part 20: 19; Ibn Khaldūn, 1966: 153; ar-Rāzī, 1906: 425; at-Ṭabarsī, 1961, part 20: 263; at-Ṭabarī, 1910: 19-20; at-Ṭabarī, undated: 199-200; Abū al-Suʿūd, 1906: 344; al-Qurṭubī, 1941: 248-249; Ibn Kathīr, 1985: 297; 1988: 607; al-Marāghī, 1946c, part 20: 33; at-Ṭabaṭabāʾī, undated: part 14: 161).

Houtman has also referred to the existence of extra-Biblical Jewish tradition in which "not Israel's phenomenal increase but Pharaoh's fear at the birth of a rival is adduced as the reason for his actions" (Houtman, 1993: 262). This is, obviously, in contradiction with the Biblical story. According to the Jewish historian Josephus, Pharaoh organized the massacre of all Israelite newborn males after he was told by one of the scribes who foretell the future this very worrying prophecy:

> About this time there would a child be born to the Israelites, who, if he were reared, would bring the Egyptian dominion low, and would raise the Israelites; that he would excel all men in virtue, and obtain a glory that would be remembered through all ages. (Josephus, *Antiquities of the Jews*, 2.205)

The concerned Pharaoh then commanded that the Israelites should throw into the river every newborn boy and destroy it. Josephus accommodates in his account the Biblical role of the Hebrew midwives.

Ramesses II could not have committed the massacre of the Israelite boys as a means to control the Israelite population. But he might well have committed that, following the advice of his foretellers, to preempt the rising of one of the Israelites and his eventual victory over him. Being a book focused on promoting the Israelites as a special ethnic group, the Bible has understandably presented the massacre as an act against the *nation* of Israel rather than one *individual* Israelite.

10.2 The Second Massacre

Another fundamental difference between the Qur'anic account of

Moses' story and its Biblical counterpart is that the Qur'an speaks of *two*, not one, campaigns by Pharaoh to kill Israelite males. The first occurred around the time of Moses' birth and aimed at killing the future leader, and the second was launched sometime after Moses' return to Egypt and the magicians' defeat and conversion:

> So the magicians were thrown down in prostration (7.120). They said: "We believe in the Lord of all peoples (7.121), the Lord of Moses and Aaron" (7.122). Pharaoh Said: "You have believed in Him before I give you permission? This is a plot that you have devised in the city to drive its people out of it, but you shall know (7.123). I will cut off your hands and legs on opposite sides, and then I will crucify you all" (7.124). They said: "We shall return to our Lord (7.125). You take revenge on us only because we have believed in the signs of our Lord when they came to us. Our Lord! Pour out on us patience and cause us to die as Muslims" (7.126). The chiefs of Pharaoh's people said: "Do you leave Moses and his people to cause corruption in the land and forsake you and your gods?" He said: "We will kill their sons but spare their women, and surely we will overpower them" (7.127).
>
> We sent Moses with our signs and clear authority (40.23) to Pharaoh, Hāmān, and Korah, but they said: "A lying magician!" (40.24). When the truth from Us came to them they said: "Kill the sons of those who are with him but spare their women." The scheming of the disbelievers is bound to fail (40.25). Pharaoh said: "Let me kill Moses and let him call on his Lord. I fear that he will change your religion or cause corruption in the land" (40.26).

Significantly, these verses speak about Pharaoh and his court's perception of Israel's danger to Egypt's religion, not to its security. It was this particular threat that Pharaoh and his court perceived Moses and his followers posed while they were within Egypt's borders (pp. 122-123). Pharaoh first felt danger coming from the Israelites when he knew of the imminent birth of an Israelite who would cause his downfall. Then, after Moses' return to Egypt, Pharaoh feared that if he would let the Israelites leave Egypt they would soon return with an invading army to overrun Pi-Ramesses. Yet keeping them in Egypt was also worrying him because Moses' religion could do to Egypt's religion even greater damage than that of the anti-Amun campaign of Akhenaten.

Pharaoh carried out the first indiscriminate massacre because he could not know the identity of the dangerous child to target him personally. But why did he launch a second massacre of Israelite males when the threat was this time clear, embodied in the person of Moses? Why did he not murder Moses himself and put an end to his own fears? He did indeed consider this solution:

> When the truth from Us came to them they said: "Kill the sons of those

who are with him but spare their women." The scheming of the disbelievers is bound to fail (40.25). Pharaoh said: "Let me kill Moses and let him call on his Lord. I fear that he will change your religion or cause corruption in the land" (40.26). Moses said: "I take refuge in my and your Lord from every arrogant person who does not believe in the Day of Reckoning" (40.27).

Pharaoh could not carry out his plan because Moses was miraculously protected by God (pp. 130-131). It is this divine protection that Moses' words about *taking refuge in God* refer to.

The six references in the Qur'an to the two killing campaigns use almost the same wording (2.49; 7.127, 141; 14.6; 28.4; 40.25). Both involved killing or slaying Israelite sons but sparing their women. The use of the same wording to describe both massacres suggests that there was no essential difference between what happened in the two cases. But there was a clear difference between the purposes of the massacres. While the first vicious campaign targeted the life of baby Moses, the second was intended to terrorize the Israelites and force them not to follow Moses (7.127; 40.25).

The suggestion of a second massacre was put forward only in response to Moses' commission — an obvious indication that it was intended to turn the Israelites away from Moses' call, not reduce their number. The fact that the second campaign of murder had this broader aim may mean that the killing was not necessarily restricted to *newborn* boys but could have claimed older male victims as well. This possibility cannot be ruled out on linguistic grounds, because all six verses use the same Arabic word, "*abnā'* (sons)", which can be used for adult males as well as young ones (e.g. 4.23). On the other hand, it is equally reasonable to argue that killing adult males would have been a loss of labor force. Probably, unlike the first killing campaign, the second massacre did not target *all* newborn boys of the Israelite families involved.

There is no *explicit* indication in the Qur'an of the duration of the second killing campaign and whether it stopped at some point or continued until the Israelites fled Egypt. But as it was launched before the plagues started hitting Pharaoh's people, it seems reasonable to suggest that Pharaoh would have abandoned his brutal persecution at some point hoping that this might stop the disasters. This is likely as these retributions had such an impact on Pharaoh and his people that he was even eventually forced to promise Moses to allow the Israelites to leave once the punishment had seized, even though he eventually did not keep his word:

> The chiefs of Pharaoh's people said: "Do you leave Moses and his

people to cause corruption in the land and forsake you and your gods?" He said: "We will kill their sons and spare their women, and surely we will overpower them" (7.127). Moses said to his people: "Ask help from Allah and be patient; surely the land is Allah's; He gives it for inheritance to whom He wills of His servants. The [best] end is for the pious" (7.128). They said: "We were harmed before you came to us and we have been harmed since then also." He said: "May your Lord destroy your enemy and make you inheritors in the land so He sees how you act" (7.129). We tested Pharaoh's people with droughts and shortage of crops that they may heed (7.130). When good befall them they would say: "This is due to us," and when evil afflicted them, they would attribute it to the ill fortune of Moses and those with him; surely their ill fortune is only from Allah, but most of them do not know (7.131). They said: "Whatever sign you may bring to bewitch us, we will not believe you" (7.132). We sent on them the flood, the locusts, the lice, the frogs, and the blood as clear signs; but they behaved arrogantly and were guilty (7.133). When the plague hit them, they said: "O Moses! Pray to your Lord for us, by whatever covenant He has with you, that if you remove the plague from us we will believe you and we will send away with you the Children of Israel" (7.134). But when We removed the plague from them till a term that they were to reach, they broke the promise (7.135).

The Israelites' complaint to Moses that they suffered before he came to them and were also suffering since referred primarily to Pharaoh's two campaigns of murder, but also to their ongoing enslavement of course.

10.3 The First Massacre: History or Literary Motif?

The historicity of Moses' birth story has been questioned because of the account of the massacre. It has been suggested that this story has been copied from other stories or created independently by its authors. The story is seen as sharing "literary motifs" with birth stories from various cultures, and is therefore considered unhistorical. A motif may be defined as "the smallest element in a tale having power to persist in tradition" (Thompson, 1946: 415).

The later Christian story of Herod's massacre of young boys in Bethlehem aside, there is no ancient story that significantly resembles the story of the indiscriminate killing of the male infants in the Biblical and Qur'anic accounts of Moses' birth. Nevertheless, similarities have been noted between certain details of this story and other ancient stories and identified as literary motifs. One such motif is "the persecuted baby" (Irvin, 1977: 191-192). One ancient story that contains this motif is the birth of Cyrus, king of Persia and Medea.

According to the historian Herodotus, the Median king Astyages saw a dream in which his daughter would pass so much water to cover all of

Asia. After having this ominous dream interpreted for him, he decided to give his daughter in marriage to a Persian man, who was much below a Mede in rank. When Astyages' daughter was pregnant, he saw another dream whereby a vine grew from the womb of his daughter and covered the whole of Asia. Dream interpreters understood the dream to mean that his daughter would give birth to a child who would become king and sit in the very room in which Astyages sat.

Astyages then called his pregnant daughter from Persia and kept her under his watchful eye to make sure that the child is killed as soon as he is born. When Cyrus was born, the king called on his most trusted relative and charged him with the horrific task of taking the child away and destroying him. This relative, however, concluded that it would not be in his very interest to be the killer of the child, so he in turn commissioned one of Astyages' herdsmen to do the dirty work for him and ordered him to abandon the child on a mountain full of beasts.

The herdsman then discovered the identity of the child from a royal servant and told the story to his wife. She tried to convince him not to kill the boy. As she had had a stillbirth when her husband was away after being summoned by Astyages' relative, she suggested swapping their dead child with Cyrus. This way, she explained, he would be seen to have obeyed the order, their dead child would get a royal burial, and the life of the living child would be spared. Her husband agreed, so he dressed his dead boy in Cyrus' royal gold ornaments and embroidered clothing, placed him in the chest in which he carried Cyrus, and abandoned him in a desolate part of a mountain. On the third day, he went to the king's relative and informed him that he can now send witnesses to see the child's dead body. The herdsman and his wife then brought up Cyrus under a different name (Herodotus, *Histories*, 1.107-113).

One significant fact about this story is that Cyrus, who went on to rule the Persians and the Medes as was predicted in the dream, lived in the 6th century BCE — almost 7 centuries after Moses. Clearly, if any story copying has taken place, then it is the Cyrus birth story that would have borrowed some details from Moses', unless one presumes that Moses' story was written later than the 6th century BCE, but scholars think that it was written down around the 10th century BCE.

Moses' story of birth has also been seen as another instance of the literary motif of a *hero cast away in infancy*. In a detailed study titled *The Literary Motif of the Exposed Child*, Donald Redford (1967) compiled 32 ancient stories, some of which are mythical and/or legendary, that share the motif of the casting away of an infant hero. He classified the reasons for exposing the child in those stories into three categories: (i) shame associated with its birth because of moral issues; (ii) threat to its life from a king fearing that, according to a prophecy, the child would overthrow him in the future; this is the case in Cyrus' story and probably Moses' story according to the Qur'an; and (iii) saving it from a general massacre.

In the latter category, Redford cites, in addition to the Bible's and Josephus' versions of Moses' birth and the New Testament's story of Jesus' birth, the stories of the Roman emperor Augustus and Pyrrhus. In Augustus' story, which circulated 2 centuries after the birth of the emperor, the Roman senate was foretold that a king of Rome was about to be born, so a decree was issued prohibiting the rearing of male children (Suetonius, *Lives of the Caesars: Augustus*, 2.94).

In Pyrrhus' story, shortly after he was born in 318 BCE, a revolt broke out against his father, who was the king of Epirus in Northern Greece. Pyrrhus' father was killed, but his only son and successor was saved by royal servants. Redford notes that this account may be historical. Pyrrhus' story does not involve a massacre targeting his life, but enemies seeking to kill him (Plutarch, *Lives: Pyrrhus*, 2).

One particular story that is often likened and linked to Moses' birth story is that of king Sargon of Akkad who lived about 11 centuries before Moses. According to the Assyrian story, Sargon's mother conceived him in secret. When she gave birth, she put her son in a basket of rushes which she sealed with pitch and cast him into the river. Little Sargon was then picked by someone who brought him up. This is the full surviving text of the story of Sargon, inscribed in the first person:

> Sargon, the mighty king, king of Agade,[16] am I.
> My mother was changeling, my father I knew not.
> The brother(s) of my father loved the hills.
> My city is Azupiranu, which is situated on the banks of the Euphrates.
> My changeling mother conceived me, in secret she bore me.
> She set me in a basket of rushes, with bitumen she sealed my lid.
> She cast me into the river which rose not (over) me.
> The river bore me up and carried me to Akki, the drawer of water.
> Akki, the drawer of water lifted me out as he dipped his e[w]er.
> Akki, the drawer of water [took me] as his son (and) reared me.
> Akki, the drawer of water, appointed me as his gardener.
> While I was a gardener, Ishtar granted me (her) love,
> And for four and [...] years I exercised kingship.

---

[16] Another spelling for Akkad.

> The black headed [people] I ruled, I gov[erned];
> Mighty [mou]tains with chip axes of bronze I conquered,
> The upper ranges I scaled,
> The lower rangers I [trav]ersed,
> The sea [lan]ds three times I circled.
> Dilmun my [hand] cap[tured],
> [To] the great Der I [went up], I [...],
> [...] I altered and [...].
> Whatever king may come up after me,
> [...],
> Let him r[ule, let him govern] the black headed peo[ple];
> [Let him conquer] mighty [mountains] with chip axe[s of bronze],
> [Let] him scale the upper ranges,
> [Let him traverse the lower ranges],
> Let him circle the sea [lan]ds three times!
> [Dilmun let his hand capture],
> Let him go up [to] the great Der and [...]!
> [...] from my city, Aga[de ...]
> [...] ... [....]. (*ANET*, 1950: 119)

Because of sharing elements with the birth stories of Sargon, Cyrus, and others, Moses' story is considered by many scholars to be unhistorical (Hyatt, 1971: 62; Rogerson & Davies, 1989: 354; Widengren, 1977: 516). This is how one scholar argued this view:

> We would be closing our eyes to well-known facts if we were unwilling to recognize that the elements in the story of the birth of Moses are themes which occur frequently in legendary stories. The world of the ancient East provides the legend of the birth of King Sargon of Akkad.... This motif is also well-known from the Cyrus legend.... It can be hardly doubted that such stories were known in the world of ancient Israel and had their effect on the development of the story of the birth of Moses. Although the individual details of these legends are developed in completely different ways, there is common to them all the basic thought that great figures, both rulers and benefactors, had stood from the beginning of their lives under the special working of a divine providence which had proved itself effective in the face of all the attacks directed against them by worldly despots. (Noth, 1962: 26-27)

Despite the assertions of its followers, motif study is a highly speculative approach that, while may have some useful applications, cannot be used to study history. We have shown elsewhere how literary motifs such as the "birth under the tree" (Fatoohi, 2007b: 180-186) or the "spurned seductress" (Fatoohi, 2007b: 14) reflect real and recurring events that can be easily verified. Similarly, the story element of *a child exposed by his mother and found and brought up by someone else* is today almost a daily item in news media. No sensible person would suggest that all reports of abandoned infants who are found and taken to be brought up by foster parents are manifestations of a literary motif!

It may be suggested that there are other similarities between Moses' and Sargon's stories that cannot be described as daily or common occurrences — namely, the way the child is rescued from a pending danger. However, despite their rarity, there is no justification to suggest that such stories *could not* have happened in reality more than once over hundreds of years across the world. There is nothing inherent in such stories that make them impossible to happen more than once in different places separated by hundreds of kilometers and centuries of time. If the infant Sargon was indeed put by his mother in a basket and cast in the river, there is no reason to think that the same could not have happened to another child over one thousand years later, hundreds of kilometers away, in a completely different environment. If the story of Sargon was completely unhistorical — whether based on another story or created independently by its authors — this would still not *necessarily* imply that Moses' was the same. We do not know whether Sargon's story was a complete legend, and similarly no one can show that Moses' story is unhistorical. The fact that there are similar ancient stories probably mean that some of them were made up, but rejecting all of them or pointing out that Moses' was unhistorical is mere speculation.

There is another important point. When the lengthy and complicated story of Moses is considered in its entirety it becomes clear that it is totally different from the stories compiled by Redford, including Sargon's. We have cited the story of Sargon in full to show how minute are its similarities with Moses' story. These similarities are virtually negligible in comparison with the differences. The attempt to deny the historicity of the stories of Moses and Joseph by motif analysis using a very small part in each of the two narratives is misleading and misguided.

We have concluded elsewhere that the alleged Herod's massacre of children in Bethlehem was copied from the Old Testament's story. But this conclusion was not reached because of the similarities between the Herodian massacre in Matthew and Pharaoh's killing of the Israelites in older records. Only after arguing that Herod could not have committed that massacre and the Christian story was therefore unhistorical it was concluded that the authors of this story probably derived it from the story of the birth of Moses (Fatoohi, 2007b: 201-207). Readers interested in a more detailed discussion of the topic of this section may consult our book *The Mystery of the Historical Jesus* (pp. 13-17).

11

Scriptural Names of the Israelites

The Bible uses the terms "Israelites" and "Hebrews" interchangeably. But there are fundamental differences between the two, which we will examine in this chapter. We will also study the terms that the Qur'an applies to the Israelites.

11.1 Who Were the 'Apiru/Habiru?

Around the end of the 19th century important documents were discovered in Middle Egypt in Amarna — the site of Akhenaten's capital. Written in Akkadian, the "Amarna letters" represented the diplomatic correspondence that Amenhotep III (1386-1349 BCE) and his son and successor Akhenaten (1350-1334 BCE) received from vassals of the Egyptian empire in Canaan.

These letters created so much excitement among Biblical scholars because they mention people called "'Apiru" who are depicted as disruptive groups involved in insurgencies against the Egyptian authorities in various cities in Canaan. This find was seized upon by Biblicists who, equating the name "'Apiru" with the Biblical term "Hebrew,"[17] saw in the Amarna letters extra-Biblical evidence on Israel's military invasion of Canaan as related in the book of Joshua. Dating the letters at the time to the end of the 15th and beginning of the 14th centuries BCE further enhanced this view, as this date was in line with what was believed for a while to be the date of the conquest of Canaan by Joshua — a view that is held today by only a very small minority of scholars (e.g. Wood, 2005).

The excitement created by the Amarna letters was to prove short-lived, as texts discovered later showed that the 'Apiru, appearing as "Habiru" in cuneiform records, were *not* "an ethnic group confined to fourteenth-century [BCE] Palestine but a social class which was present throughout the second millennium BCE and throughout the ancient Near East" (Miller, 1977: 249). Greenberg (1955) has compiled a large number of ancient documents containing the term 'Apiru. These texts originate

---

[17] The words for "Hebrew" and "Hebrews" in the Hebrew language are *'ivri* or *'ibri* and *'ivrim* or *'ibrim*, respectively.

from various places in the Near East, including Egypt, and cover the whole of the 2nd millennium BCE. Particularly significant is the fact that the 'Apiru were still in Egypt as late as the reign of Ramesses IV (1151-1145 BCE) — some five decades after the exodus — as attested by the mention of "800 'Apiru" among men sent by that Pharaoh to quarry in Wadi Hammamat (Greenberg, 1955: 57).

Miller (1977: 279) notes that the "presumption that 'Apiru,' 'Hebrew,' and 'Israelite' were virtually synonymous terms is, at the very least, probably an oversimplification." He reckons that "the relationship (if any) between the 'Apiru and the Hebrews seems less clear now than it did at any earlier stage of research" (p. 267).

Dever (1977: 118) is also dismissive of equating the Hebrews with the 'Apiru:

> In addition to problems of etymology and ethnic identification there is the larger question of whether the patriarchs pictured in Genesis resemble the Amarna Age 'Apiru as a socio-economic class. The former are peaceful nomadic pastoralists (except in Genesis 14),[18] while the latter are freebooters, usually in conflict with the urban authorities.

Thompson (1977: 156) stresses that "the 'Apiru ought not be too facilely identified as Semitic; nor is the basis for their identification with the Biblical 'Hebrew' very substantial." He also points out that the 'Apiru were in Egypt as slaves from at least the time of Amenhotep II (1453-1419 BCE) and were still there during the reign of Ramesses IV.

The overwhelming majority of scholars now reject the view that "Hebrew" and "'Apiru" are synonymous. On the other hand, many scholars view the apparent similarity between *'Apiru* and *Hebrew* as significant rather than fortuitous. This view finds support in Ramesside documents that show 'Apiru having their share of enslavement as forced labor in building sites — exactly as the Bible says about the Israelites. Of particular significance are documents from the era of Ramesses II, the builder of Pi-Ramesses. One such document from this Pharaoh's middle years, which Abraham Malamat sees as "probable evidence of the Israelite servitude in Egypt," is Papyrus Leiden 348 from Memphis. In this document, the scribe cites previously received instructions from his lord — an official of Ramesses II — concerning construction work at the new capital of Pi-Ramesses:

---

[18] In Genesis 14, Abraham is seen fighting to free his nephew Lot from captivity.

> I have received the letter which my lord sent to (me) to say: 'Give corn-rations to the soldiers and the 'Apiru who are dragging stone to the great pylon of Ramesse-miamun [life, prosperity, health!] 'Beloved-of-Maet' which is under the authority of the chief of Medjay Amenemone.' I am giving them their corn-rations every month according to the manner which my lord told me. (*LEM*, 1954: 491)

Cazelles, who identifies "Hebrew" with "'Apiru" as a sociological phenomenon not an ethnic group, points out to an ostracon from the 19th Dynasty which mentions the 'Apiru being engaged in the handling of stones (Cazelles, 1973: 14). Kitchen has no doubt as to the implications of these documents:

> Lumped in with the 'Apiru generally were doubtless those who in the Bible appear as the Hebrews, and specifically the clan-groups of Israel, resident in the east Delta since the distant days when their forefathers Joseph and Jacob had first come to Egypt to escape famine. (Kitchen, 1982: 70)

Like many other scholars (e.g. Noth, 1962: 21-22), Malamat also agrees that there are some ethnic and linguistic links between the Hebrews and the 'Apiru. However, he thinks the Hebrews designate a broader ethnicity than the Biblical Israelites, so every Israelite is a Hebrew and likely an 'Apiru but, contrary to what Kitchen above suggests, not every Hebrew or 'Apiru is necessarily an Israelite. He concludes that the fact that 'Apiru and Hebrews were employed as slave labor in building Pi-Ramesses does not necessarily mean that the Israelites were also engaged in the building work (Malamat, 1997: 18). So, the relation, if any, between the Hebrews and the 'Apiru is difficult to define clearly, and the difference, if any, between Hebrew and Israelite is also unclear. Houtman (1993: 123), on the other hand, takes the view that since the Bible uses "Hebrew" as a gentilic noun, it must be synonymous with "Israelite."

In summary, most scholars agree that the 'Apiru where a socio-economic class rather than an ethnic group, but there is no consensus on the nature of the relationship between the Hebrews and the 'Apiru.

11.2 Hebrews Hijack 'Apiru

There are at least two good reasons to believe that the terms "Hebrew" and "'Apiru" are related. **First**, there is clear phonetic similarity between the two terms. **Second**, the Hebrews and the 'Apiru were both used as slaves in Egypt. We do not have 'Apiru sources to interrogate about the Hebrews, but we have the Hebrew Bible to examine to try and understand this link. But the Bible does not give a clear or straightforward answer.

The Bible uses "Hebrew" and "Children of Israel" or "Israelites" interchangeably (e.g. Exo. 1:7, 9, 15, 16 & 19). It does not indicate any differences between the two. Yet looking from outside, there is a significant difference between the two. The origin of "Israelite" is clear, as "Israel" was Jacob's later name (Gen. 32:28) so "Israelite" denoted all his offspring. But the Bible is completely silent on the etymology of the supposedly synonymous term "Hebrew." In the 19th century, Biblical scholars suggested that the word *'Ivri* was derived from *ever* which means "across" or "other side" because the Bible states that Abraham *crossed* into Canaan from Mesopotamia, i.e. from the *other side* of the Euphrates or the Jordan River. This view is still held by a minority of scholars (e.g. McCarter, 1992).

One problem with this theory is the Biblical phrase "Abraham the Hebrew" (Gen. 14:13). In our view, this application of the term to Abraham eliminates any possible etymological relation with the name "Abraham." It looks like a case of an already existing term being used to describe Abraham rather than a new term being created for Abraham. The attempt to force the Bible to tell us what "Hebrew" means is futile. The complete disinterest of this ethnocentric book in explaining the second name it applies to the people it focuses on must point to something; but what is it?

Our following analysis is partly speculative — something that no attempt to establish a link between "Hebrew" and "'Apiru" can escape, given the lack of direct and sufficient information. But it is based on direct, substantial observations from the Bible. The conclusion that we draw is that "Hebrew" and "'Apiru" are one and the same term that the Biblical writers applied *exclusively* to the Israelites for reasons that are not unexpected.

The use of "Hebrew" in the Bible looks rather vexing. It is first used when applied to Abraham. But it is not used again until it appears 5 times in the story of Joseph. Three of these are applied to Joseph (Gen. 39:14, 17; 41:12). In one of the remaining two Joseph calls his homeland "the land of the Hebrews" (Gen. 40:15), and in the other Joseph's brothers are called "Hebrews" (Gen. 43:32). Now, given that "Hebrew" was at least as old as Abraham and that he was described as a Hebrew, why is it almost ignored early on and not used more often in a book that follows the history of the patriarchs so closely? Why does it then appear as many as 5 times in the story of Joseph in Egypt? Also, why does it occur even much more — namely, 16 times — in the story of Moses in the Book of Exodus? This peculiar pattern of the appearance of the term "Hebrew" in the Bible is instructive.

The story of Moses is where the Israelites are shown to be working as slaves. Interestingly, all but one of the occurrences of "Hebrew" in this story appear when the Israelites were still *slaves* under Pharaoh. Significantly, the one exception and last appearance of this term in Exodus (21:2), which is after the Israelites had earned their freedom, is in a divine legislation about how long the Israelites should keep a "Hebrew servant" before freeing him. In other words, it also talks about a *slave*.

The same link between "slavery" and "Hebrew" is also seen in the story of Joseph. In the three times in which Joseph is described as "Hebrew" he was a *slave* (Gen. 39:19), i.e. before he was freed and honored by the king. One of the other two appearances of the term in Joseph's story is this: "The Egyptians are not able to eat with Hebrews, for the Egyptians think it is disgusting to do so" (Gen. 43:32). The Egyptian's attitude is explained in another passage: "everyone who takes care of sheep is disgusting to the Egyptians" (Gen. 46:34). But ancient historians have reported that Egyptians found eating with *foreigners* in general disgusting. What underlines this attitude is probably a form of racism which is not that far from the view that the Egyptians are *masters* and foreigners are *slaves*. We have already seen that Egyptians used to send military campaigns to bring captives from abroad to enslave. The other use in the "the land of the Hebrews" is neutral but was spoken by Joseph when he was in jail, so it could have meant "the land of the slaves."

Given that Joseph was first a slave in Egypt and that the Israelites later and during Moses' time suffered servitude there, the use of the term "Hebrew" in these stories suggests a very strong link between this term and "slavery." So, "Hebrew" meant "slave," and it and "'Apiru" were one and the same. But if that is true, how did this term come to be used by the Bible as a gentilic name for the Israelites?

We know that the Israelites were enslaved in Egypt, exactly as the 'Apiru were. Yet when detailing the suffering of the Israelite slaves, the Bible does not make any reference to any group other than the ethnic Hebrews/Israelites being subjected to the same bad treatment by the Egyptians. But we know for sure that the Israelites were not alone in their suffering. It is also inconceivable that Ramesses II would have employed the Israelites in places where they would have been the only slave workers (pp. 127-128).

The writers of Exodus were aware of some specific details of the nature of the building work that the Israelites were engaged in, such as the use of straw in making bricks and the imposing of a target-quota system. They must have been equally aware of the fact that non-Israelite slaves did take part in that building work. The Biblical writers' omission of any reference to those people could not have been an innocent mistake. The question is not whether or not the writers of Exodus were deliberate in giving the impression that only the Israelites were employed as slaves — indeed, they presented the enslavement of Israel as a means to control the population of this specific nation not as a general Egyptian practice — but what motive stood behind this intentional omission. Why is the Bible completely silent on any other ethnic group sharing with the Israelites their sufferings? The answer to this question lies in the nature of the Bible itself.

Conceding that non-Israelites were also used by Pharaoh as slave labor would have only served to deprive the horrific experience of Israel of its *uniqueness*. This would have been a very unwelcome consequence for the redactors of the Bible, as the singling out of Israel by Pharaoh for harsh treatment was an essential ingredient of the Biblical story of the slavery of the Israelites. If other peoples were also treated as badly by Pharaoh, what happened to Israel would have looked less dramatic. It would not have been a story of a *wronged people* as much as a story of a *wrongful Pharaoh*. But the Bible is about that people, not Pharaoh or other peoples.

This very attitude is what stands behind the misleading presentation of Pharaoh's killing of the Israelite newborn males as at attempt to control the growth of the Israelite *people* rather than targeting one Israelite *individual* who was destined to be the source of grave danger to Pharaoh in the future. This manipulation of history with the aim of placing the Israelite *people* at the center of events is also responsible for the Biblical misrepresentation of the fact that God *preferred the Israelite people over other peoples.*

The *uniqueness* of the Egyptian experience of the Israelite *people* as portrayed in the Bible is very much in line with the *uniqueness* of the position of this *people* as the *chosen people* of God. In reality, what was unique about the Israelites was due to the appearance among them of certain *individuals* — prophets — not because of something special about Israel as a nation (pp. 77-78).

The redactors of the Bible were well aware that the term 'Apiru was used in Egypt to refer to slaves irrespective of their ethnic origins, and was therefore applied to the Israelites also. They decided to hijack this term, which read "Hebrew" for the Biblical authors, and relaunch it as another gentilic name for the Israelites. Interestingly, the Egyptian term

'Apiru went out of currency around the 10th century BCE, i.e. before the Bible is thought to have been written. So the Biblical writers were able to claim the term for the Israelites without fear of confusing them with other peoples.

The Biblical authors found themselves facing the problem that the Israelites could not have suddenly become "Hebrews" in Egypt. This was dealt with by applying the term "Hebrew" to Abraham, the forefather of all Israelites. If Abraham was a Hebrew and this is an ethnic term, then naturally all the Israelites were also Hebrews. But this ad-hoc fix was rather clumsy, because it also meant that *all* of Abraham's descendants, not only the Israelites, are Hebrews. Yet this inevitable implication is totally neglected in the Bible where there are no Hebrews other than the Israelites and where "Hebrew" and "Israelite" are used synonymously.

In a nutshell, the Bible's editors could not have confused the 'Apiru and the Israelites innocently. The whole atmosphere is one of a conspiracy than a muddle.

It is significant that Merneptah's stela does not refer to "Israel" with the term "'Apiru," despite the fact that the latter term was used in Egypt at the time. The reason is that "'Apiru" was a generic term that was applied to all slaves, yet the writers of the stela wanted to identify the Israelites specifically.

This view of how the term "Hebrew" became a synonym for "Israelite" explains well all of the following facts:

(1) The close phonetic similarity between the terms "Hebrew" and "'Apiru."

(2) The Israelites and 'Apiru were both used as slaves.

(3) Abraham is called "Hebrew" yet this term is applied only to Jacob's descendants.

(4) Excluding the lone application of this term to Abraham, the Bible starts applying it to the first Israelite slave in Egypt.

(5) This term makes by far its most appearances in the story of Moses, where the Israelites lived as slaves.

(6) The absence of any etymology for the term "Hebrew" in the Bible.

(7) The Bible's silence on the enslavement of ethnic groups other than the Israelites.

(8) The obvious redundancy of the term "Hebrews" given that it is equivalent to "Israelites" or "Children of Israel."

(9) The appearance of "Hebrew" 35 times only in the whole Bible whereas "Israelite" is used well over 700 times.

(10) The reference of the Merneptah stela to the Israelites with

"Israel" rather than "'Apiru."

It is quite clear that the term "Hebrew" is a misnomer. It should not be used to refer to Israel exclusively.

Significantly, the Qur'an does not apply to the Israelite a term that is equivalent to "Hebrew." It also does not use Jacob's name "Israel" to refer to all of his descendants. The Qur'an refers to the Israelites with the exclusive term "Children of Israel" and with the broader term "People of the Book." The latter is applied to the people who had in their possession a divine book when the Qur'an was revealed. It is applied to the Jews who had the Torah, the book that was revealed to Moses, and the Christians who had the Injīl, the book of Jesus:[19]

> Say [O Muhammad!]: "O People of the Book! You do not stand on anything until you observe the Torah, the Injīl, and what has been revealed to you from your Lord." But what has been revealed to you from your Lord will only increase many of them in insolence and disbelief. Do not feel sorry for the disbelieving people (5.68).

The use of the word "Book" rather than its plural case "Books" in a verse that talks about both the Jews and the Christians reflects the fact that all divine books have essentially the same message and have come from the same source.

The Qur'an also uses the term "Jews" for the Israelites, which we shall study next to complete this investigation of the names of the Israelites.

11.3 Jews: Moses' Followers

The Hebrew word for "Jew" is *Yehudi*. Scholars believe that this term is derived from the name of one of Jacob's twelve sons, *Yehudhah* (Judah). According to the Bible, the child's mother chose this name to praise the Lord. The *NET* Bible states that the name means "he will be praised." *Yehudi*, thus, is taken to have originally referred to a member of the tribe of Judah. This etymology is reiterated by some Muslim writers as well (e.g. Ṭabbārah, undated: 11).

The term was then applied to the inhabitants of the southern kingdom of Judah or Judea, which consisted of the tribes of Judah and his half brother Benjamin. It is in this broader sense of inhabitants of the kingdom of Judah that the term "Jew" makes its first appearance in the

---

[19] For a detailed study of the "Injīl," see our book *The Mystery of the Historical Jesus: The Messiah in the Qur'an, the Bible, and Historical Sources*, pp. 357-388.

Bible late in 2 Kings 16:6.

The popular explanation of how the term "Jew" came to denote all adherents of Judaism is based on the Biblical narrative. When the Assyrians attacked the northern state of Israel in 721 CE after its revolt they took its inhabitants captives and scattered them (2 Kings 18:9-11). The Babylonian king Nebuchadnezzar attacked Judea three times in the first two decades of the 6th century BCE and took captives to Babylon (Jer. 52:28-30). Half a century later the two captive tribes of Judea were then allowed to return to their homeland by the Persian king Cyrus. Judea was reestablished. The scattered ten tribes of Israel did not have such luck because they had already been assimilated by other peoples and were lost. So the inhabitants of Judea in exile were the only Israelites who retained their distinctive identity.

In the Qur'an, the Arabic masculine singular for "Jew" is *Yahūdī*, whose plural cases are *Yahūd* or *Hūd*. But the Qur'an gives *Yahūdī* a different etymology. The verb is *hāda* which means "repented" or "returned to the right path." This name comes sometimes in the plural verbal form of *Allathīna hādū* which means "those who repented."

The Qur'an implies that the term "Jew" did not exist before Moses or, more accurately, the Torah. In other words, it was coined by God Himself, as He coined the term "Muslim" (22.78). The following verses confirm this fact by stressing that neither Abraham nor any of his sons and grandsons, including Israel, could have been a "Jew" or "Naṣrānī/Christian," because both the Torah and the Injīl, where these terms came from, were revealed after them:

> O People of the Book! Why do you argue about Abraham, when the Torah and the Injīl were not sent down till after him? Have you no sense (3.65)? You have argued about things that you have knowledge of, so why do you argue about what you have no knowledge of? Allah knows and you do not know (3.66). Abraham was not a Jew or Christian, but he was upright, a Muslim (someone who surrenders to God), and he was not one of the polytheists (3.67). The people who are most worthy of Abraham are those who followed him, this Prophet (Muhammad), and those who believed [in Muhammad]. Allah is the patron of the believers (3.68).
>
> They said: "Be Jews or Christians so that you may be guided." Say [O Muhammad!]: "Not so, but follow the religion of Abraham who was upright and was not one of the polytheists" (2.135).
>
> Or do you [O People of the Book!] say that Abraham, Ishmael, Isaac, Jacob, and the Asbāṭ (Jacob's sons) were Jews or Christians? Say [O Muhammad!]: "Do you know best or Allah does?" And who is more of a wrongdoer than he who conceals a testimony that he has from Allah? Allah is not unaware of what you do (2.140). This is a nation that has

passed away. Theirs is what they gained, and yours is what you gain. You shall not be asked about what they have done (2.141).

The fact that the forefathers of the Israelites were not "Jews" leaves no doubt that this term, unlike "the Children of Israel," is not gentilic. It is a name for those who believed in Moses' message and embraced his religion, regardless of their ethnic origin. Although Moses' main goal was to deliver the Israelites and take them out of Egypt, his prophetic mission had a wider scope and his religious message did not target the Israelites only. Non-Israelite people in Canaan, for instance, would have converted to the new religion of Moses and become as much Jews as the Israelite believers. The domain of the activity of any prophet might well be limited for practical reasons, but not so as a matter of principle. For example, when two prison inmates in polytheistic Egypt asked Joseph to interpret their dreams he started first by preaching about his monotheistic religion, obviously hoping to convert them (12.35-41). The Qur'an also tells us, in addition to Pharaoh's wife (66.11), of an Egyptian man who believed in Moses:

> A believing man from Pharaoh's people who concealed his faith said: "Will you kill a man for saying 'my Lord is Allah' when he has come to you with manifest proofs from your Lord? If he is a liar then his lie would be against him, and if he is truthful then some of what he has threatened you with would fall on you. Allah does not guide one who is an extravagant liar" (40.28).

Significantly, the Qur'an does not describe this non-Israelite who believed in Moses' message as a "Jew" but rather a "believer." Even more telling is the fact that throughout Moses' struggle with Pharaoh, only the term "Children of Israel" is used for Moses' people. At no point during the confrontation the Israelites were called Jews. This is due to the fact that the Torah had not been revealed then so those who believed in Moses had not been called Jews yet.

The earliest historical event in which the Qur'an calls the followers of Moses "Jews" is after the exodus when seventy of Moses' people went with him to the mount where he used to converse with God in order to hear His words. A verse in one of the two accounts of this event reveals the Qur'anic etymology of the word "Jew":

> Moses chose from his people seventy for our appointment. When the earthquake overtook them he said: "My Lord! Had you willed, you could have killed them and me before. Would You kill us for what the fools among us have done? This is not but Your trial with which You send astray whom You will and guide whom You will. You are our guardian, so forgive us and show mercy to us, and You are the best of forgivers (7.155). Write down for us good in this world and in the hereafter. *We*

have repented to You." He said: "I will strike with My torment whom I will, and My mercy embraces everything, so I shall write it down for those who are pious, give alms, and believe in Our signs" (7.156).

In 7.156, Moses prays to God saying *"innā hudnā ilayka"* which means "we have repented to You." According to the Qur'an, this event occurred after Moses' reception of the *Tablets* which were inscribed by God. In his appeal to God, Moses used a term that was already coined by God in the Torah.

To sum up, the Qur'an refers to the Israelites with three terms each of which has a clear etymology: "the Children of Israel," "People of the Book," and *"Yahūd/Hūd."* But the Qur'an does not have a word corresponding to "Hebrew." This totally agrees with the fact that the word "Hebrew" is a misnomer which was chosen by the Biblical authors as a name for the Israelites for the purpose of presenting the horrific experience of Israel in Egypt as unique.

12

The Historical Exodus

This short chapter summarizes our findings, telling the story of the exodus using the Qur'an and archaeological and historical sources.

Around the middle of the 17th century BCE, Joseph, while a young child, was taken to the eastern Delta which was then under the rule of the Hyksos. The child who arrived as a slave rose in his youth to a high position, probably second only to the king. His father Jacob, his mother, and his eleven brothers and their families later came and settled in that part of Egypt. The expulsion of the Hyksos by Pharaoh Ahmose I around the middle of the 16th century BCE resulted in the Israelites being enslaved, like many other foreigners on Egyptian soil. They were deployed individually and in groups to various parts of Pharaonic Egypt wherever their service was needed.

Sometime in the 13th century BCE, Israelite and other slaves were gathered from various parts of Egypt and sent to where the Israelites' ancestors used to live in the eastern Delta. Ramesses II had decided to build a new city on the same site of ancient Avaris, once the capital of the Hyksos and city of residence of the first Israelites in Egypt. After the building of the new capital, Pi-Ramesses, the slaves were redeployed to other parts of Egypt according to the needs for labor force. Some slaves, including Israelites, were left in the city to provide services and to take part in further building work. Moses' family was living with the Israelite community at Pi-Ramesses.

At some point, Pharaoh knew somehow of the imminent birth of an Israelite boy who would grow up to become the leader of his enslaved people and cause his downfall and defeat his army. To head off this gloomy scenario, Pharaoh launched a brutal campaign to kill every Israelite newborn boy. Moses, the targeted boy, however, escaped death. When she felt that her child's life was in danger, Moses' mother, as instructed by God, put him in a coffin and sent it floating down the river. The child was then picked up by Pharaoh's people and brought up in his palace.

Sometime in his early twenties, Moses intervened in a fight between an Israelite and an Egyptian, killing the latter. As a result, a plot to kill Moses was worked out by Egyptian courters, so he had to escape to Midian. He lived there for less than 10 years before leaving with his family. While on the road, Moses was spoken to by God and made a prophet. He was commanded to return to Egypt to call Pharaoh to believe in God and ask him to release the Israelites from their bondage. God wanted the Israelites to live in the holy land which He had ordained that they would occupy for centuries. Moses asked for his brother Aaron to assist him in his mission — a request that God granted.

After the arrogant Pharaoh turned down Moses' request to free Israel, the messenger tried to make Ramesses II change his mind by performing miracles. Moses then was ordered by God that he and his brother Aaron should live in the eastern Delta and make their area of residence a gathering point for the Israelites from all parts of Egypt.

Having found himself unable to cause any harm to Moses and Aaron who were under God's protection, Pharaoh then started a new campaign of killing Israelite males to deter the Israelites from following Moses. The Israelites resumed their grumbly attitude, accusing Moses of being the cause of their new misery. This second massacre probably stopped when the Egyptians started to suffer episodes of divine punishment in the form of plagues. After the last plague, Ramesses II gave in and promised Moses that he would let his people go with him if Moses asked God to end the plague. But when this happened, Pharaoh broke his promise. Having had enough of Moses and his people and refusing to put up with them any longer, Pharaoh took the decision to disperse the gathered Israelites once again. Forestalling Pharaoh's plan, God ordered Moses to lead his people out of Egypt in the night.

After finding out about the Israelites' unauthorized departure, Ramesses II gathered an army and in probably a few weeks he was after the escapees. The small number of fleeing Israelites would have stood no chance in the face of the much superior Pharaonic army. Pharaoh and his soldiers caught up with the Israelites who had reached the sea. God intervened again, enabling Moses to part the sea for his people who crossed to the other side. When Pharaoh and his army pursued them on that dry path, the sea returned to its normal state and they all drowned. When he found himself on the verge of death, Ramesses II declared his belief in Moses' God; only too late. God saved Ramesses II's dead body to make it a sign for people. Indeed, it has been witnessed by countless people from various generations and places.

After the exodus, the disobedient Israelites went on to cause all sorts of troubles for Moses. The Israelites' 4-century long sojourn in Egypt had left its mark on them, making them accommodate polytheistic beliefs and practices. More than once they worshipped or tried to worship an idol. In one instance their disobedience led them to reject the divine command to enter the holy land. God punished them for the disloyalty and disobedience, banning them from entering the holy land for forty years they had to spend wandering in other lands.

The Qur'anic story of Moses, including the exodus, has similarities with its Biblical counterpart, but there are substantial differences between the two. There are more differences than similarities between the two accounts. This book has shown how the Qur'anic account is consistent and that its details are either corroborated by independent evidence or at least not contradicted by it. The Biblical narrative, on the other hand, contains many internal discrepancies as well as a lot of details that are at odds with archaeological evidence.

If the Qur'an was derived from the Bible, as Western scholars believe, then it would have inherited those many Biblical errors. Yet the Qur'an is amazingly free of those Biblical problems. If the Qur'an was copied from the Bible then why, for instance, does it describe the Israelites as a small nation rather embrace the Bible's claim that they were 2-3 million — an enormously inflated number that no scholar would accept? The picture of a huge number of Israelites being a danger to Egypt is so appealing to the minds of people who are not aware of historical facts that even Muslim exegetes have accepted it! Why does the Qur'an not go along the Biblical, and indeed much more likely, scenario that Pharaoh was swallowed for good by the sea, to state instead that Ramesses II's "body" was rescued? Why does the Qur'an say this about Ramesses II in particular but not about other people who were also destroyed by God? Why does "Hāmān," whose name we can now relate to the Egyptian god Amun, appear in Moses' story in New Kingdom Egypt not in Biblical Persia? Why does the Qur'an totally ignore the erroneous but otherwise very attractive Biblical etymology of "Moses"? Why does it contain no equivalent of the Biblical name "Hebrew" which is a misnomer?

The Qur'an does not accept these and many more wrong Biblical claims. How come this *filtration* process? Why does the Qur'an agree with Biblical details that have no historical problems but reject problematic ones? The popular view that the Qur'an is derived from the Bible is categorically rejected by the facts. This 14-century old claim is often the result of ignorance of the Qur'an and sometimes even of the Bible, but it is usually driven by prejudice also. This is how the Qur'an challenged its rejectionists then — a challenge that remains equally valid today:

> Can they not consider the Qur'an? If it was from someone other than Allah they would have found so much discrepancy in it (4.82).

Appendix A

Qur'anic Verses on Moses

The Qur'an recounts details of the story of Moses in a number of chapters. For easy reference, this appendix compiles the longest of these accounts, presented in ascending order of length.

We have not included the story of Moses' spiritual journey looking for a certain wise man (18.60-82). This journey, in which he was accompanied with an unnamed assistant, is rather unrelated to the history of the nation of Israel.

Passing references to Moses' story are found in other Qur'anic chapters also.

A.1 The Chapter of al-A'rāf (the Heights) (7.103-137, 7.159-166)

> Then we sent after them (the messengers) Moses with Our signs to Pharaoh and his chiefs, but they disbelieved in them; so see what the end of the corrupters was (7.103). Moses said: "O Pharaoh! I am a messenger from the Lord of all peoples (7.104). It is a duty on me to say nothing about Allah but the truth; I have come to you with clear proof from your Lord, therefore send with me the Children of Israel" (7.105). He said: "If you have come with a sign, then produce it, if you are one of the truthful" (7.106). So he threw his staff down, and it became a manifest serpent (7.107). And he took his hand out and lo! it was white to the beholders (7.108). The chiefs of Pharaoh's people said: "This is an accomplished magician (7.109) who would like to drive you out of your land; what is your advice" (7.110)? They said: "Let him and his brother wait, and send to the cities summoners (7.111) to bring to you every accomplished magician" (7.112). The magicians came to Pharaoh and said: "We will have a reward if we are the victorious" (7.113). He said: "Yes, and you will be considered with those who are brought close [to me]" (7.114). They said: "O Moses! Either you throw down [your staff] or we will be the first to throw down" (7.115). He said: "You throw [first]". So when they threw, they deceived peoples' eyes, frightened them, and they produced a mighty feat of magic (7.116). We revealed to Moses: "Throw your staff"; then lo! it devoured what they faked (7.117). So the truth was established, and what they did became null (7.118). Thus they were vanquished there, and they turned abased (7.119). So the magicians were thrown down in prostration (7.120). They said: "We believe in the Lord of all peoples (7.121), the Lord of Moses and Aaron" (7.122). Pharaoh Said: "You have believed in Him before I give you permission? This is a plot that you have devised in the city to drive its people out of it,

but you shall know (7.123). I will cut off your hands and legs on opposite sides, and then I will crucify you all" (7.124). They said: "We shall return to our Lord (7.125). You take revenge on us only because we have believed in the signs of our Lord when they came to us. Our Lord! Pour out on us patience and cause us to die as Muslims" (7.126). The chiefs of Pharaoh's people said: "Do you leave Moses and his people to cause corruption in the land and forsake you and your gods?" He said: "We will kill their sons but spare their women, and surely we will overpower them" (7.127). Moses said to his people: "Ask help from Allah and be patient; surely the land is Allah's; He gives it for inheritance to whom He wills of His servants. The [best] end is for the pious" (7.128). They said: "We were harmed before you came to us and we have been harmed since then also." He said: "May your Lord destroy your enemy and make you inheritors in the land so He sees how you act" (7.129). We tested Pharaoh's people with droughts and shortage of crops that they may heed (7.130). When good befalls them they would say: "This is due to us," and when evil afflicts them, they would attribute it to the ill fortune of Moses and those with him; surely their ill fortune is only from Allah, but most of them do not know (7.131). They said: "Whatever sign you may bring to bewitch us, we will not believe you" (7.132). We sent on them the flood, the locusts, the lice, the frogs, and the blood as clear signs; but they behaved arrogantly and were guilty (7.133). When the plague hit them, they said: "O Moses! Pray to your Lord for us, by whatever covenant He has with you, that if you remove the plague from us we will believe you and we will send away with you the Children of Israel" (7.134). But when We removed the plague from them till a term that they were to reach, they broke the promise (7.135). Therefore We took vengeance on them and drowned them in the sea because they denied Our signs and were heedless of them (7.136). We made the people who used to be oppressed to inherit the eastern and western parts of the land that We have blessed. The good word of your Lord was fulfilled for the Children of Israel because of their patience, and We destroyed what Pharaoh and his people wrought and what they built (7.137). We made the Children of Israel cross the sea. They came upon a people who worshipped idols they have created. They said: "Moses, create for us a god as they have gods." He said: "You are ignorant people (7.138). What they are engaged in shall be destroyed and what they are doing is in vain" (7.139). He said: "What, shall I seek for you a god other than Allah when He has preferred you above all peoples" (7.140)? [Remember, O Children of Israel!] when we rescued you from Pharaoh's people who subjected you to the worse torment, killing your sons and sparing your women. There was a great trial from your Lord in this (7.141). We appointed for Moses thirty nights and then completed them with another ten, so the appointed time of his Lord was completed to forty nights. Moses said to his brother Aaron: "Take my place among my people, act rightly, and do not follow the path of the corrupting ones" (7.142). When Moses came to our appointment and was spoken to by his Lord he said: "My Lord, enable me to see You." He said: "You shall not see Me, but look at the mountain; if it remains steady, you shall see Me."

When his Lord manifested Himself to the mountain He turned it into dust, and Moses fell down in a swoon. When he regained consciousness he said: "Glory be to You! I repent to You, and I am the first of the believers" (7.143). He said: "O Moses! I have chosen you over people for My messages and words, so take what I have given you and be among the thankful" (7.144). We wrote for him on the Tablets an admonition concerning everything and a detailing of everything. [We said to him:] "Take them firmly and command your people to observe their most excellent teachings. I will show you the abode of the ungodly (7.145). I will turn away from My signs those who unjustly behave with arrogance in the earth so if they see any sign they do not believe it, if they see the path of righteousness they do not take it for a path, and if they see the path of transgression they take it for a path. This is so because they have rejected Our signs and have been heedless of them (7.146). The works of those who rejected Our signs and the encounter of the hereafter will be in vain. Shall they be rewarded other than for what they have done" (7.147)? The people of Moses took to themselves [as a god] after him a lowing corporeal calf made of their ornaments. Did they not see that it did not speak to them and did not guide them in the path? They took it and were wrongdoers (7.148). When they realized what they have done and saw that they have sinned they said: "If our Lord does not show mercy to us and forgive us we will be among the losers" (7.149). When Moses returned to his people angry and grieved he said: "Evil is what you have done after me. Would you hasten your Lord's matter?" He threw down the Tablets and seized his brother by the head, dragging him. He said: "O son of my mother! The people weakened me and almost killed me. Do not make my enemies gloat over me and do not consider me with the wrongdoing people" (7.150). He said: "My Lord! Forgive me and my brother and admit us into Your mercy; You are the most merciful of the merciful" (7.151). Those who took the calf [as a god] shall have wrath from their Lord and humiliation in the life of this world, and so do We reward the forgers (7.152). As for those who commit evil things then repent after that and believe, Your Lord will be to them, after that, forgiving, merciful (7.153). When Moses' anger calmed down, he took the Tablets, in the inscription of which there are guidance and mercy for those who fear their Lord (7.154). Moses chose from his people seventy for our appointment. When the earthquake overtook them he said: "My Lord! Had you willed, you could have killed them and me before. Would You kill us for what the fools among us have done? This is not but Your trial with which You send astray whom You will and guide whom You will. You are our guardian, so forgive us and show mercy to us, and You are the best of forgivers (7.155). Write down for us good in this world and in the hereafter. We have repented to You." He said: "I will strike with My torment whom I will, and My mercy embraces everything, so I shall write it down for those who are pious, give alms, and believe in Our signs" (7.156).

From Moses' people there is a nation who guide by the truth and measure with it (7.159). We divided them into twelve tribes — nations. We inspired Moses when his people asked him for drink: "Strike the rock with your staff," so twelve springs burst forth. Every people knew their drinking place. We overshadowed them with the clouds and sent down on them the manna and the quails, [saying]: "Eat of the good things We have given you." They did not wrong Us but they were wronging themselves (7.160). When it was said to them: "Live in this town and eat from wherever you like. Say '*ḥiṭṭatun*' and enter the gate prostrating so that We forgive your sins and give increase to the good-doers" (7.161). The wrongdoers among them then changed what had been said to them with another saying, so We sent down on them a punishment from heaven because of their wrongdoing (7.162). Ask them about the town on the sea when they transgressed during the Sabbath, as their fish would come to them on the day when they observe the Sabbath, appearing openly, and on the day they do not observe the Sabbath they would not come. So We tested them because of their rebellion (7.163). When a group from them said: "Why do you admonish a people whom Allah will destroy or punish severely?" They said: "For our own excuse with your Lord, and that they may become pious to Allah" (7.164). When they forgot what they had been reminded of we saved those who forbade evil and we overtook those who did wrong with a severe torment because of their rebellion (7.165). But when they arrogantly persisted in that which they were forbidden We said to them: "Be despised apes" (7.166).

A.2 The Chapter of Ṭāhā (20.9-97)

Has the story of Moses come to you [O Muhammad!] (20.9)? When he saw a fire he said to his family: "Stay here, for I have perceived a fire, that I may bring to you therefrom a brand or find a guidance [to the road] at the fire" (20.10). When he reached it, he was called: "O Moses! (20.11). It is Me, your Lord, so take off your sandals; you are in the sacred valley Ṭūwā (20.12). I have chosen you, so listen to what is revealed (20.13). I am Allah; there is no god save Me. Therefore worship Me and keep up prayer for My remembrance (20.14). The Hour [of Judgment] is coming; I keep it almost hidden, so that every soul will be rewarded according to its deeds (20.15). Let not the person who does not believe in it and follows his own passion turn you away from it so that you perish (20.16). What is that in your right hand, O Moses" (20.17)? He said: "This is my staff; I recline on it, I beat down with it tree leaves for my sheep, and I use it for other things" (20.18). He said: "Throw it down, O Moses!" (20.19). So he threw it down; and behold! it became a crawling serpent (20.20). He said: "Seize it and fear not. We will restore it to its former state (20.21). Draw your hand to your side, and it will come out white without harm, as another sign (20.22). To show you of Our great signs (20.23). Go to Pharaoh, for he has transgressed" (20.24). He said: "O my Lord! Expand my breast (20.25), ease my task for me (20.26), and loosen the knot of my tongue (20.27) so that they may understand what I say (20.28). Appoint for me a vizier from my family (20.29): Aaron, my brother (20.30). Strengthen my back with him (20.31) and let him share my task (20.32). So that we shall glorify You so much (20.33) and remember You so much (20.34). You have been caring to us" (20.35). He said: "You have been granted your request, O Moses! (20.36). We have thus conferred favor on you again (20.37). [The first was] when We revealed to your mother that which is revealed (20.38), saying: 'Put him in a coffin, then throw him in the river. The river shall throw him onshore; there shall take him up one who is an enemy to Me and an enemy to him.' And I threw over you love from Me, and that you should be brought up according to My will (20.39). When your sister came walking and said: 'Shall I direct you to one who will take custody of him?' So We brought you back to your mother, that her eye might be cooled and that she should not grieve. You killed a soul, then We delivered you from the grief, and We tried you with a severe test. Then you stayed for years with the people of Midian, then you came [here] as ordained, O Moses! (20.40). I have prepared you for Myself (20.41). Go you and your brother with My signs and do not slacken in remembering Me (20.42). Go both to Pharaoh; he has transgressed all bounds (20.43). Speak to him gentle words that he may remember or fear" (20.44). They said: "O our Lord! We fear that he may hasten to do evil to us or that he may play the tyrant" (20.45). He said: "Do not fear; I am with you, hearing and seeing (20.46). So go you both to him and say: 'We are two messengers of your Lord; therefore send the Children of Israel with us and do not torment them; we have brought to you a sign from your Lord; peace be upon him who follows right guidance (20.47). It has been revealed to us that the torture will come upon him who rejects and turns back'" (20.48). He (Pharaoh) said: "So who is your Lord, O Moses" (20.49)? He said: "Our Lord is He Who created everything, then guided it [to its course]" (20.50). He said: "Then what about the past generations" (20.51)? He said: "The knowledge of them is with my Lord, in a book; my Lord neither errs nor forgets" (20.52). [It is He] who made the earth for you an expanse and made for you in it paths, and sent down from the sky water with which We have brought forth pairs of diverse species of vegetation (20.53). Eat and pasture your cattle; there are signs in this for people of intellect (20.54). From it We created you, into it We shall return you, and from it We will bring you forth a second time (20.55). We showed him all Our signs, but he rejected and refused (20.56). He said: "Have you come to us to drive us out of our land by your magic, O Moses (20.57)? We too shall produce to you magic like it. Set an appointment between us and you, which neither we nor you shall break, in a place where both shall have even chances" (20.58). He said: "Your appointment shall be the day of decoration, and let the people be gathered together in the early afternoon" (20.59). Pharaoh went and made his arrangement, then came [to the agreed place] (20.60). Moses said to them (the magicians): "Woe to you! Do not invent lies about Allah, lest He destroy you by a punishment, and he who invents lies is doomed to fail" (20.61). So they disputed with one another about their affair and kept the discourse secret (20.62). They said: "These are two magicians who wish to drive you out of your land by their magic and to take away your ideal tradition (20.63). Therefore concert your plan, then come as one. He shall prosper this day who gains the upper hand" (20.64). They said: "O Moses! Either you throw down [your staff] or we will be the first to throw down" (20.65). He said: "No, you throw down"; then lo! their cords and staffs looked to him, because of their magic, as if they were moving (20.66). So Moses felt inside fear (20.67). We said: "Do not fear; you have the upper hand (20.68). Throw down what is in your right hand, and it shall devour what they have worked; that which they have made is a magician's work, and the magician shall not be successful wherever he may go" (20.69). So the magicians were thrown down in prostration; they said: "We believe in the Lord of Aaron and Moses" (20.70). He said: "You have believed in him before I give you permission? He must be your master who taught you magic. I shall cut off your hands and feet on opposite sides, and I will crucify you on the trunks of palm trees. You shall know who of us can give the more severe and lasting punishment" (20.71). They said: "We shall not prefer you to what has come to us of manifest signs and to He Who made us. Decide whatever you like to do; you can only decide about this world's life (20.72). We have believed in our Lord that He may forgive us our sins and the magic that you compelled us to perform, and Allah is better and more lasting" (20.73). Whoever comes to his Lord as guilty he shall have hell where he shall not die or live (20.74). Whoever comes to Him as a believer who has done righteous deeds, for such are the high states (20.75). The gardens of Eden underneath which rivers flow, wherein they will abide forever. This is the reward of he who purified himself (20.76). We revealed to Moses: "Take away My servants by night, then strike for them a dry path in the sea. Do not be afraid of being overtaken or have any fear" (20.77). Pharaoh then followed them with his soldiers, so there came upon them of the sea that which came upon them (20.78). Pharaoh led his people astray and he did not guide [them] aright (20.79). O Children of Israel! We have rescued you from your enemy, appointed a meeting for you on the right side of the mountain, and sent down on you the manna and the quails (20.80), [saying]: "Eat of the good things We have given you, but do not transgress in them, otherwise My wrath would fall on you. Whoever My wrath falls on he would perish (20.81). I am forgiving to the person who repents, believes, does good works, and is guided" (20.82). [We said]: "What have made you rush away from your people, O Moses" (20.83)? He said: "They are hard on my footsteps, but I have rushed to you, My Lord, that You might be pleased" (20.84). He said: "We have tempted your people after you and the Sāmirī has misled them" (20.85). Moses went back angry and sad to his people and said: "O my people! Has your Lord not promised you a good promise? Has the time been too long for you, or did you want wrath from your Lord to fall on you so you broke my appointment" (20.86)? They said: "We did not break your appointment of our volition, but we were made to carry loads of people's ornaments, and we threw them, and so did the Sāmirī" (20.87). He (the Sāmirī) produced for them a calf — a body that lowed, and said: "This is your god and Moses' god," and he forgot (20.88). Could they not see that it did not return any speech and could not help or harm them (20.89)? Aaron had told them before: "O my people! You have been tempted by it and your Lord is Allah, so follow me and obey my commands" (20.90). They said: "We will not cease our devotion to it until Moses comes back to us" (20.91). He (Moses) said: "O Aaron! What prevented you, when you saw that they have gone astray (20.92), from following me? Have you disobeyed my command" (20.93)? He said: "O son of my mother! Do not seize me by the beard or head. I feared that you may say 'you have divided the Children of Israel and have not observed my word'" (20.94). He (Moses) said: "What is the matter with you, O Sāmirī" (20.95)? He said: "I saw what they did not see, so I grasped a handful from the messenger's track and cast it; so did my soul suggest to me" (20.96). He said: "Go then, you are doomed in this life to say 'do not touch me,' and you will have an appointment that you will not miss. Look to your god which you remained devoted to, we shall burn it and scatter its ashes into the sea" (20.97).

A.3 The Chapter of al-Qaṣaṣ (the Stories) (28.2-46)

Those are verses of the manifest Book (28.2). We narrate to you [O Muḥammad!] parts of the story of Moses and Pharaoh in truth, for people who believe (28.3). Pharaoh exalted himself in the earth and made its people castes, oppressing one group of them, slaying their sons and sparing their women; he was one of the corrupters (28.4). We desired to show favor to those who were oppressed in the earth, make them leaders, make them the inheritors (28.5), establish them in the earth, and show Pharaoh, Hāmān, and their soldiers from them that which they feared (28.6). We inspired Moses' mother: "Suckle him, and when you fear for him, cast him into the river and do not fear or grieve; We shall bring him back to you and make him one of the messengers" (28.7). Then the people of Pharaoh picked him up [from the river], to become for them an enemy and a sorrow; Pharaoh, Hāmān, and their soldiers were sinful (28.8). The wife of Pharaoh said: "[He will be] a delight for the eye for me and you. Do not kill him. He may be useful for us, or we may take him as a son," while they were unaware [of what was going to happen] (28.9). The heart of Moses' mother became void; she would have revealed it (the secret) had We not strengthened her heart to be one of the believers (28.10). She said to his sister: "Trace him," so she observed him from afar while they [with whom Moses was] were unaware (28.11).

We had forbidden foster-mothers for him before. She (his sister) said: "Shall I show you a household who could rear him for you and take good care of him" (28.12)? So We returned him to his mother so that she be comforted and not grieve, and to know that Allah's promise is true, but most of them (people) do not know (28.13). When he attained his full strength and settled, We gave him Wisdom and Knowledge; thus do We reward the good-doers (28.14). He entered the city at a time of unawareness by its people, and he found there two men fighting — one of his own people and the other of his enemies. He who was of his people asked him for help against him who was of his enemies. So Moses struck and killed him. He said: "This is of Satan's doing; he is a manifest misleading enemy" (28.15). He said: "My Lord! I have wronged myself, so forgive me." Then He forgave him; He is the Forgiving, the Merciful (28.16). He said: "My Lord! Forasmuch as You have favored me, I will nevermore be a supporter of the guilty" (28.17). And morning found him in the city, fearing, vigilant, when he who had appealed to him the day before cried out to him for help; Moses said to him: "You are indeed a manifest lurer" (28.18). When he was to assault the man who was an enemy to them both, he said: "O Moses! Is it your intention to kill me as you killed a person yesterday? Your intention is none other than to become a powerful tyrant in the land, and not to be one of the reformers" (28.19). A man came from the uttermost part of the city, running; he said: "O Moses! The chiefs are plotting against you to kill you, therefore leave [the city]; I am of those who give you good advice" (28.20). So he left it, fearing, vigilant; he said: "My Lord! Save me from the wrongdoing people" (28.21). When he turned his face toward Midian, he said: "May my Lord guide me to the right way" (28.22). When he came to the water of Midian he found at it a group of people watering [their flocks], and he found apart from them two women keeping back [their flocks]; he said: "What is the matter with you?" They said: "We cannot water [our flocks] till the shepherds return from the water, and our father is a very old man" (28.23). So he watered [their flocks] for them; then he turned aside into the shade, and said: "My Lord! I stand in need of whatever good You would send down to me" (28.24). Then one of them (the two women) came to him walking shyly; she said: "My father invites you to reward you for having watered [the flocks] for us." When he came to him (their father) and told him his story he said: "fear no more; you have escaped from the wrongdoing people" (28.25). One of the two women said: "O my father! Hire him, for the best [man] that you can hire is one who is strong and trustworthy" (28.26). He said: "I would like to marry you to one of my two daughters and in return you hire yourself to me for eight years, and it is up to you if would make it ten, for I do not want to make it hard for you; Allah willing, you will find me one of the righteous" (28.27). He said: "This is [a contract] between me and you; whichever of the two terms I fulfill, there shall be no wrongdoing on my part, and Allah is a witness on what we say" (28.28). When Moses fulfilled the term and left in the night with his family, he perceived a fire at the side of the mountain. He said to his family: "Stay here; I have perceived a fire that I might bring you tidings from or a firebrand that you might warm yourselves" (28.29). When he came to it (the fire), he was called from the right side of the valley in the blessed spot at the tree: "O Moses! I am Allah, the Lord of all peoples" (28.30). And [that]: "Throw down your staff." When he saw it moving like a snake he fled without tracing his steps. "O Moses! Draw near and do not fear for you are one of the secure ones (28.31). Enter your hand to your bosom and it will come forth white without harm; and do not show fear. These shall be two proofs from your Lord to Pharaoh and his chiefs; they are a rebellious people" (28.32). He said: "My Lord! I have killed a person from them and I fear that they will kill me (28.33). My brother Aaron is more eloquent than me, so make him a messenger with me — a helper to confirm me; I fear that they will accuse me of telling lies" (28.34). He said: "We will strengthen you with your brother, and We will give you both authority so that they shall not be able to reach you [for harm] on account of Our signs. You both and those who follow you will be the victorious" (28.35). When Moses brought to them Our clear signs, they said: "This is nothing other than invented magic, and we have never heard of this among our forefathers" (28.36). Moses said: "My Lord knows best him who has come with guidance from Him and whose will be the best end; the wrongdoers will not be successful" (28.37). Pharaoh said: "O chiefs! I know no god for you other than me, so kindle for me [a fire], O Hāmān, to bake the mud, and set up for me a lofty tower that I may look at Moses' god; I believe he is one of the liars" (28.38). He and his soldiers behaved arrogantly in the earth without right, and they thought that they would not be brought back to Us (28.39). Therefore We seized him and his soldiers, and flung them into the sea. So see how the end of the wrongdoers was (28.40). We made them leaders who invite to the Fire, and on the Day of Resurrection they will not be helped (28.41). We followed them up with a curse in this world, and on the Day of Resurrection they will be among the hated (28.42). We gave Moses the Book after We had destroyed the generations of old, as clear testimonies for the people, guidance, and mercy, that they may remember (28.43). And you [O Muhammad!] were not on the western side [of the mountain] when We handed to Moses the matter, and you were not one of the witnesses (28.44). But We brought forth generations, and their lives dragged on for them. You were not dwelling with the people of Midian reciting to them Our verses, but We have sent [you as] a Messenger (28.45). You were not on the side of the mountain when We called [Moses], but this [knowledge that We have revealed to you] is a mercy from your Lord so that you warn a people to whom no warner before you came, that they may give heed (28.46).

A.4 The Chapter of ash-Shu'arā' (the Poets) (26.10-66)

When your Lord [O Muhammad!] called Moses [saying]: "Go to the wrongdoing people (26.10) — the people of Pharaoh. Will they not be pious" (26.11)? He said: "My Lord! I fear that they will accuse me of telling lies (26.12), my breast will be straitened, and my tongue will not speak plainly, so call Aaron [to help me] (26.13). They also have a charge of crime against me, so I am afraid that they will kill me" (26.14). He said: "By no means. Go you both with Our signs; We shall be with you, hearing (26.15). Go to Pharaoh and say: 'We are messengers of the Lord of all peoples (26.16). Let the Children of Israel go with us'" (26.17). [Pharaoh] said [to Moses]: "Did we not rear you among us as a child, you lived a number of years among us (26.18), and then you committed what you did, being one of the ungrateful" (26.19)? He said: "I did it when I was one of those who are astray (26.20). Then I fled from you when I feared you, so my Lord granted me Wisdom and appointed me one as of the messengers (26.21). Is it a favor you remind me of that you have enslaved the Children of Israel" (26.22)? Pharaoh said: "Who is the Lord of all peoples" (26.23)? He (Moses) said: "The Lord of the heavens and the earth and all that is between them, if you would be sure" (26.24). He (Pharaoh) said to those around him: "Do you not hear" (26.25)? He (Moses) said: "Your Lord and the Lord of your forefathers" (26.26). He (Pharaoh) said: "Your messenger who has been sent to you is a madman" (26.27). He (Moses) said: "The Lord of the East and the West and what is between them, if you would understand" (26.28). He (Pharaoh) said: "If you choose a god other than me, I shall imprison you" (26.29). He (Moses) said: "Even if I show you clear evidence" (26.30)? He (Pharaoh) said: "Produce it then, if you are of one the truthful" (26.31). So he threw his staff down, and it became a manifest serpent (26.32). And he took his hand out and, lo! it was white to the beholders (26.33). He (Pharaoh) said to the chiefs around him: "This is an accomplished magician (26.34) who would like to drive you out of your land by his magic; what is your advice" (26.35)? They said: "Let him and his brother wait, and send to the cities summoners (26.36) who shall bring to you every skilled magician" (26.37). So the magicians were gathered together at the set time on an appointed day (26.38). It was said to the people: "Will you gather together (26.39)? So that we may follow the [evidence of the] magicians if they are the victorious" (26.40). When the magicians came, they said to Pharaoh: "Shall we get a reward if we are the victorious" (26.41)? He said: "Yes, and you will be considered with those who are brought close [to me]" (26.42). Moses said to them: "Throw down what you are going to throw" (26.43). They threw down their cords and staffs and said: "By Pharaoh's might, we shall be the victorious" (26.44). Then Moses threw down his staff, and it swallowed that which they falsely showed (26.45). So the magicians were thrown down in prostration

(26.46). They said: "We believe in the Lord of all peoples (26.47), the Lord of Moses and Aaron" (26.48). He Said: "You have believed in him before I give you permission? He must be your master who taught you magic, so you shall know. I will cut off your hands and feet on opposite sides, and I shall crucify you all" (26.49). They said: "It is no harm, for to our Lord we shall return (26.50). We hope that our Lord will forgive us our sins that we are the first believers" (26.51). We revealed to Moses: "Take away My servants by night; you will be pursued" (26.52). Then Pharaoh sent into the cities summoners (26.53) [saying] that: "These are a small isolated group (26.54), they have angered us (26.55), and we are apprehensive of a coalition" (26.56). So We removed them from gardens, springs (26.57), treasures, and a fair abode (26.58); and We caused the Children of Israel to inherit them (26.59). Then they pursued them eastward (26.60). When the two gatherings became close enough to see each other, those who were with Moses said: "We will be caught" (26.61). He said: "No way! My Lord is with me; He will show me a way out" (26.62). We revealed to Moses: "Strike the sea with your staff," so it split, and each part was like a huge mountain (26.63). We brought near the others (Pharaoh and his army) (26.64). We saved Moses and all those who were with him (26.65). Then We drowned the others (26.66).

A.5 The Chapter of Baqara (The Cow) (2.47-71)

O Children of Israel! Remember My favor to you and that I preferred you above all peoples (2.47). Fear a day on which no soul shall pay any recompense for another, no intercession will be accepted from it, no compensation will be taken from it, and they will not be helped (2.48). [Remember] when We rescued you from Pharaoh's people who subjected you to the worst torment, slaying your sons and sparing your women. There was a great trial from your Lord in this (2.49). When We parted the sea for you, so we saved you and drowned Pharaoh's people while you look (2.50). When We appointed for Moses forty nights, then you took the calf [for a god] after him, and you were wrongdoers (2.51). Then We forgave you after it that you may give thanks (2.52). When We gave Moses the Book and the Discrimination [between right and wrong] that you may be guided (2.53). When Moses said to his people: "O my people! You have wronged yourselves by taking the calf [for a god], so repent to your Creator and kill yourselves (those who have been guilty of the crime); that is better for you in the eyes of your Creator." So He pardoned you; He is the forgiving, the merciful (2.54). When you said: "O Moses! We will not believe you until we see Allah plainly," so the thunderbolt caught you while you were looking on (2.55). Then We resurrected you after your death that you may give thanks (2.56). We overshadowed you with the clouds and sent down on you the manna and the quails, [saying]: "Eat of the good things We have given you." They did not wrong Us but they were wronging themselves (2.57). When We said: "Enter this town and eat from wherever you like as much as you like. Enter the gate prostrating and say ʿ*ḥiṭṭatun*' so that We forgive your sins and give increase to the good-doers" (2.58). The wrongdoers then changed what had been said to them with another saying, so We sent down on those who did wrong a punishment from heaven because of their rebellion (2.59). When Moses asked for drink for his people We said: "Strike the rock with your staff," so twelve springs burst forth. Every people knew their drinking place. [We said]: "Eat and drink of what Allah has provided and do not cause corruption on the earth" (2.60). When you said: "O Moses! We cannot endure one kind of food. Pray to your Lord to produce for us of what the earth grows — its beans, cucumbers, garlic, lentils, and onions." He said: "Would you exchange that which is better for that which is meaner? Go down to some town and you shall have what you asked for." Humiliation and abasement were stamped on them and they incurred wrath from Allah, because they used to deny Allah's signs and unjustly kill prophets. That is because they disobeyed and transgressed (2.61). Those who believe, the Jews, the Christians, and the Sabaeans — whoever believe in Allah and the Last Day and does good — they shall have their reward from their Lord, and there is no fear for them, nor shall they grieve (2.62). When We took a covenant with you and raised the mountain above you [saying]: "Take firmly what We have given you and remember what is in it that you may become pious" (2.63). Then you turned away after that; had it not for Allah's favor on you and His mercy you would have been among the losers (2.64). You knew about those of you who transgressed during the Sabbath; We said to them: "Be despised apes" (2.65). We made it a punishment at the time and later (for those who do the same) and an admonition to the pious (2.66). When Moses said to his people: "Allah commands you to slaughter a cow." They said: "Are you making fun of us?" He said: "I take refuge with Allah from being one of the ignorant" (2.67). They said: "Pray to your Lord for us to clarify to us what she is." He said: "He says she is neither old nor a heifer but middle-aged between the two, so do what you are commanded" (2.68). They said: "Pray to your Lord for us to clarify to us her color." He said: "He says she is a yellow cow, bright is her color, and she is pleasing to the beholders" (2.69). They said: "Pray to your Lord for us to clarify to us what she is, for the cows look the same to us; Allah willing, we shall be guided" (2.70). He said: "He says that she is a cow that is not used to plough the land or water the field. She is sound, blemishless." They said: "Now you have brought the truth." They slaughtered her, but they nearly did not do (2.71).

A.6 The Chapter of Ghāfir (Forgiver) (40.23-46)

We sent Moses with our signs and clear authority (40.23) to Pharaoh,

Hāmān, and Korah, but they said: "A lying magician!" (40.24). When the truth from Us came to them they said: "Kill the sons of those who are with him but spare their women." The scheming of the disbelievers is bound to fail (40.25). Pharaoh said: "Let me kill Moses and let him call on his Lord. I fear that he will change your religion or cause corruption in the land" (40.26). Moses said: "I take refuge in my and your Lord from every arrogant person who does not believe in the Day of Reckoning" (40.27). A believing man from Pharaoh's people who concealed his faith said: "Will you kill a man for saying 'my Lord is Allah' when he has come to you with manifest proofs from your Lord? If he is a liar then his lie would be against him, and if he is truthful then some of what he has threatened you with would fall on you. Allah does not guide one who is an extravagant liar (40.28). O my people! Today kingship is yours and you are in control in the land. But who would help us against the might of Allah if it comes on us?" Pharaoh said: "I let you see only what I see. I will guide you only in the right direction" (40.29). The one who believed said: "O my people! I fear for you the like of the day of the parties (40.30) — the like of the case of the people of Noah, 'Ād, Thamūd, and those after them. Allah does not desire any injustice for His servants (40.31). O my people! I fear for you the Day of Crying Out (40.32) — the day when you turn away in retreat, with none to defend you from Allah. Whomever Allah leads astray, he has no guide (40.33). Surely Joseph came to you in times gone by with clear proofs, but you ever remained in doubt about what he brought to you. When he died, you said: 'Allah will not send a messenger after him.' Thus does Allah cause to err him who is an extravagant doubter" (40.34). Those who dispute about the signs of Allah without any authority has come to them — that is very hateful in the sight of Allah and the believers. Thus does Allah set a seal on every arrogant, tyrant heart (40.35). Pharaoh said: "Hāmān, build for me a tower that I may be able reach the ways (40.36) — the ways of heavens to look at Moses' god. I believe he is a liar." Pharaoh's evil work was made to look fair to him and he was turned away from the straight path. Pharaoh's scheming is bound to fail (40.37). The one who believed said: "O my people! Follow me so that I can guide you to the right path (40.38). O my people! The life of this world is temporary and it is the hereafter that is the final abode (40.39). Whoever does evil he will only be recompensed with the like of it." Whoever does good, whether a male or female while being a believer — those will enter Paradise and be provided for without count (40.40). [The one who believed said]: "O my people! How is it that I call you to salvation yet you call me to the Fire (40.41)? You call me to disbelieve in Allah and to associate with Him gods whom I have no knowledge of yet I call you to the Impregnable, the Forgiving One! (40.42). No doubt that what you call me to has no real call in this world or in the hereafter. Our return will be to Allah and the extravagant are the people of the Fire (40.43). You shall remember what

I am saying and I shall commit my case to Allah. Allah sees the servants" (40.44). So Allah protected him from the evil of their scheming, and the woe of the torment encompassed the people of Pharaoh (40.45). They are all exposed to the fire in the morning and evening, and when the Hour comes [it will be said]: "Admit the people of Pharaoh to the worst torment" (40.46).

A.7 The Chapter of Yūnus (Jonah) (10.75-93)

Then We sent after them Moses and Aaron to Pharaoh and his chiefs with Our signs, but they showed arrogance and they were a guilty people (10.75). When the truth came to them from Us they said: "This is surely clear magic" (10.76). Moses said: "This is what you say of the truth when it has come to you? Is it magic? Magicians cannot succeed" (10.77). They said: "Have you come to turn us away from what we found our fathers do, and so that greatness in the land should be for you two? We are not going to believe you two" (10.78). Pharaoh said: "Bring to me every skilled magician" (10.79). When the magicians came, Moses said to them: "Cast down what you have to cast" (10.80). So when they cast, Moses said: "What you have performed is magic; Allah will make it vain; Allah does not allow the work of corrupters to thrive (10.81). Allah will show the truth to be the truth by His words however much the guilty may hate it" (10.82). But none believed in Moses except some offspring of his people while full of fear of Pharaoh and their chiefs that he would persecute them. Surely Pharaoh was lofty in the land; and surely he was one of the extravagant (10.83). Moses said: "O my people! If you believe in Allah, then rely on Him, if you are Muslims" (10.84). They said: "On Allah we rely; Our Lord! Do not make us subject to the persecution of the unjust people (10.85) and deliver us by Your mercy from the disbelieving people" (10.86). We revealed to Moses and his brother: "Take you both, for your people, houses in Egypt; make your houses *qibla*; and perform the prayer. Do give good tidings to the believers" (10.87). Moses said: "Our Lord! You have given to Pharaoh and his chiefs finery and riches in this world's life, our Lord, that they may lead [people] astray from Your way. Our Lord! Destroy their riches and harden their hearts so that they do not believe until they see the painful punishment" (10.88). He said: "The prayer of you both has been accepted, so keep to the straight path and do not follow the path of those who do not know" (10.89). We made the children of Israel to pass through the sea, then Pharaoh and his soldiers followed them in transgression and oppression. When the drowning overtook him, he said: "I believe that there is no god but He in whom the children of Israel believe and I am one of the Muslims" (10.90). Now, having disobeyed before and having been one of the corrupters (10.91)? Today We shall save you in the body that you may be a sign to those after you. Surely many people are heedless of Our signs (10.92).

We lodged the children of Israel in a goodly abode and We provided them with good things. They did not differ until the knowledge came to them; your Lord will judge between them on the Day of Resurrection about what they differed about (10.93).

A.8 The Chapter of Isrā' (The Night Journey) (17.4-7, 17.101-104)

We decreed to the Children of Israel in the Book: "You will cause corruption in the earth twice and you will show great loftiness (17.4). When the first of the two promises comes to pass, We will send against you servants of Ours with great might who will invade your dwellings; this promise is certain to be fulfilled (17.5). Then We will make it your turn to prevail over them and supply you with a lot of wealth and children and make you more enormous (17.6). If you do good work you do so for your own souls, and if you commit evil you do so to your own detriment. When the second promise comes to pass, they will make your faces full of grief, enter the mosque as they did the first time, and destroy what they control" (17.7).

We gave Moses nine manifest signs. Ask the Children of Israel about when he came to them, and Pharaoh said to him: "Moses, I think you are bewitched" (17.101). He said: "You know that none sent these down other than the Lord of the heavens and earth as proofs; I think, O Pharaoh, that you are cursed" (17.102)! So he sought to drive them out of the land but We drowned him and all those who were with him (17.103). We said to the Children of Israel after him: "Dwell in the land. When the last promise comes to pass, We will bring you in a mixed crowd" (17.104).

A.9 The Chapter of Dukhān (Smoke) (44.17-33)

We tried the people of Pharaoh before them and there came to them a noble messenger (44.17), [saying]: "Deliver to me Allah's servant; I am a trustworthy messenger to you (44.18). Do not exult yourselves above Allah; I have come to you with a manifest authority (44.19). I seek refuge in my and your Lord that you do not stone me (44.20). If you do not believe me then leave me alone" (44.21). Then he prayed to his Lord that these are a sinful people (44.22). [We told him]: "Take away My servants by night. You will be followed (44.23). Leave the sea dry; they are a host to be drowned" (44.24). They left behind many gardens (44.25), crops, a noble dwelling (44.26), and favors in which they enjoyed themselves (44.27). Thus, We made another people inherit them (44.28). The heaven and the earth did not weep for them, and they were not respited (44.29). We saved the Children of Israel from the degrading torment (44.30) — from Pharaoh; he was haughty; one of the extravagant (44.31). We chose them knowingly above all peoples (44.32). We gave them signs in which there was a manifest trial (44.33).

A.10 The Chapter of Zukhruf (Ornaments) (43.46-55)

We also sent Moses with Our signs to Pharaoh and his chiefs, and he said: "I am the messenger of the Lord of all peoples" (43.46). But when he came to them with Our signs, they laughed at them (43.47). We did not show them a sign but it was greater than its fellow, and We seized them with a torment that they may return (43.48). They said: "O you magician! Pray to your Lord for us, by whatever covenant He has with you, and we shall be guided" (43.49). But when We removed the torment from them they broke the promise (43.50). Pharaoh proclaimed among his people: "O my people! Do I not possess the kingdom of Egypt, and these rivers flow beneath me? Do you not see (43.51)? Am I not better than this fellow (Moses) who is contemptible and can hardly speak clearly (43.52)? Why then have bracelets of gold not been cast on him or angels not come with him conjoined" (43.53)? He fooled his people so they obeyed him. They were ungodly people (43.54). When they angered Us, We took revenge on them and drowned them all (43.55).

A.11 The Chapter of Ma'ida (The Table) (5.20-26)

When Moses said to his people: "O my people! Remember the favor of Allah on you when He made prophets among you and made you kings and gave you what He has not given to any of the other peoples (5.20). O my people! Enter the holy land which Allah has decreed for you and do not turn back, otherwise you would turn about losers" (5.21). They said: "O Moses! There is a mighty people in it; we will not enter it until they go out of it. If they go out, we will enter it" (5.22). Then two men who fear [God] whom Allah has given favor to said: "Enter on them by the gate. Once you have entered you will be victorious. Put your trust in Allah if you are believers" (5.23). They said: "O Moses! We will never enter it as long as they are in it. Go you and your Lord and fight. We will sit here" (5.24). He said: "My Lord! I do not control other than myself and my brother, so separate between us and the rebellious people" (5.25). He said: "It shall then be forbidden for them for forty years in which they shall wander in the earth, so do not grieve for the rebellious people" (5.26).

A.12 The Chapter of Naml (Ants) (27.7-14)

When Moses said to his family: "I have perceived a fire that I might bring you tidings from or a burning brand that you might warm yourselves" (27.7). When he came to it (the fire), he was called that "blessed is that who is in the fire and that who is around it, and glory be to Allah the Lord of all peoples (27.8). O Moses! It is Me, Allah, the Mighty, the Wise (27.9). Throw down your staff." When he saw it moving like a snake he fled without tracing his steps. [He was called]: "O Moses! Do not fear for messengers are not to fear in My presence (27.10). As for the others, those who do wrong and then substitute good for evil, I am forgiving, merciful (27.11). Enter your hand to your bosom and it will come forth white without harm. These are among nine signs to Pharaoh and his people; they are a rebellious people" (27.12). When Our clear signs came to them, they said: "This is a manifest magic" (27.13). They denied them while their souls were certain they were true, out of wrongdoing and arrogance. See what the end of the doers of corruption was (27.14).

A.13 The Chapter of An-Nāzi'āt (The Snatchers) (79.15-25)

Has the story of Moses reached you (79.15)? When his Lord called him in the holy valley of Ṭuwā (79.16): "Go to Pharaoh; he has transgressed (79.17). Say to him: 'Do you have the will to purify yourself (79.18) and to let me guide you to your Lord so that you become pious to Him'" (79.19)? He showed him the great sign (79.20) but he denied [it] and disobeyed (79.21). Then he went to plan (79.22) so he gathered and proclaimed (79.23), saying: "I am your Lord supreme" (79.24). So Allah seized him with the punishment of the hereafter and this world (79.25)

Appendix B

Egyptian Dynasties and Kingdoms

Manetho, the 3rd century BCE High Priest of Heliopolis, was the first to divide the history of Egypt, which for him begins with the unification of Upper and Lower Egypt under one king, into Dynasties in the king lists in his book *Aegyptiaca* (*History of Egypt*). This list survived in the writings of Christian chronographers such as Eusebius of Caesarea. Thirty Pharaonic Dynasties are today recognized from the unification of Egypt in around 3100 BCE to the death of the last native Egyptian Pharaoh, Nectanebo II, in 343 BCE. Sometimes two other Dynasties are added after this date.

Modern Egyptologists group the Pharaonic Dynasties into longer periods. The three major periods are known as the "Old Kingdom," "Middle Kingdom," and "New Kingdom." Each of the three Kingdoms ends with an "Intermediate Period" of decline. The third Intermediate Period is followed by the "Late Period." The Pharaohs of the 31st Dynasty were Persians. The dates of these periods and the Dynasties they covered are listed below:

Period	Date (BCE)	Dynasties
Early Dynastic Period	3150-2686	0th-2nd
Old Kingdom	2686-2181	3rd-6th
First Intermediate Period	2181-2040	7th-10th
Middle Kingdom	2040-1782	11th and 12th
Second Intermediate Period	1782-1570	13th-17th
New Kingdom	1570-1070	18th-20th
Third Intermediate Period	1069-525	21st-26th
Late Period	525-332	27th-31st

The following table lists the dates and Kingdoms of the 11th-20th Dynasties which are particularly relevant to the subject of the book:

Dynasty	Date (BCE)	Kingdom
11th	2134-1991	Middle Kingdom
12th	1991-1782	Middle Kingdom

13th	1782-1650	2nd Intermediate Period
14th	uncertain	2nd Intermediate Period
15th (Hyksos)	1663-1555	2nd Intermediate Period
16th	1663-1555	2nd Intermediate Period
17th	1663-1570	2nd Intermediate Period
18th	1570-1293	New Kingdom
19th	1293-1185	New Kingdom
20th	1185-1070	New Kingdom

The following table shows the pharaoh's of the 19th Dynasty during which the exodus took place:

Pharaoh	Date (BCE)
Ramesses I	1293-1291
Seti I	1291-1278
Ramesses II	1279-1212
Merneptah	1212-1202
Amenmesses	1202-1199
Seti II	1199-1193
Siptah	1193-1187
Queen Twosret	1187-1185

Researchers differ slightly on the exact dates of the reigns of Pharaohs, with some scholars shifting dates toward a lower or higher chronology than others. The above dates of Ramesses II's reign are according to the "low chronology" which is used by researchers more than the "middle chronology" and "high chronology" whose corresponding dates are 1290-1223 and 1304-1237, respectively. For consistency, we have followed throughout this book the chronological scheme used by Clayton (1994).

References

Works in English

Al-Jilani, 'A. (2008). *Purification of the Mind (Jila' al-Khātir)*, translated from Arabic by S. Al-Dargazelli and L. Fatoohi, Luna Plena Publishing: UK.

ANET (1950). *Ancient Near Eastern Texts Relating to the Old Testament*, edited by J. B. Pritchard, Princeton University Press: Princeton.

ANETS (1968). *The Ancient Near Eastern Supplementary Texts and Pictures Relating to the Old Testament*, edited by J. B. Pritchard, Princeton University Press: Princeton.

Breasted, J. H. (1912). *Development of the Religion and Thought in Ancient Egypt*, London. (cited in Syed, 1984.)

Bimson, J. J. (1991). "Merneptah's Israel and Recent Theories of Israelite Origins." *Journal for the Study of the Old Testament*, 49, 3-29.

Bucaille, M. (1995). *The Bible, The Qur'an and Science: The Holy Scriptures Examined in the Light of Modern Knowledge*, translated from the French by A. D. Pannell & M. Bucaille, Millat Book Centre: New Delhi.

Clayton, P. A. (1994). *Chronicle of the Pharaohs: The Reign-By-Reign Record of the Rulers and Dynasties of Ancient Egypt*, Thames & Hudson: Slovenia.

Cazelles, H. (1973). "The Hebrews." In: D. J. Wiseman (ed.), *Peoples of Old Testament Times*, The Clarendon Press: Oxford, 1-28.

Colenso, J. W. (1862). *The Pentateuch and the Book of Joshua, I*, London. (cited in Houtman, 1993: 70.)

Dever, W. G. (1992). "How to Tell a Canaanite From an Israelite." In: H. Shanks (ed.), *The Rise of Israel*, Biblical Archaeological Society: Washington, 27-56.

Dever, W. G. (1977). "Palestine in the Second Millennium BCE: The Archaeological Picture." In: J. H. Hayes & J. M. Miller (eds.), *Israelite and Judaean History*, SCM Press: London, 70-120.

Dever, W. G. (1997). "Is There Any Archaeological Evidence for the Exodus?" In: E. S. Frerichs & L. H. Lesko (eds.), *Exodus: The Egyptian Evidence*, Eisenbrauns: Indiana, 67-86.

Dever, W. G. (2003). *Who Were the Early Israelites and Where Did They Come From?*, Wm. B. Eerdmans Publishing Company: Cambridge.

Fatoohi, L (2007a). *Prophet Joseph in the Qur'an, the Bible, and History: A New Detailed Commentary on the Qur'anic Chapter of Joseph*, Luna Plena Publishing: UK.

Fatoohi, L (2007b). *The Mystery of the Historical Jesus: The Messiah in the Qur'an, the Bible, and Historical Sources*, Luna Plena Publishing: UK.

Fouts, D. M. (1997). "A Defense of The Hyperbolic Interpretation of Large Numbers in the Old Testament." *Journal Of The Evangelical Theological Society*, 40/3, 377–387.

Greenberg, M. (1955). *The Hab/piru*, American Oriental Society: New Haven, Connecticut.

Halpern, B. (1992). "The Exodus From Egypt: Myth or Reality?" In: H. Shanks (ed.), *The Rise of Ancient Israel*, Biblical Archaeology Society: Washington, DC, 87-113.

Harris, J. E. & Weeks, K. R. (1973). *X-Raying the Pharaohs*, Charles Scribner's Sons: New York.

Hayes, J. H. (1977). "The History of the Study of Israelite and Judaean History." In: J. H. Hayes & J. M. Miller (eds.), *Israelite and Judaean History*, SCM Press: London, 1-69.

Herodotus (2004). *The Histories*, translated By R. Waterfield, Oxford University Press: USA.

Hoffmeier, J. (1999). *Israel in Egypt: The Evidence for the Authenticity of the Exodus Tradition*, Oxford University Press: New York.

Houtman, C. (1993). *Exodus*, vol. I, translated from the Dutch by J. Rebel & S. Woudstra, Kok Publishing House: Kampen.

Houtman, C. (1996). *Exodus*, vol. II, translated from the Dutch by S. Woudstra, Kok Publishing House: Kampen.

Husain, A. (1994). *Moses Versus Pharaoh*, Adam Publishers: India.

Hyatt, J. P. (1971). *Commentary on Exodus*, Oliphants: London.

Irvin, D. (1977). "The Joseph and Moses Stories As Narrative in the Light of Ancient Near Eastern Narrative." In: J. H. Hayes & J. M. Miller (eds.), *Israelite and Judaean History*, SCM Press: London, 180-209.

Josephus, F. (1998a). *Against Apion*, translated by W. Whiston, Thomas Nelson Publishers: Tennessee.

Josephus, F. (1998b). *Antiquities of the Jews*, translated by W. Whiston, Thomas Nelson Publishers: Tennessee.

Kempinski, A. (1985). "Some Observations on the Hyksos (XVth) Dynasty and Its Canaanite Origins." In: S. Israelit-Groll (ed.), *Pharaonic Egypt: The Bible and Christianity*, The Magnus Press: Jerusalem, 129-137.

Kitchen, K. A. (1966). *Ancient Orient and Old Testament*, the Tyndale Press: London.

Kitchen, K. A. (1977). The *Bible in its World: The Bible and Archaeology Today*, The Paternoster Press: Exeter.

Kitchen, K. A. (1982). *Pharaoh Triumphant: The Life and Times of Ramesses II King of Egypt*, Aris & Phillips ltd: Warminster.

LEM (1954). *Late-Egyptian Miscellanies*, translated by R. A. Caminos, Oxford University Press: London.

Levenson, J. D. (1997). *Esther: A Commentary*, Westminster John Knox Press: Kentucky.

Lewis, B. (1948). *Land of Enchanters: Egyptian Short Stories From the Earliest Times to the Present Day*, The Harvill Press: London.

Malamat, A. (1997). "The Exodus: Egyptian Analogies." In: E. S. Frerichs & L. H. Lesko (eds.), *Exodus: The Egyptian Evidence*, Eisenbrauns: Indiana, 15-26.

McCarter, P. K. (1992). "Panel Discussion." In: H. Shanks (ed.), *The Rise of Ancient Israel*, Biblical Archaeology Society: Washington.

Miller, J. M. (1977). "The Israelite Occupation of Canaan." In: J. H. Hayes & J. M. Miller (eds.), *Israelite and Judaean History*, SCM Press: London, 213-284.

Montet, P. (1974). *Lives of the Pharaohs*, Spring Books: London.

Noth, M. (1962). *Exodus: A Commentary*, translated from the German by J. S. Bowden, SCM Press: London.

Partridge, R. B. (1996). *Faces of Pharaohs: Royal Mummies and Coffins From Ancient Thebes*, The Rubican Press: London.

Petrie, W. M. F. (1924). *Religious Life in Ancient Egypt*, London. (cited in Syed, 1984.)

Pritchard, J. B. (1950) (ed.). *Ancient Near Eastern Texts Relating to the Old Testament*, Princeton University Press: Princeton.

Plutarch (1920). *Lives*, IX, Loeb Classical Library.

Ray, P. J. (1986). "The Duration Of The Israelite Sojourn In Egypt." *Andrews University Seminary Studies*, Autumn 1986, Vol. 24, No.3, 231-248.

Redford, D. B. (1967). "The Literary Motif of the Exposed Child (cf. Ex. ii 1-10)." *Numen*, 14, 209-228.

Redford, D. B. (1992). *Egypt, Canaan, and Israel in Ancient Times*, Princeton University Press: Princeton.

Redford, D. B. (1997). "Observations on the Sojourn of the Bene-Israel." In: E. S. Frerichs & L. H. Lesko (eds.), *Exodus: The Egyptian Evidence*, Eisenbrauns: Indiana, 57-66.

Rendsburg, G. A. (1992). "The Date of the Exodus and the Conquest/Settlement: The Case for the 1100s." *Vetus Testamentum*, 42, 510-527

Riggs, J. R. (1971). "The Length of Israel's Sojourn in Egypt." *Grace Theological Journal*, 12.1, 18-35.

Rogerson, J. & Davies, P. (1989). *The Old Testament World*, Cambridge University Press: Cambridge.

Van Seters, J. (1966). *The Hyksos: A New Investigation*, Yale University Press: New Haven.

Siddiqi, M. (1994). *The Qur'anic Concept of History*, Adam Publishers, India.

Steindorff, G. (1905). *Religion of the Ancient Egyptians*, New York. (cited in Syed, 1984.)

Suetonius (2004). *Lives of the Caesars*, translated by J. C. Rolfe, Kessinger Publishing: Montana.

Syed, S. M. (1984). "Haman in the Light of the Qur'an." *Hamdard Islamicus*, 7(4), 83-92.

Thompson, S. (1946). *The Folktale*, Holt, Rinehart, & Winston: New York. (cited in Irvin, 1977.)

Thompson, T. L. (1977). "The Joseph and Moses Narratives: Historical Reconstructions of the Narratives." In: J. H. Hayes & J. M. Miller (eds.), *Israelite and Judaean History*, SCM Press: London, 149-166.

Vajda, G. (1971). *The Encyclopedia of Islam, vol. 3*, edited by B. Lewis, Ch. Pellat, & J. Schacht, E. J. Brill: Leiden, 110.

Ward, W. A. (1997). "Summary and Conclusions." In: E. S. Frerichs & L. H. Lesko (eds.), *Exodus: The Egyptian Evidence*, Eisenbrauns: Indiana, 105-112.

Weinstein, J. (1997). "Exodus and Archaeological Reality." In: E. S. Frerichs & L. H. Lesko (eds.), *Exodus: The Egyptian Evidence*, Eisenbrauns: Indiana, 87-103.

Widengren, G. (1977). "The Jewish Community Under the Persian." In: J. H. Hayes & J. M. Miller (eds.), *Israelite and Judaean History*, SCM Press: London, 515-538.

Wood, B. G. (2005). "The Rise and Fall of the 13th-Century Exodus-Conquest Theory." *Journal of the Evangelical Theological Society*, 48(3), 475-489.

Yurco, F. J. (1997). "Merenptah's Canaanite Campaign and Israel's Origins." In: E. S. Frerichs & L. H. Lesko (eds.), *Exodus: The Egyptian Evidence*, Eisenbrauns: Indiana, 27-55.

Works in Arabic

Abu al-Suʻūd (1906). *Tafsīr Abī Al-Suʻūd (The Interpretation of Abī Al-Suʻūd)*, vol. 7, Al-Matbaʻa al-ʻAmira al-Sharqiyyah.

Al-Jalālayn [J. al-Mahallī & J. as-Suyūtī] (1982). *Tafsīr al-Jalālayn (The Interpretation of al-Jalālayn)*, Dar al-Maʻrifa: Beirut.

Al-Marāghī, A. (1946b). *Tafsīr al-Marāghī (The Interpretation of al-Marāghī)*, vol. 1-5, Maktabat wa Matba'at Mustafā al-Bābī al-Halabī wa Awlāduh: Egypt.

Al-Marāghī, A. (1946c). *Tafsīr al-Marāghī (The Interpretation of al-Marāghī)*, vol. 16-20, Maktabat wa Matba'at Mustafā al-Bābī al-Halabī wa Awlāduh: Egypt.

Al-Qurtubī, M. (1941). *Al-Jāmi' li Ahkām al-Qur'an (The Collection of the Rules of the Qur'an)*, vol. 13-14, Dār al-Kutub al-Misriyyah: Egypt.

An-Najjār, 'A. (1986). *Qisas al-Anbiyā' (The Stories of Prophets)*, Dār Al-Kutub Al-'Ilmiyyah: Beirut.

Ar-Rāzī, M. (1906). *Mafātīh al-Ghayb (The Keys of the Unknown)*, known as Al-Tafsīr al-Kabīr (The Great Interpretation), al-Matba'a al-'Āmira al-Sharqiyyah.

At-Tabarī, M. (1910). *Jami' al-Bayān fī Tafsīr al-Qur'an (The Compiler of Clarity in Interpreting the Qur'an)*, Al-Matba'a al-Kubrā al-Amīriyyah Bibūlāq: Egypt.

At-Tabarī, M. (undated). *Tarīkh al-Umam wa al-Mulūk (History of Nations and Kings)*, vol. 1, Al-Matba'a al-Husayniyyah al-Misriyyah: Egypt.

At-Tabarsī, F. (1961). *Majma' al-Bayān fī Tafsīr al-Qur'an (The Focus of Clarity in Interpreting the Qur'an)*, vol. 5, Maktabat al-Hayāt: Beirut.

At-Tabatabā'ī, M. (undated). *Al-Mīzān fī Tafsīr Al-Qūr'an (The Scale in Interpreting the Qur'an)*, Dār Al-Kutub Al-Islāmiyyah: Tehran.

Hijāzī, M. (1954). *Al-Tafsīr al-Wādhih (The Clear Interpretation)*, vol. 11-20, Dār al-Kitāb al-'Arabī: Egypt.

Ibn al-Athīr, 'A. (1929). *Al-Kāmil fī al-Tārīkh (The Complete Book About History)*, vol. 1, al-Matba'a al-Munīriyyah.

Ibn Kathīr, 'A. (1985). *Qisas al-Anbiyā' (The Stories of Prophets)*, Isha'at al-Islam: Delhi.

Ibn Kathīr, 'A. (1988). *Tafsīr al-Qur'an al-'Adhīm (Interpretation of the Great Qur'an)*, Dār al-Kutub al-'Ilmiyya: Beirut.

Ibn Khaldūn, A. (1966). *Tārīkh Ibn Khaldūn (The History of Ibn Khaldūn)*, part 1, vol. 2, Dār al-Kitāb al-Lubnānī: Beirut.

Tabārah, A. (undated). *Al-Yahūd fī Al-Qur'an (The Jews in the Qur'an)*, Dār al-'Ilm Lilmalāyīn: Beirut.

Index of Qur'anic Verses

2.47	77, 203	7.108-111	39, 193
2.48	203	7.112-115	193
2.49	171, 203	7.116-117	116, 193
2.50	142, 203	7.118	193
2.51	147, 203	7.119	193
2.51-54	145	7.120-122	39, 107, 170, 193
2.52-54	203	7.123, 39	107, 170, 194
2.55-56	160, 203	7.124, 107	170, 194
2.57	159, 204	7.125-126	170, 194
2.58-59	154, 204	7.127	104, 131, 170, 171, 172, 194
2.60	160, 204	7.127-129	104
2.61	155, 165, 204	7.128	104, 142, 172, 194
2.62	79, 204	7.129	104, 172, 194
2.63	151, 204	7.130-131	73, 104, 172, 194
2.64-66	204	7.132-134	73, 104, 136, 172, 194
2.67-71	148, 204	7.135	104, 136, 172, 194
2.87	77	7.136	104, 136, 155, 194
2.93	145, 151	7.137	152, 156, 194
2.115	138	7.138-139	144, 194
2.135	185	7.140	77, 144, 194
2.140	185	7.141	171, 194
2.141	186	7.142	149, 194
2.258	42	7.143	150, 161, 195
3.65-68	185	7.144-148	150, 195
4.6	102	7.148-153	145
4.23	171	7.149	150, 195
4.48	145	7.150-151	146, 150, 195
4.53	45	7.152-154	150, 195
4.82	191	7.155-156	161, 186, 195
4.116	145	7.159	195
4.153	145, 160	7.160	159, 160, 196
4.154	151, 154	7.161-162	154, 196
5.20	44, 45, 77, 153, 208	7.163-166	196
5.21	151, 152, 153, 157, 208	7.171	151
5.22	153, 208	10.75-77	206
5.23	153, 154, 208	10.78	133, 206
5.24-26	153, 208	10.79	206
5.68	184	10.80-82	130, 206
5.69	79	10.83	105, 130, 131, 206
5.70	77	10.84-86	105, 130, 206
6.84	20	10.87	41, 105, 130, 132, 206
6.152	101, 102	10.88-89	206
7.74	109	10.90	74, 112, 137, 142, 206
7.85	103	10.91-92	112, 206
7.103	193	10.93	207
7.104-105	76, 193	11.84	103
7.106	193	12.4	24
7.107	39, 116, 193		

12.11-12	23	20.40-41	197
12.18	25	20.42	131, 197
12.19	23	20.43-44	76, 131, 197
12.21	41, 115, 132	20.45-46	131, 197
12.22	23, 102	20.47	75, 76, 197
12.25	26	20.48	75, 197
12.30	43	20.49	75, 76, 197
12.31	115	20.50-52	75, 197
12.35	26	20.53-55	197
12.35-41	186	20.56	39, 197
12.42	23	20.57	39, 115, 197
12.43	41	20.58-59	115, 197
12.50	41, 45	20.60-62	197
12.51	43, 45	20.63	39, 123, 198
12.54	38, 41	20.64-65	198
12.55-56	38	20.66	116, 198
12.58-61	43	20.67-68	198
12.59-61	43	20.69	116, 198
12.62	27	20.70-71	107, 198
12.65-66	27	20.72-76	198
12.69	28	20.77	74, 136, 137, 198
12.70-71	43	20.78	74, 137, 198
12.72, 41	43	20.79	198
12.76	41	20.80-81	144, 159, 198
12.78	29, 42	20.82-89	144, 198
12.88	42, 45	20.90	144, 146, 199
12.99	28, 41, 132	20.91-92	144, 199
12.100	44, 45, 142	20.93-97	145, 199
12.101	44, 45	20.97-98	147
13.3	108	21.31	108
14.6	171	21.36-45	43
15.16	108	21.50-51	44
15.19	108	21.71	152
15.66	137	21.81	152
15.73	137	22.5	102
16.15	108	22.78	185
16.97	79	23.20	150
17.4	156, 207	25.37	114
17.5-7	157, 207	26.10-11	100, 202
17.34	101, 102	26.12-15	100, 131, 202
17.101-102	73, 133, 207	26.16-17	100, 202
17.103	134, 156, 207	26.18-22	99, 202
17.104	156, 157, 207	26.23-28	75, 202
18.60-82	193	26.29-31	202
18.82	102	26.32	39, 116, 202
19.52	150	26.33-35	39, 202
20.9-19	196	26.36	202
20.20	116, 196	26.37	39, 202
20.21-31	196	26.38-44	202
20.32-36	197	26.45	116, 202
20.37-38	168, 197	26.46-48	203
20.39	115, 168, 197	26.49	107, 203

26.50-51	203	29.39-40	119
26.52	74, 136, 137, 141, 203	31.10	108
26.53	138, 141, 203	32.26	113
26.53-54	142	38.10-13	107
26.54-56	137, 141, 203	40.23	119, 126, 170, 204
26.57-59	137, 156, 203	40.24	119, 126, 170, 205
26.60	137, 138, 203	40.25	126, 170, 171, 205
26.61	137, 140, 203	40.26	75, 76, 123, 131, 170, 171, 205
26.62	137, 203	40.27	75, 171, 205
26.63-66	74, 137, 203	40.28	186, 205
26.146-149	109	40.29-33	205
27.7	208	40.34	20, 35, 40, 41, 114, 205
27.8-9	209	40.35	205
27.10	116, 209	40.36	123, 205
27.11	209	40.37	76, 123, 205
27.12	73, 209	40.38-43	205
27.13-14	209	40.44-46	206
27.51-52	113	40.67	102
27.61	108	41.10	108
28.2	199	43.46-48	136, 208
28.3	98, 119, 121, 168, 199	43.49	76, 136, 208
28.4	98, 120, 121, 168, 169, 171, 199	43.50	136, 208
28.5	98, 120, 155, 168, 199	43.51	41, 133, 136, 208
28.6	98, 119, 120, 121, 168, 199	43.52	133, 136, 208
		43.53-55	136, 208
28.7	70, 98, 120, 168, 199	44.17-19	75, 207
28.8	98, 119, 120, 121, 168, 199	44.20	76, 207
		44.21-22	207
28.9	98, 115, 168, 199	44.23	136, 137, 207
28.10-11	199	44.24	137, 207
28.12-13	200	44.25	156, 207
28.14	101, 102, 200	44.26	156
28.15-21	200	44.27-29	156, 207
28.24-26	200	44.30-31	207
28.27	103, 200	44.32-33	208
28.28-29	103, 201	45.16	77
28.29-30	150	46.15	102
28.30	201	50.7	108
28.31	116, 201	66.11	111, 186
28.32-34	100, 201	70.40	139
28.35	100, 131, 201	77.27	108
28.36-37	201	78.6-7	108, 109
28.38	76, 123, 201	79.15-19	76, 209
28.39-45	201	79.20-25	209
28.46	150, 201	88.17-18	108
28.76-82	119	88.19-20	108, 109
29.36	103	89.6-13	107, 109
29.38	113	95.1-2	150

Index of Biblical Passages

Gen. 12:4	53	Gen. 43:26	24, 42
Gen. 12:10	34	Gen. 43:28	42
Gen. 12:15	41	Gen. 43:29-31	28
Gen. 12:17	41	Gen. 43:32	180, 181
Gen. 12:18	41	Gen. 44:14-16	29
Gen. 12:20	41	Gen. 44:33	29
Gen. 14:13	180	Gen. 45:25-28	26
Gen. 15:13	51	Gen. 46:4	29
Gen. 15:13-16	53, 55	Gen. 46:26-27	19, 57
Gen. 15:16	56	Gen. 46:30	29
Gen. 21:5	53	Gen. 46:34	181
Gen. 25:26	53	Gen. 47:4	34
Gen. 26:2	34	Gen. 47:9	53
Gen. 32:28	180	Gen. 47:11	84
Gen. 37:2	22	Gen. 48:10	29
Gen. 37:9	24	Gen. 50:4	42
Gen. 37:10	24	Gen. 50:7	42
Gen. 37:21-22	25	Gen. 50:24	19
Gen. 37:26	25	Exo. 1:5	57
Gen. 37:28	37	Exo. 1:7	57, 62, 180
Gen. 37:33-35	26	Exo. 1:8	41, 47, 114, 128
Gen. 37:36	38	Exo. 1:9	180
Gen. 39:11	26	Exo. 1:10	47, 63
Gen. 39:14	180	Exo. 1:11	35, 41, 82, 84, 128
Gen. 39:17	180	Exo. 1:11-14	63
Gen. 39:19	181	Exo. 1:14	88
Gen. 39:20	41	Exo. 1:15	41, 180
Gen. 40:1	41	Exo. 1:16	180
Gen. 40:3	43	Exo. 1:17	41
Gen. 40:5	41	Exo. 1:19	41, 64, 180
Gen. 40:13	41	Exo. 1:22	41, 167
Gen. 40:14	41	Exo. 2:1-2	68
Gen. 40:15	180	Exo. 2:1-10	65
Gen. 40:17	41	Exo. 2:3	48
Gen. 41:12	180	Exo. 2:10	48, 65, 72
Gen. 41:41	42	Exo. 2:11	92
Gen. 41:41-44	37	Exo. 2:11-15	68
Gen. 41:43	42	Exo. 2:15	48
Gen. 41:46	22, 42	Exo. 2:16-22	68
Gen. 41:57	34	Exo. 2:18	66
Gen. 42:6	24, 42	Exo. 2:23	67, 85, 97
Gen. 42:24	27	Exo. 3:1	66
Gen. 42:25	27	Exo. 3:4	48
Gen. 42:35	27	Exo. 3:8	48
Gen. 42:36	28	Exo. 3:9-10	66
Gen. 43:1	28	Exo. 3:17	152
Gen. 43:1-3	28	Exo. 3:21-22	73
Gen. 43:11	28		

Exo. 4:8	68	Exo. 14:21-23	111
Exo. 4:16	48	Exo. 14:26-30	112
Exo. 4:18	66	Exo. 14:28	50, 85
Exo. 4:18-20	66	Exo. 14:30	112
Exo. 4:19	48, 67, 85, 93, 97, 100	Exo. 15:21	111
		Exo. 16:10	159
Exo. 4:20	68	Exo. 16:13-15	159
Exo. 4:24-25	68	Exo. 16:31	159
Exo. 5:1	89, 90	Exo. 16:35	159
Exo. 5:1-3	75	Exo. 17:5-6	160
Exo. 5:3	135	Exo. 18:1	66
Exo. 5:6	89	Exo. 21:2	181
Exo. 5:6-13	88	Exo. 24:12-18	149
Exo. 5:6-18	49	Exo. 31:18	149
Exo. 5:8	89	Exo. 32:1-5	145
Exo. 5:10	89	Exo. 33:18-23	161
Exo. 5:11	89	Num. 1:1-46	58
Exo. 5:13-14	89	Num. 1:2	59
Exo. 6:8	151	Num. 1:21	59
Exo. 6:14-26	55	Num. 1:45-46	57
Exo. 6:20	56	Num. 1:46	61
Exo. 6:25	56	Num. 2:9	58
Exo. 7:7	67, 68	Num. 3:22	57
Exo. 7:12	49	Num. 3:28	54, 57
Exo. 7:16	90	Num. 3:34	57
Exo. 7:20	49	Num. 3:39	57, 58
Exo. 7:22	68	Num. 10:29	66
Exo. 8:6	49	Num. 11:21-22	57
Exo. 8:7	68	Num. 13:28	153
Exo. 8:24	49	Num. 13:30	153
Exo. 9:6	49	Num. 13:33	153
Exo. 9:10	49	Num. 14:6-9	153
Exo. 9:23	49	Num. 14:11-38	153
Exo. 10:13	49	Num. 14:26-35	50
Exo. 11:2 3	73	Num. 14:33-34	67
Exo. 12:31-32	50	Num. 19:1-10	149
Exo. 12:29	49	Num. 26:57-60	54, 55
Exo. 12:29-32	135	Num. 33:3	83, 84
Exo. 12:33	74	Num. 33:5	83, 84
Exo. 12:35-36	74	Num. 33:5-15	139
Exo. 12:37	57, 82, 83, 84, 139	Deu. 7:1-2	60
		Deu. 7:17	60
Exo. 12:37-38	50	Deu. 7:7	60
Exo. 12:38	88	Deu. 9:1	60
Exo. 12:40	51, 52	Deu. 11:23	60
Exo. 12:40-41	58	Deu. 23:19-20	74
Exo. 12:41	51	Deu. 34:5	153
Exo. 13:20	139	Deu. 34:7	50
Exo. 14:2	139	Jos. 1:1	67
Exo. 14:5-6	135	Jos. 1:1-2	103
Exo. 14:13-14	50	Jud. 1:16	66
Exo. 14:21	96	Jud. 4:11	66

1 Kings 6:1	91	Jer. 52:28-30	157
1 Kings 12:1-32	146	Acts 7:6	51
2 Kings 16:6	185	Acts 7:23-24	67
2 Kings 18:9-11	185	Acts 7:29-30	67
1 Chr. 6:1-3	54, 55	Acts 13:17-20	52
Ps. 106:11	111	Gal. 3:16-18	52
Ps. 136:13-15	111		

Index of Names and Subjects

'Abd al Qadir al Jilani (shaikh), 115
'Ād, 107, 109, 113, 205
1 Kings (book), 91, 92, 146
Abraham (prophet), 17, 19, 20, 31, 32, 34, 41, 51-54, 90, 151, 152, 178, 180, 183, 185
Abu Simbel, 87, 110, 111
Acts (book), 52, 67
Ahasuerus (king), 124, 125
Ahmose I (pharaoh), 36, 129, 189
Akhenaten (pharaoh), 106, 123, 170, 177
Akhetaten, 123
Akkad, 32, 174, 175
Al-Jalālayn, 101, 115, 134, 137, 152, 216
al-Madīna, 20
Al-Qurṭubī, 72, 101, 109, 115, 134, 137, 138, 142, 147, 152, 156, 169
Amarna letters, 158, 177
Amen (see Amun), 121
Amen hir khopshef (Ramesses II's son), 94, 95
Amenhotep II (pharaoh), 112, 178
Amenhotep III (pharaoh), 105, 106, 177
Amenhotep IV (see also Akhenaten), 123
Amenmesses (pharaoh), 65, 85, 92, 212
Amon (see Amun), 83, 121
Amun, 83, 87, 88, 121-123, 126, 170, 191
Anastasi (papyri), 34, 83, 88-90
Ashkelon, 162, 163, 165
Assyrians, 185
Astyages (king), 172, 173
Aten, 123
Aṭ-Ṭabarī, 72, 110, 142, 147, 169
Aṭ-Ṭabaṭabā'ī, 115, 137, 169
Augustus (emperor), 174
Avaris, 33, 36, 40, 83, 128, 129, 189
Babylon, 157, 185
Benjamin (Joseph's brother), 18, 19, 21, 22, 27-29, 43, 45, 47, 184
Bethlehem, 176
Bitter Lakes, 140

Bucaille (Maurice), 97, 98, 106, 113, 166, 213
Contextual displacement, 125, 126, 149
Cyrus (king), 157, 172-175, 185
David (prophet), 20, 59
Deuteronomy (book), 47
Esther (book), 124, 125, 126
Eusebius of Caesarea, 211
Exodus (book), 41, 47, 54, 66-68, 83, 84, 86, 92, 124, 181, 182
Gebel el Silsila, 87, 110
Genesis (book), 17, 28, 32, 41, 47, 51, 53, 54, 58, 84, 178
Genesis, Biblical book of, 28
Gezer, 162-165
Hatshepsut (queen), 106
Heliopolis, 211
Herodotus, 172, 173
Horemheb (pharaoh), 83
Hyksos, 32, 33, 35-38, 40, 41, 44, 53, 83, 91, 106, 114, 122, 128, 129, 132, 167, 189, 212
Ibn 'Abbās, 109, 142
Ibn Kathīr, 74, 98, 99, 101, 115, 138, 142, 156, 169, 217
Injīl (book), 184, 185
Isaac (prophet), 19, 20, 31, 34, 37, 53, 151, 185
Ishmael (prophet), 31, 37, 185
Jacob (prophet), 17-31, 33-35, 37, 47, 52-55, 57, 61, 77, 78, 81, 82, 84, 127, 144, 151, 179, 180, 183-185, 189
Jeroboam (king), 146
Jerusalem, 81, 90, 146, 157, 158
Jesus (prophet), 9, 69, 78, 125, 156, 174, 176, 184
Job (prophet), 20
Jordan (river), 60, 103, 180
Josephus, 32, 35, 91, 169, 174
Joshua (book), 143, 155, 177
Joshua (son of Nun), 50, 53, 67, 103, 143, 149, 153, 177
Judah (Jacob's son), 184
Judah (Joseph's brother), 29
Judea, 146, 157, 184, 185
Ka'ba, 133

Kamose (pharaoh), 33, 36
Karnak, 87, 110, 162, 163, 164
Korah, 119, 120, 126, 170, 205
Leviticus (book), 47
Luxor, 110
magicians (Egyptian), 39, 40, 49, 68, 71, 105, 107, 115-117, 130, 170, 193, 198, 202, 206
Manetho, 32, 35, 61, 91, 211
manna, 144, 155, 159, 160, 196, 198, 203
Matthew (evangelist), 176
Makkah, 20, 133
Memphis, 34, 83, 85, 89, 122, 178
Mesha (king), 162
Mesopotamia, 180
Midian, 48, 66-68, 70, 71, 85, 92-94, 97-101, 103, 105, 151, 189, 197, 200, 201
midwives (Hebrew), 47, 60, 63, 64, 72, 127, 167, 169
Muhammad (prophet), 20, 44, 77, 79, 147, 148
Near East, 13, 32, 177
Nebuchadnezzar (king), 157, 185
Nectanebo II (pharaoh), 211
Nefertari (queen), 111
New Testament, 174
Noah (prophet), 20, 107, 114, 205
Nubia, 87, 88, 110, 163
Numbers (book), 47, 57-59, 139
Old Testament, 29, 32, 43, 52, 54, 61, 76, 86, 140, 176
Palestine, 13, 31, 62, 83, 84, 91, 139, 152, 157, 158, 162-164, 177, 185
Patriarchs, 47
Paul (apostle), 52
Pentateuch, 47, 52
Persia, 124, 125, 126, 172, 173, 191
Pithom, 62, 82, 85, 91, 93, 128, 129
plagues, 49, 68, 71, 73, 74, 81, 94, 95, 103, 104, 133, 166, 171, 190
Plutarch, 174, 215
Potiphar, 18, 26, 38
Qantir, 81, 83
quails, 144, 155, 159, 160, 196, 198, 203
Ramesses I (pharaoh), 212
Ramesses III (pharaoh), 158
Ramesses IV (pharaoh), 178
Ramesseum, 87, 110
Red Sea, 61, 139, 140

Reed Sea, 140
Rehoboam (king), 146
Reuben (Joseph's brother), 25
Sabbath, 154, 196, 204
Sais, 86
Ṣāliḥ (prophet), 109
Samaria, 146, 147
Samaritan Pentateuch, 52, 53
Samaritans, 52, 146, 147
Sāmirī, 144-148, 198, 199
Sargon (king), 174-176
Septuagint, 52, 53, 140
Seqenere Tao (pharaoh), 36
Setau (viceroy), 87, 88
Seti I (pharaoh), 83, 110, 212
Seti II (pharaoh), 212
Shabtaka (pharaoh), 125
Shalmaneser III (king), 162
Shasu, 34
Sheshi (king), 37
Shu'ayb (prophet), 103
Simeon (Joseph's brother), 28
Sinai, 35, 57, 58, 62, 67, 91, 139, 149, 150
Siptah (pharaoh), 212
Solomon (prophet), 20, 81, 91, 92, 146, 152
Succoth (Sukkoth), 139
Suetonius, 174, 216
Suez, 140
Sukkoth, 50, 139
Tablets (Torah), 146, 149-151, 187, 195
Tell el-Dab'a, 33, 83
Tell el-Maskhuta, 82
Tell el-Retabe, 82
Thamūd, 107, 109, 110, 113, 205
Thebes, 35, 83, 84, 87, 90, 110, 112, 117, 121, 122, 161, 215
Titus, 157, 158
Torah, 47, 149, 151, 184-187
Tuthmosis II (pharaoh), 106
Tuthmosis III (pharaoh), 41, 86, 105, 106
twosret (queen), 212
Valley of the Kings, 112
Wadi es-Sebua, 87, 110
Wellhausen (Julius), 96
Xerxes (king), 125
Ya'qub her (king), 37
Yakobaam (king), 37
Yanoam, 162, 163, 165

The Mystery of the Crucifixion
The Attempt to Kill Jesus in the Qur'an, the New Testament, and Historical Sources

• Flaws of the Gospel accounts of the crucifixion

• Does history really support the crucifixion tradition?

• The Qur'an's explanation of the crucifixion

• The origin of the theology of the cross

• The reality of Jesus' appearances after the crucifixion

Publication Date: November 2008
ISBN: 978-1-906342-04-3
Available from Amazon and other bookstores

Numerous books and articles have been published about the crucifixion. Western studies have focused on the Christian narratives and historical sources, but most of them have completely ignored the Qur'an, which denies that Jesus was crucified. Muslim scholars have also studied the Qur'an's account but mostly in exegetical works that focused on the Qur'an's version of the story, with some comparative references to the Gospel narratives but almost no consideration of historical sources.

This book takes a new approach by considering the crucifixion in the Qur'an, Christian writings, and early historical sources. It discusses the serious flaws in the Gospel accounts and the unreliability of the few non-scriptural sources. The book also challenges common modern alternative readings of the history of that event. One new contribution that this study makes to the literature of the crucifixion is its new interpretation of all related Qur'anic verses. It also presents a coherent explanation of the development of the fictitious story of the crucifixion of Jesus.

The theology of the cross that Paul developed is also examined. The book shows that the doctrine of the atonement conflicts with the Gospel teachings and is refuted in the Qur'an.

The Mystery of the Historical Jesus
The Messiah in the Qur'an, the Bible, and Historical Sources

- Jesus in the Qur'an, Christian writings, and historical sources
- The scriptural Jesus in the light of history
- The life and teachings of the historical Jesus
- The time and places in which Jesus lived
- Jesus and the Jews and the Romans
- The historical Jesus versus the theological one

Publication Date: September 2007
ISBN: 978-1-906342-01-2
Available from Amazon and other bookstores

Jesus remains one of the most studied characters in history. In the two millennia since his birth, countless writers have published numerous books and articles on every aspect of his life, personality, teachings, and environment. Depending on the backgrounds, goals, and trainings of their respective authors, these works relied on the New Testament, other Christian sources, Jewish writings, or other historical sources, or on combinations of these writings. The Qur'an is rarely mentioned, let alone seriously considered, by the mainly Christian authors of these studies. This explicit or implicit neglect reflects a presumed historical worthlessness of the Qur'an.

Muslim scholars have also written extensively about Jesus. Contrary to their Western counterparts, they have studied in detail what the Qur'an and other Islamic sources say about Jesus. The Christian image of Jesus is often cited to be dismissed, usually on the basis of what Islamic sources say, but at times also because of its incoherence and inconsistency. Like Western scholars who have ignored the Qur'an, Muslim writers have shown no interest in independent historical sources.

This book fills a gap in the literature on the historical Jesus by taking the unique approach of considering together the Qur'an, the Gospels, and other religious and historical sources. This genuinely new contribution to the scholarship on the historical Jesus shows that, unlike the New Testament accounts, the Qur'anic image of Jesus is both internally consistent and reconcilable with known history. While showing that our understanding of how the New Testament was formed and our growing knowledge of history confirm that the Christian Jesus is unhistorical, this study makes a strong case for the historicity of the Jesus of the Qur'an.

The Prophet Joseph in the Qur'an, the Bible, and History
A new, detailed commentary on the Qur'anic Chapter of Joseph

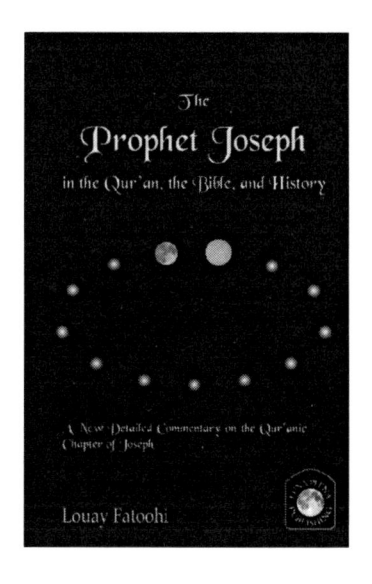

- Modern and comprehensive interpretation of the sūra of Joseph

- Verse by verse analysis and commentary

- Comparative references to classical interpretations

- Comparison between the story in the Qur'an and its Biblical counterpart

- Examination of the historical time and place where Joseph lived

- Explanation of the Qur'an's style in relating history

Publication Date: August 2007
ISBN: 978-1-906342-00-5
Available from Amazon and other bookstores

    The Qur'anic sūra (chapter) of Joseph deals almost entirely with the story of this noble Prophet, his brothers, and their father Prophet Jacob. Since the revelation of the Qur'an fourteen centuries ago, there have been numerous attempts to interpret this sūra. The present study is a genuinely new look at the sūra — including careful examination of the historical background of its story and detailed comparison with the corresponding Biblical narrative. While referring to interpretations from classical exegetical works, this book offers new insights into the meanings and magnificence of this Qur'anic text.

    The author is not only concerned with analysing the individual verses; he is equally focused on showing how various verses are interrelated, explicitly and subtly, to form a unique textual unit. He shows particular interest in unveiling subtle references and meanings that are often overlooked or missed by exegetes. Through this comprehensive study, the author elucidates why the Qur'an has always been firmly believed to be a unique book that could have only been inspired by Allah.